A NEW DICTIONARY OF ART

A NEW DICTIONARY OF

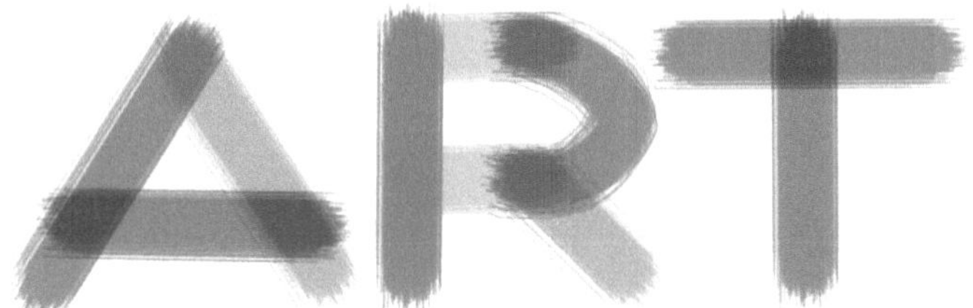

ART

one word
3000 definitions

ROBERT GOOD

Design: Jane Glennie

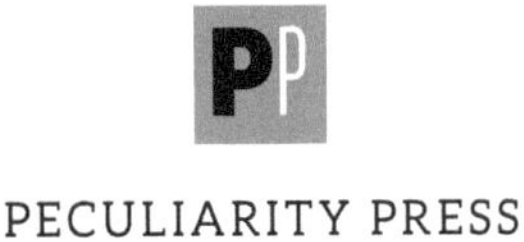

PECULIARITY PRESS

What is art?

No-one seems to know,

but everyone has an opinion.

CONTENTS

FOREWORD

BY PROFESSOR DEREK MATRAVERS

THE noted philosopher and fare-dodger of the 1930s, C.E.M. Joad, would always begin an answer to a question with the words 'It all depends on what you mean by...'. Defining your terms before entering into a discussion is thought to be a necessary part of making progress, and this need to define terms explains the popularity of subject dictionaries. This is particularly so when it comes to the arts, discussion of which employs confusing terms from 'abstraction' to 'zeitgeist'. Indeed, in a book that is a significant milestone in the history of thought on the subject, Clive Bell wrote that 'either all works of visual art have some common quality, or when we speak of 'works of art' we gibber' (Bell, 1987/1914:7). Finding this common quality, this essence of art, is the Holy Grail of philosophical aesthetics.

Thus Robert Good's *A New Dictionary of Art* follows in a great tradition of helpful reference books for the tidy minded. Except, of course, it doesn't. Rather than defining terms, it has over 3,000 entries for a single term - 'art' - each presented with meticulous scholarly apparatus. The various definitions from noted philosophers are offered (Bell's first appears on page 159 with a variant on page 184 - some definitions, including those listed here, appear in multiple entries each with a slightly different emphasis and so nicely adding a further layer of complexity). There are current contenders at definition from the likes of George Dickie (p.1), Arthur Danto (p.207), Jerrold Levinson (p.227), and Robert Stecker (p.60). However, these are overwhelmed by other definitions, pillaged from all manner of gibbering, including academic tomes, chat-rooms, and ordinary conversation. The serious point, if one wanted to dredge up a serious point in the face of all this wanton frivolity, is that there really, really is no hope at all in coming up with a definition that will capture all uses of this rattlebag of a term. It is an overwhelming proof from a plethora of fact.

The compilation is strangely compelling. Various things emerge quite quickly. One is that policing the boundaries of art excites passion – it matters to people what other people count as art. We have here (unsurprisingly) all views, from art as 'a manifestation of genius' (p.194) to 'a copout term used by professional and amateur masturbators alike in a desparate attempt to give value to otherwise worthless vomit' (p.10). The other is that definitions cover the waterfront of human endeavour. There is the attempt at parsimony – 'x is an artwork if and only if x is an object which a person or persons non-passingly intends for regard as a work of art' – to the more liberal 'everything' (p.99). Pretty much all human life is here in some form or another and, if talk about 'art' is a fair reflection of the practice of art, this tells us something about the boundless fecundity of that practice.

What are we to make of the book itself? Well, there is certainly a story to be told about its own credentials as art. There is, in modernist literature, a concern for lists and classifications, whether Samuel Beckett's *Watt* going through endless pointless permutations and combinations or Borges's *'Library of Babel'* (which contains all possible books) or *'Funes the Memorious'* (who remembers everything). Part of the story of *A New Dictionary of Art* is that it appears as a serious and scholarly attempt to cover everything that is art in our society. However, as with a lot of art (oh, beware of these essentialist claims) its real message is its reflective commentary on itself – by taking the attempt to absurd lengths it makes a mockery of the modern world's desire to systematise, to classify, and to control. In particular, it mocks the modern world's desire to put a boundary on creativity. Reflexivity abounds – the attempt is not just any definition, but a definition of 'art'. Hence, it is a work of art that is about 'art' (and so about art) with some nice little reflections on this reflexivity in its content (see, for example, a definition on page 9: 'a confusing subject; *and difficult to define, is it not?*') I say 'part of this story' because there is so much else besides; it sets hares running about (amongst other things) the nature of dictionaries, the nature of philosophy, the role of scholarly apparatus, the nature of artistic work, and the point of art and indeed of any human endeavour.

It might come as a relief, however, that one does not have to think of *A New Dictionary of Art* in the august company of the likes of Beckett and Borges. Instead one can place it in the company of people such as Philip Warren who spent 60 years creating scale models of all Royal Navy ships out of matchsticks, or Lluis Carreras, who, in the course of a lifetime, collected over 5000 small things (some of which can be seen in the utterly splendid Museu de Miniatures I Microminiatures in Besalú, Spain). For as one reads through the definitions - some good, some terrible, some po-faced, some vulgar abuse - one is awe-struck at the thought that *someone went to the trouble of assembling all this*. Robert Good needs to take his place in the long and distinguished list of obsessive, eccentric collectors who have done so much to brighten the world. However, unlike some of those collections this one can bear serious reflection. Also unlike some of those collections, it is screamingly funny.

Bell, Clive. 1987/1914. *Art*. (Oxford: OUP).

PREFACE

As an artist I am fascinated by the question of 'What is Art?' and mesmerised by the hive mind of the internet, so I began to collect online definitions as a way to explore both these ideas in one project. Initially I had no idea where this might lead me, but they kept on accumulating. I tried a five-hour rolling slide show (exhibited in 2015 as a library intervention at Leeds College of Art), but eventually it became clear that a faithfully realised dictionary format, with full, obsessive editing and annotation, was conceptually the best way to set out the claims being made and to evaluate their status as potential purveyors of knowledge. The work excludes the name of each contributor as I did not want the classification of authorship to interrupt or colour the reader's assessment of the ideas being proposed (doesn't everyone check the label in a museum before deciding how much time to devote to a particular picture?).

So I wanted to ask 'What is Art?' as directly as possible, and the results do not disappoint. I am fascinated by the ferocity with which people defend their idea of 'art' and how upset some become when certain things (very often urinals, sharks and beds) are put into galleries. On the flipside I am also intrigued by the attempts made by art theorists and cultural commentators to define (and constrict?) the potentials of art. But above all, the breadth and creativity of the responses is energising and inspirational. Perhaps the conclusion to be drawn is that art is 'all of the above': a glorious, inclusive cacophony of possibility, contradiction and furious debate.

Many thanks to everyone who has contributed to this project and helped it see the light of day. Particular thanks to Jane Glennie for tireless work on design and production, and to Derek Matravers for a most insightful foreword. For advice and encouragement along the way (even if, in some cases, rejection as well), and for help with the launch, thanks go to: Amanda Crawley Jackson, Ann and Bob Good, Bryan Eccleshall, Chris Owen, Claire Koch, Fiona Coffey, Henry Lydiate, Joe Banks, John Clark, Jonnie Howard, Judith Weik, Helen Sudell, Hugh Merrell, Lara Speicher, Miriam Berg, Natalie Kay, Nicholas Alexander, Paul Sammut, Roger Conover, Rossella Black, Samantha Rayner, Simon Morris and many others.

RG

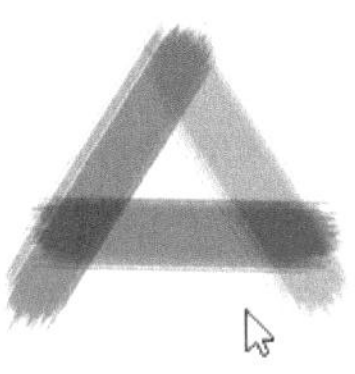

art */ärt/ n* **1** a creation of the human mind **2** the creator has labelled it 'art' **3** it is accepted by the recipient as art. [L *ars, artis*]

art */ärt/ n* **1** a creative expression of thoughts, feelings and messages that the artist wants to convey **2** *usu* involves a certain amount of skill **3** *usu* provokes thought in audience **4** commonly refers to visual arts, such as paintings, sculptures *etc* **5** most importantly, interpretation and judgment of art tends to be controversial. [L *ars, artis*]

art */ärt/ n* **1** aesthetics **2** purpose **3** is interpretable. [L *ars, artis*]

art */ärt/ n* **1** an agent A grows up in an environment that includes a category of artefacts which the community categorizes as 'art' **2** these artefacts have the peculiarity – in the current Western environment at least – of being able to fulfil a variety of functions; *moreover, many of these artefacts can fulfil several functions at once* **3** growing up in such an environment, A progressively stores a set of functions in memory that can be fulfilled by the artefacts that she accepts as representative of the category of art based on the fact that people she trusts categorize these artefacts as art **4** when A later infers that an artefact is intended to fulfil one or more of these functions, she spontaneously categorizes it as art. [L *ars, artis*]

art */ärt/ n* **1** an artefact **2** upon which some society or some subgroup of a society has conferred the status of candidate for appreciation. [L *ars, artis*]

art */ärt/ n* **1** an (original) artefact **2** a set of the aspects of which has had conferred upon it the status of candidate for appreciation by some person or persons acting on behalf of a certain social institution (the artworld). [L *ars, artis*]

art */ärt/ n* **1** created by a HUMAN **2** experienced by a DIFFERENT human **3** ENJOYED by the second human to the extent that they want more **4** NOT weakened by (geographical) separation of the two humans. [L *ars, artis*]

art */ärt/ n* **1** created from a set of mediums that are recognized through consensus to be artistic mediums **2** serving a primarily aesthetic goal. [L *ars, artis*]

art */ärt/ n* **1** has a subject **2** about which it projects some attitude or point of view *(has a style)* **3** by means of rhetorical ellipsis *(usu metaphorical)* which ellipsis engages audience participation in filling in what is missing **4** where the work in question and the interpretations thereof require an art historical context. [L *ars, artis*]

art */ärt/ n* **1** made by a human being **2** created to have an impact, to change someone else **3** a gift; *you can sell the souvenir, the canvas, the recording… but the idea itself is free and the generosity is a critical part of making art.* [L *ars, artis*]

art */ärt/ n (inf)* **1** manipulation of human systems **2** doing stuff so fucking well that people take notice. [L *ars, artis*]

art */ärt/ n* **1** means different things to different people **2** evolves. [L *ars, artis*]

art */ärt/ n* **1** must be about something **2** must embody its meaning. [L *ars, artis*]

art */ärt/ n* **1** must be the indescribable **2** must be inimitable. [L *ars, artis*]

art */ärt/ n* **1** must have emotion; *be it stoic or edgy* **2** must be cogent to the times; *to the 21st century, if it's contemporary art* **3** must be technically proficient; *and not what elephants and chimps do.* [L *ars, artis*]

art */ärt/ n* **1** must have meaning; *doesn't have to be deep meaning, just some kind of meaning* **2** must require technical skill to create; *no black dots on white canvas* **3** must be the artist's own work; *no 'found' objects – sorry Picasso, that bull's head is just a bicycle seat;* or the work of a collaborative team; *but you can't put your name on something made entirely by other people – even if the original idea was yours* (Pablo Ruiz y Picasso, *(1881–1973), Sp painter, sculptor, printmaker, ceramicist and stage designer).* [L *ars, artis*]

art */ärt/ n (inf)* **1** NOT about skill, NOR a competition; *that crazy guitar shredder who can play a thousand scales in a minute is not necessarily a better artist than the guy who can play only chords; Caravaggio is* *not necessarily a better painter than Picasso; get this in your minds: technical skill is a tool to help you to make art, not art itself* **2** NOT only about the 'beautiful'; *Marilyn Manson or your average death metal singer are not necessarily worse artists than Pavarotti or your average pop singer because they sing in a 'ugly' way; some art is mean to be horrible, disgusting, or shocking* **3** NOT necessarily about complicated and expensive materials put together; *so what if it's only a pile of dirt? the fact that it's so simple doesn't make it any more or any less artistic than a tree made of, I don't know, fucking M&M™s* **4** NOT necessarily legal; *there's a lot of graffiti that even the most conservative and narrow-minded of all people would find stunning and artistic; guess what, the huge majority of them are illegal* **5** NOT necessarily made to please the viewer; *when a rock band makes a fucking disco-funk album, they should not receive hate for their decision; it's the artist's job to decide what kind of art he wants to do, not the viewer (*Michelangelo Merisi *or* Amerighi da Caravaggio *(1571–1610), It artist active in Rome, Naples, Malta and Sicily;* Pablo Ruiz y Picasso *(1881–1973), Sp painter, sculptor, printmaker, ceramicist and stage designer;* Brian Hugh Warner *known as* Marilyn Manson *(1969–), Am musician, actor, painter, multimedia artist and former music journalist;* Luciano Pavarotti, *Cavaliere di Gran Croce OMRI (1935–2007), It operatic tenor;* M&M™s, *colourful button-shaped candies produced by Mars™, Inc.).* [L *ars, artis*]

art */ärt/ n* **1** possessing positive aesthetic properties **2** being expressive of emotion **3** being intellectually challenging **4** being formally complex and coherent **5** having the capacity to convey complex meanings **6** exhibiting an individual point of view **7** being original **8** being an artefact or performance which is the product of a high degree of skill **9** belonging to an established artistic form **10** being the product of an intention to make a work of art. [L *ars, artis*]

art */ärt/ n* **1** possessing positive aesthetic properties; *such as being beautiful, graceful, or elegant (properties which ground a capacity to give sensuous pleasure)* **2** being expressive of emotion **3** being intellectually challenging *(ie questioning received views and modes of thought)* **4** being formally complex and coherent **5** having a capacity to convey complex meanings **6** exhibiting an individual point of view **7** being an exercise of creative imagination *(being original)* **8** being an artefact (or performance) which is the product of a high degree of skill **9** belonging to an established artistic form *(music, painting, film,* etc*)* **10** being the product of an intention to make a work of art. [L *ars, artis*]

art */ärt/ n* **1** produced with the aim of eliciting a defined mental response **2** succeeds in eliciting that response from the target audience **3** requires diligent effort and skill to produce. [L *ars, artis*]

art */ärt/ n* **1** requires creative perception both by the artist and by the audience **2** elusive **3** communicates on many levels and is open to many interpretations **4** connotes a sense of ability **5** interplay between the conscious and unconscious part of our being, between what is real and what is an illusion **6** any human creation which contains an idea other than its utilitarian purpose. [L *ars, artis*]

art */ärt/ n* **1** skill in controlling materials **2** ability to create form or patterns that hold attention **3** creative manipulation and innovation **4** functional utility **5** appropriateness for ritual or ceremony **6** all the above. [L *ars, artis*]

art */ärt/ n (inf)* **1** something that evokes feelings or thoughts to the viewer/listener *etc* **2** is the result of conscious or subconscious planning of a creator, an array of arranged *(yay alliteration)* elements in a purposeful or at least interpretable fashion that evokes said emotions/thoughts. [L *ars, artis*]

art */ärt/ n* **1** something which is produced primarily with the intention of rewarding aesthetic contemplation **2** exhibits value-features whose presence in the work is owing *(in some degree)* to an artist *(or artists), ie* someone who acts primarily with the aforesaid intention. [L *ars, artis*]

art */ärt/ n (derog)* **1** stuff people do **2** overrated **3** what people unable to deal with their inadequacies grasp onto in the hope that they will appear to be more interesting. [L *ars, artis*]

art */ärt/ n* (*biol*) a baby, as a creation; *authors: parents, tools: organic material, creative process: sex, biological processes,* etc, *medium: reality (just like in performance art), the audience: anyone that gets to see the baby.* [L *ars, artis*]

art */ärt/ n* (*interj*) a bang! [L *ars, artis*]

art */ärt/ n* a beautiful abstract form of expression that displays its unlimited creativity and symbolizing depth. [L *ars, artis*]

art */ärt/ n* a beautiful object or a stimulating experience that is considered by the audience to have artistic merit. [L *ars, artis*]

art */ärt/ n* a beautiful painting or a drawing hung on the wall of an art gallery. [L *ars, artis*]

art */ärt/ n (fig)* a big bus and everybody is free to ride; *inside the bus, there is a steering wheel to every seat; still the bus drives one way; some passengers just sit and watch the landscape rolling by; others talk, discuss and criticize; there are bus-riders staring into a void, keeping themselves in a shell, focus on their own stuff; a few of the passengers are sleeping; 2 are getting carsick and puke out the window; 'did you see that?' yells one of them 'that is art, – right there'; the discussion panel turns its attention to the carsick; a man sitting in the back is scribbling in his notebook; there are passengers who want to get off the bus; passengers who insist that they are steering the bus; passengers hanging on the outside of the bus with spray cans in their hands; passengers that are on for the ride; blind passengers; some passengers, crawling around inside the bus, tearing out seats to make a sculpture in the middle section, coming up with crazy ideas on how to change the whole outlook of the bus; making strange designs; should I change into a submarine? banana? airplane? UFO? naked woman? penis? a cookie? a cartoon character?* etc… *(finally) there are passengers unsatisfied with the landscape outside, but they'll have to be patient, 'cus the bus is driving in its own pace; it'll eventually reach new territory.* [L *ars, artis*]

Art */ärt/ n (joc)* a big, fat arse-crack-showing mechanic. [Arthur]

art */ärt/ n* a big, fat question mark; *there is no specific answer; nor a right or wrong answer.* [L *ars, artis*]

art */ärt/ n* a big umbrella. [L *ars, artis*]

art */ärt/ n* a bit of a pretentious word. [L *ars, artis*]

art */ärt/ n* a blanket term for anything a person makes. [L *ars, artis*]

art */ärt/ n* a body of knowledge. [L *ars, artis*]

art */ärt/ n* a boost of energy that is not controlled by reason and consciousness. [L *ars, artis*]

art */ärt/ n* a borderline useless word. [L *ars, artis*]

art */ärt/ n* a boring version of something else. [L *ars, artis*]

art */ärt/ n (inf)* a brain fart enacted under the creative muse with relevancy to the previous brain farts that have come before it. [L *ars, artis*]

art */ärt/ n* a branch of learning. [L *ars, artis*]

art */ärt/ n* a branch of learning; **1** one of the humanities **2** *pl* liberal arts. [L *ars, artis*]

art */ärt/ n* a branch of learning; *esp* one of the liberal arts; *as in faculty of arts, master of arts.* [L *ars, artis*]

art */ärt/ n* a branch of learning regarded as an instrument of thought, or as something the knowledge of which is to be acquired in order to be applied or practised. [L *ars, artis*]

art */ärt/ n* a break from the difficulties in life. [L *ars, artis*]

art */ärt/ n* a break from the norm. [L *ars, artis*]

Art */ärt/ n* a bricklayer I worked with over the years; *he was about 5ft 3in and would regularly wave his hand about 3in above his head while saying 'I've had it up to here with the short jokes'.* [Arthur]

art */ärt/ n* a brief encounter with a fictitious thought. [L *ars, artis*]

art */ärt/ n* a broad topic fulfilling links to artists, paintings, sculptures, music, physical and emotional aspects too. [L *ars, artis*]

art */ärt/ n* a broader category than people imagine. [L *ars, artis*]

art */ärt/ n (derog)* a bunch of drugged-out, conceptual crap. [L *ars, artis*]

art */ärt/ n* a bunch of scribbles some person sees a picture in; *as in 'look at those blobs: they remind me of rain, it must be art'.* [L *ars, artis*]

art */ärt/ n* a business, craft. [L *ars, artis*]

art */ärt/ n* a business, occupation, or pursuit that depends upon a skill. [L *ars, artis*]

art */ärt/ n (econ)* a capitalist concept. [L *ars, artis*]

art */ärt/ n (econ)* a capitalist conspiracy. [L *ars, artis*]

art */ärt/ n (neg)* a car cannot be art; *nor can a hammer or a chair, unless it has a single nail protruding up from the centre of the seat.* [L *ars, artis*]

art */ärt/ n* a career that if followed may not reap so much of a benefit financially. [L *ars, artis*]

art */ärt/ n (fig)* a carrot tantalizingly placed in front of a donkey's face; *if the carrot is too far away, then the donkey will not want to chase it; however, if it's too close, then the donkey will eat the carrot and no longer care about it; art is the carrot and the viewer is the donkey; art must be just far enough to seduce the viewer into desiring it; as in 'that artwork nearby looks tasty'.* [L *ars, artis*]

art */ärt/ n (inf)* a cat's butthole, blossoming. [L *ars, artis*]

art */ärt/ n* a category defined by the ruling class; *always has been, always will be.* [L *ars, artis*]

art */ärt/ n* a category of object – like 'wood' – rather than a medal of praise that we bestow on stuff we think is really peachy; *a Rodin sculpture and a crass naked zombie torso thing are both forms of self-expression and I guarantee you that someone spent a decent amount of time labouring over that torso and trying to get it just right, but being art isn't a magic shield that protects the zombie torso from criticism* (François-Auguste-René Rodin *(1840–1917), Fr sculptor).* [L *ars, artis*]

art */ärt/ n (neg)* a chair is not art; *and I will never accept it as art, regardless of the idiots that will.* [L *ars, artis*]

art */ärt/ n* a circuit of power, money and influence. [L *ars, artis*]

art */ärt/ n (educ)* a class I failed in grade 10. [L *ars, artis*]

art */ärt/ n* a close approximation of an unknown quality. [L *ars, artis*]

art */ärt/ n (photog)* a collage of photographs. [L *ars, artis*]

art */ärt/ n* a collection of certain rules for doing anything in a set form. [L *ars, artis*]

art */ärt/ n* a collection of patterns which evoke a directed change in the mental state of a person perceiving them; art has degrees of precision and accuracy; *precision* is a measure of how repeatable the evoked mental change is from person to person; *accuracy* is a measure of how closely the mental change comes to what the artist had intended. [L *ars, artis*]

art */ärt/ n* a collective reality; *when we look at a Rembrandt, we all know we are looking at the same thing, responding to the same source of experience outside ourselves: we might respond slightly differently, according to our natures, but the heart of what Rembrandt has given us is something we know we can share* (Rembrandt Harmenszoon van Rijn *(1606–69), Du painter and etcher).* [L *ars, artis*]

art */ärt/ n* a collective understanding. [L *ars, artis*]

art */ärt/ n* a combination of colours and lines. [L *ars, artis*]

art */ärt/ n* a combination of thought and craft. [L *ars, artis*]

art */ärt/ n (interrog)* a comic strip? [L *ars, artis*]

art */ärt/ n* a commitment. [L *ars, artis*]

art */ärt/ n* a common sense to describing everything for everyone. [L *ars, artis*]

art */ärt/ n* a communication of emotion; *be it rage, beauty, wonder, tranquility or dismay*. [L *ars, artis*]

art */ärt/ n* a communication that evolves by co-evolution between the observed and the observer, a performance and an audience, through sensory evaluation. [L *ars, artis*]

art */ärt/ n* a communicative work that exists for itself and is a total human creation, as close as possible to a completely intended work that is the product of one unbroken creative vision; *the artist first intends to create art, then finds a concept, message and audience to communicate with and executes that message to the smallest detail.* [L *ars, artis*]

art */ärt/ n* a complex system of qualities with a structure characterized by a combination of cognitive, evaluative, creative *(spiritual and material)* and symbolically communicative elements *(or subsystems).* [L *ars, artis*]

art */ärt/ n* a complexity and a simplicity; *just like life.* [L *ars, artis*]

art */ärt/ n* a component of culture, reflecting economic and social substrates in its design. [L *ars, artis*]

art */ärt/ n* a component of the spiritual culture of mankind. [L *ars, artis*]

art */ärt/ n (comput)* a compressed image format from AOL™ (AOL™ Inc, *Am multinational mass media corp).* [L *ars, artis*]

art */ärt/ n* a compulsion that sometimes I wish I didn't have. [L *ars, artis*]

art */ärt/ n* a concept created by the powerful to serve their own purposes; *an investment, a possession, something you can be knowledgeable about, an expert about and gain status thereby; something you can use to manipulate others, or something you can use to overawe etc etc.* [L *ars, artis*]

art */ärt/ n* a concept in the sense that it's the product of thought; *but must also be a creation, it can't just be a projected thought.* [L *ars, artis*]

art */ärt/ n* a concept of appreciation; *it's like asking 'does everything have meaning?'; well, from one person, no; but from every living thing (from all possible opinions), yes; we all judge things differently and art is one of them.* [L *ars, artis*]

art */ärt/ n* a concept that was created to describe man-made objects, markings or sounds that were used socially rather than in a completely utilitarian way. [L *ars, artis*]

art */ärt/ n* a conceptual manifestation that has been deemed as a work of art by the creating artist and the greater art community. [L *ars, artis*]

art */ärt/ n* a conceptual public debate. [L *ars, artis*]

art */ärt/ n* a concern with change and variety. [L *ars, artis*]

art */ärt/ n (philos)* a concretization of metaphysics. [L *ars, artis*]

art */ärt/ n (interrog)* a confusing subject; *and difficult to define, is it not?* [L *ars, artis*]

art */ärt/ n* a conscious attempt to communicate beyond words. [L *ars, artis*]

art */ärt/ n* a conscious effort to portray an emotion or an image. [L *ars, artis*]

art */ärt/ n* a conspiracy between rich people and artists to make poor people think they are dumb. [L *ars, artis*]

art */ärt/ n* a constant reminder that there is nothing, no reality, no truths. [L *ars, artis*]

art */ärt/ n* a continuum within which all participate. [L *ars, artis*]

art */ärt/ n* a controlled accident. [L *ars, artis*]

art */ärt/ n* a conversation between the artist and the world. [L *ars, artis*]

art */ärt/ n* a conversation between the artist and viewer. [L *ars, artis*]

art */ärt/ n* a conversation that is multidimensional. [L *ars, artis*]

art */ärt/ n (derog, vulg)* a copout term used by professional and amateur masturbators alike in a desperate attempt to give value to otherwise worthless vomit. [L *ars, artis*]

art */ärt/ n* a copy or a new impression of our souls and the nature. [L *ars, artis*]

art */ärt/ n (fig)* a cornerstone of all our lives. [L *ars, artis*]

art */ärt/ n (fig)* a crack in our minds; *like humour.* [L *ars, artis*]

art */ärt/ n* a creation for the eye; *and can only be hinted at with words.* [L *ars, artis*]

art */ärt/ n (meteorol)* a creation inspired by a weather map. [L *ars, artis*]

art */ärt/ n* a creation of human hands. [L *ars, artis*]

art */ärt/ n* a creation of the human mind. [L *ars, artis*]

art */ärt/ n* a creation which is intended to inspire emotions and reflections. [L *ars, artis*]

art */ärt/ n* a creation with visual appeal and effort put into it; *not limited to paints and pens, but then again, EVERYTHING IS NOT ART; whoever thought up that idea is a moron.* [L *ars, artis*]

art */ärt/ n* a creative act. [L *ars, artis*]

art */ärt/ n* a creative communication of subjective truth. [L *ars, artis*]

art */ärt/ n* a creative development expressed through the filter of its creator and shared with others. [L *ars, artis*]

art */ärt/ n* a creative endeavour that will be appreciated by most people. [L *ars, artis*]

art */ärt/ n* a creative expression. [L *ars, artis*]

art */ärt/ n* a creative expression which can mirror reality or propose new ideas. [L *ars, artis*]

art */ärt/ n* a creative idea expressed in a way that others can see. [L *ars, artis*]

art */ärt/ n* a creative medium for one to express him or herself; *can be audio, visual, or sensual, often two or more of the above three.* [L *ars, artis*]

art */ärt/ n* a creative object that comes from imagination and passion. [L *ars, artis*]

art */ärt/ n* a creative product. [L *ars, artis*]

art */ärt/ n* a creative statement. [L *ars, artis*]

art */ärt/ n* a creative work that incorporates elements of the artist's own psyche. [L *ars, artis*]

art */ärt/ n* a creative work that requires skill and imagination to produce. [L *ars, artis*]

art */ärt/ n* a creatively inspired manifested thought. [L *ars, artis*]

art */ärt/ n (appar fig)* a creature of hate and loathing, only meant to torture those who would dare create it and confound those who follow it. [L *ars, artis*]

art */ärt/ n* a critical point of view of the world the artist is living in. [L *ars, artis*]

art */ärt/ n* a cry for help. [L *ars, artis*]

art */ärt/ n* a cultural expression of excess. [L *ars, artis*]

art */ärt/ n* a cultural form of expression of human beings. [L *ars, artis*]

art */ärt/ n* a daily companion, refreshing, human and rich. [L *ars, artis*]

art */ärt/ n* a debate rather than an absolute quality. [L *ars, artis*]

art */ärt/ n* a deceptive yet honest look at the world that we live in. [L *ars, artis*]

art */ärt/ n* a decoration or symbol. [L *ars, artis*]

art */ärt/ n* a degraded reflection of the world. [L *ars, artis*]

art */ärt/ n* a deliberate human action that explores existence through a visual, verbal or sound language using craftsmanship. [L *ars, artis*]

art */ärt/ n* a delusion of infinite measure washed down with cheap wine and dreams of clarity on the cave's wall. [L *ars, artis*]

art */ärt/ n* a demonstration of the ability to act. [L *ars, artis*]

art */ärt/ n* a deployment of will. [L *ars, artis*]

art */ärt/ n (vulg)* a derived consequence of life experiences; *I consider a dick in a wall art; screenshots are art; AMVs, art* (**AMV**, *proprietary video file format).* [L *ars, artis*]

art */ärt/ n* a description of this life, this movement. [L *ars, artis*]

art */ärt/ n* a desire to convey meanings. [L *ars, artis*]

art */ärt/ n (sculpt)* a detailed sculpture. [L *ars, artis*]

art */ärt/ n* a device to save us from the chaos we so well see and try to dim. [L *ars, artis*]

art */ärt/ n* a dim mirror for the human condition. [L *ars, artis*]

art */ärt/ n (relig)* a direct interactive man and God dialogue. [L *ars, artis*]

art */ärt/ n* a direct route, process or path that meanders a bit. [L *ars, artis*]

art */ärt/ n* a discovery and development of elementary principles of nature into beautiful forms suitable for human use. [L *ars, artis*]

art */ärt/ n* a distant window into some other detached individual's 'useless' labours. [L *ars, artis*]

art */ärt/ n* a distinctive way of looking at the world. [L *ars, artis*]

art */ärt/ n* a diverse range of human activities and the products of those activities. [L *ars, artis*]

Art */ärt/ n* a dog. [poss *Arthur*]

art */ärt/ n* a drawing, sculpture, model, *etc* that describes a person's feelings, creativity and imagination. [L *ars, artis*]

art */ärt/ n* a dress made from a tasty dessert. [L *ars, artis*]

art */ärt/ n* a family resemblance term. [L *ars, artis*]

art */ärt/ n (inf)* a fart in the dark. [L *ars, artis*]

art */ärt/ n (inf)* a fart when you dart. [L *ars, artis*]

art */ärt/ n* a fascinating subject; *which everyone seems to admire and praise, although art has no word to explain what it really is, you can only know what it is by making art and surrounding yourself with art.* [L *ars, artis*]

art */ärt/ n* a feeling expressed. [L *ars, artis*]

art */ärt/ n (photog)* a fictionalization of reality in order to convey an idea; eg *a photographer who distorts reality by using a wide angle lens to include enough in his photo to say 'large', or 'towering' or 'warped lines' or whatever, or who uses gels to manipulate a scene to look cold or hot in order to enhance their subject more for a specific purpose; an artist diminishes elements that detract from an intended purpose, further manipulating reality; a novice, amateur does none of this and it shows in their work consistently and without fail UNLESS they happen to get lucky and 'accidently' snap a good shot.* [L *ars, artis*]

art */ärt/ n* a field or category of art; *dance is an art.* [L *ars, artis*]

art */ärt/ n* a field or category of art; *such as music, ballet, or literature.* [L *ars, artis*]

art */ärt/ n* a field or category of art; *such as painting, sculpture, music, ballet, or literature.* [L *ars, artis*]

art */ärt/ n (fig)* a fight to the finish between black charcoal and white paper. [L *ars, artis*]

art */ärt/ n* a figment of the imagination made comprehensible by those who can sense such to transcend its earthly physical medium. [L *ars, artis*]

art */ärt/ n* a figurative method for the evaluation of reality and the assertion of a definite system of values. [L *ars, artis*]

art */ärt/ n* a finely crafted table. [L *ars, artis*]

art */ärt/ n* a fly in the teeth of safe conventionality. [L *ars, artis*]

art */ärt/ n* a focus and a discipline; *allowing a lack of either to slither in under the definition of art is a travesty and an insult to history's great works as well as the work of today's great artists, whether they are known as such yet or not.* [L *ars, artis*]

art */ärt/ n* a force for our uninterrupted control by the almost-global forces of mass uniformity and of capital. [L *ars, artis*]

art */ärt/ n* a form of action that is not required for survival. [L *ars, artis*]

art */ärt/ n* a form of communicating the inexpressible; *such as emotion and ideas that are simply beyond words.* [L *ars, artis*]

art */ärt/ n* a form of communication. [L *ars, artis*]

art */ärt/ n* a form of communication; *best expressed by those who not only have a strong sense of recognition of their emotions, but the discipline to express them clearly to others.* [L *ars, artis*]

art */ärt/ n* a form of communication between the individual and the world as a whole. [L *ars, artis*]

art */ärt/ n* a form of communication between the viewer and the artist. [L *ars, artis*]

art */ärt/ n* a form of communication of deep non-verbal ideas but trying not to involve the use of words; *in some ways I am trying not to bring literature into this discussion as I think it will just complicate matters.* [L *ars, artis*]

art */ärt/ n* a form of communication produced through an admirable level of technical skill which can be appreciated for its message, high level of technical expertise or emotional impact. [L *ars, artis*]

art */ärt/ n* a form of communication that touches on some common or universal sensibility in mankind. [L *ars, artis*]

art */ärt/ n* a form of communication that touches on some common sensibility in mankind. [L *ars, artis*]

art */ärt/ n* a form of communication to transmit otherwise incommunicable feelings to others. [L *ars, artis*]

art */ärt/ n (photog)* a form of communication which transcends the spoken and written language and expresses ideas and concepts which often cannot be put into words; *the 'artistic nude' is more than just desaturating a colour glam photo and pumping up the contrast; it is more than taking a really poorly lit photograph with horrible shadows for 'artistic reasons'.* [L *ars, artis*]

art */ärt/ n* a form of emotional communication similar to the intellectual communication of a text book. [L *ars, artis*]

art */ärt/ n* a form of emotional expression; *and nobody has the right to denigrate or define another person's expression.* [L *ars, artis*]

art */ärt/ n* a form of emotional human communication. [L *ars, artis*]

art */ärt/ n* a form of expression. [L *ars, artis*]

art */ärt/ n (relig)* A FORM OF EXPRESSION… ALMOST LIKE A RELIGION IN SOME ASPECTS, A DEFI-

NITE CORRELATION BETWEEN THE TWO. [L *ars, artis*]

art */ärt/ n (relig)* A FORM OF EXPRESSION... ALSO IT IS LIKE A RELIGION OR THERAPY AS WELL; LIKE RELIGION, EVERYONE HAS THEIR OWN VIEW WHICH IS BEST FITTING FOR THEIR LIFESTYLE. [L *ars, artis*]

art */ärt/ n (relig)* A FORM OF EXPRESSION... LIKE RELIGION, EVERYONE HAS THEIR OWN VIEW WHICH IS BEST FITTING FOR THEIR LIFESTYLE. [L *ars, artis*]

art */ärt/ n* a form of expression; *normally, only control freaks try to define what is and is not art, like Hitler and such (*Adolf Hitler *(1889–1945), Aust-born Ger politician).* [L *ars, artis*]

art */ärt/ n* a form of expression from the creator to the audience; *in order for that language, that form of expression, to have effect it must be a closed sentence; a statement.* [L *ars, artis*]

art */ärt/ n* a form of expression that we experience in its creation and in its consumption as art. [L *ars, artis*]

art */ärt/ n* a form of imitation. [L *ars, artis*]

art */ärt/ n* a form of kettling; *like the police tactic, it contains and channels our capacities for creativity into a cordoned, sanitised zone, leaving the rest of social and cultural and political life free of such unpredictable, such potentially revolutionary, capacities.* [L *ars, artis*]

art */ärt/ n* a form of political protest. [L *ars, artis*]

art */ärt/ n* a form of politics without using words. [L *ars, artis*]

art */ärt/ n* a form of representation; *it may represent what we wish and what others wish.* [L *ars, artis*]

art */ärt/ n* a formal dexterity from which it all gels together and evokes an emotional response. [L *ars, artis*]

art */ärt/ n* a formed statement created from focused observations and inner reflection. [L *ars, artis*]

art */ärt/ n (interrog)* a four-dimensional feeling? [L *ars, artis*]

art */ärt/ n (m)* a fragment of the cosmical balance of the whole universe where all the humanity reconnects with himself. [L *ars, artis*]

art */ärt/ n (psychol)* a frame of mind. [L *ars, artis*]

art */ärt/ n* a free fall into the ambivalent and the unknown. [L *ars, artis*]

Art */ärt/ n* a friend of mine in Tulsa, Oklahoma, when I was about eleven years old. [Arthur]

art */ärt/ n* a function of celebrity; *especially a kind of celebrity that platforms multiple selves.* [L *ars, artis*]

art */ärt/ n* a function that embodies both the natural and unnatural. [L *ars, artis*]

art */ärt/ n* a fusion of beauty and talent and emotion. [L *ars, artis*]

art */ärt/ n* a futile attempt to communicate reality. [L *ars, artis*]

art */ärt/ n* a game between people of all ages. [L *ars, artis*]

art */ärt/ n* a general term used in publishing and printing for the illustrative matter in a book or other publication for which no setting of type is required; *including any hand lettering, photographs, reproductions of drawings, prints and paintings,* etc. [L *ars, artis*]

art */ärt/ n* a generic term for any product of the creative impulse, out of which sprang all other human pursuits; *such as science via alchemy and religion via shamanism.* [L *ars, artis*]

art */ärt/ n (mus)* a gentle hum, or whisper of a melody in one's own head. [L *ars, artis*]

art */ärt/ n* a gentle smile. [L *ars, artis*]

art */ärt/ n* a gift cherished, abused, obsessed over, argued about, lusted after, discovered and forgotten. [L *ars, artis*]

art */ärt/ n* a gift for every human being. [L *ars, artis*]

art */ärt/ n* a gift from artist to viewer; *and that gift is at least sensed and hopefully treasured; intention, for better or worse, is somehow infused into the work.* [L *ars, artis*]

art */ärt/ n (relig)* a gift from the gods; *which must be honoured and offered back to them.* [L *ars, artis*]

art */ärt/ n (relig)* a gift given by God; *and God gave it to a special person to do something different in the world.* [L *ars, artis*]

art */ärt/ n* (*relig, poss theol*) a gift of the Holy Spirit; *when this light shines through the mind of a musician, it manifests itself in beautiful harmonies; again, shining through* *the mind of a poet, it is seen in fine poetry and poetic prose; when the light of the Sun of Truth inspires the mind of a painter, he produces marvellous pictures; these gifts are fulfilling their highest purpose when showing forth the praise of God.* [L *ars, artis*]

Art */ärt/ n* a glimpse at the human soul... *then again, it's also my neighbour.* [Arthur]

art */ärt/ n (poss euphem)* a glimpse into the human soul in all it's glory; *also known as my little friend.* [L *ars, artis*]

art */ärt/ n* a good diversion to skip unwanted things even temporarily. [L *ars, artis*]

art */ärt/ n* a good story. [L *ars, artis*]

art */ärt/ n* a good way to express your feelings. [L *ars, artis*]

art */ärt/ n* a gratuitous act, done for its own sake. [L *ars, artis*]

art */ärt/ n* a great arena to play with ideas, stories and thoughts; *provided we recognise the limitations and the necessity to always, always, verify ideas through reasoned, critical analysis.* [L *ars, artis*]

art */ärt/ n* a great expression of self. [L *ars, artis*]

art */ärt/ n* a great healer. [L *ars, artis*]

art */ärt/ n* a great many things both different yet the same. [L *ars, artis*]

art */ärt/ n* a great stress reliever. [L *ars, artis*]

art */ärt/ n* a great way to engage children and adults with their imagination. [L *ars, artis*]

Art */ärt/ n (appar joc)* a guy with 1 arm and 1 leg hanging on the wall. [Arthur]

art */ärt/ n* a gypsy over the face of the earth. [L *ars, artis*]

art */ärt/ n (inf)* a half-assed attempt at grabbing attention; *but a very cheap way of doing so.* [L *ars, artis*]

art */ärt/ n (theol)* a half-effaced recollection of a higher state from which we have fallen since the time of Eden. [L *ars, artis*]

art */ärt/ n* a half-insult. [L *ars, artis*]

art */ärt/ n* a handiwork. [L *ars, artis*]

art */ärt/ n* a hateful exhibit such as a hate message on a wall, that demeans and belittles. [L *ars, artis*]

art */ärt/ n* a hateful splash of paint on a canvas, later painted over never to be seen. [L *ars, artis*]

art */ärt/ n* a heart to heart connection that we simply do; *almost like magic.* [L *ars, artis*]

art */ärt/ n* a higher truth than what happened. [L *ars, artis*]

art */ärt/ n (hist)* a historically evolved system of various concrete and artistic methods of apprehending the world; *each of these methods shares common features with others; at the same time, each has individual and distinctive characteristics.* [L *ars, artis*]

art */ärt/ n (derog)* a hoax perpetrated on the public by so-called 'artists' who set themselves up on a pedestal and by decadent, ivory tower 'critics' who think the world owes them a living. [L *ars, artis*]

art */ärt/ n (perh milit)* a huge explosion that you put your everything into just for that one moment. [L *ars, artis*]

art */ärt/ n* a human act to relate the artist with the viewer. [L *ars, artis*]

art */ärt/ n* a human activity consisting in this, that one consciously, by means of certain external symbols, conveys to others the feelings one has experienced, whereby people so infected by these feelings, also experience them. [L *ars, artis*]

art */ärt/ n* a human activity consisting in this, that one man consciously, by means of certain external signs, hands on to others feelings he has lived through and that other people are infected by those feelings and also experience them. [L *ars, artis*]

art */ärt/ n* a human construct. [L *ars, artis*]

art */ärt/ n* a human experience that often results in disagreements about its nature. [L *ars, artis*]

art */ärt/ n* a human expression open to interpretation. [L *ars, artis*]

art */ärt/ n (relig)* a human expression that reflects the nature of God that persists from within. [L *ars, artis*]

art */ärt/ n* a human product designed both to produce sensual pleasure through the visual or auditory modalities and to increase one's capacity to experience sensual pleasure through those modalities in response to an ever wider range of stimuli. [L *ars, artis*]

art */ärt/ n* a human propensity for goal directed play, with the intent of making objects special and supporting a culture's ceremonies. [L *ars, artis*]

art */ärt/ n* a human representation of something that exists in the world. [L *ars, artis*]

art */ärt/ n* a human vision. [L *ars, artis*]

art */ärt/ n (fig)* a jealous mistress. [L *ars, artis*]

art */ärt/ n* a joy of living and a hate for life. [L *ars, artis*]

art */ärt/ n (mus)* a joyful song, never recorded, played alone and only once. [L *ars, artis*]

art */ärt/ n* a judgment that exceeds numerical quantities and objective measures. [L *ars, artis*]

art */ärt/ n* a key to another person's life *or their universe.* [L *ars, artis*]

art */ärt/ n* a kind of communication; *so we could say that the first necessary condition for the 'happening' of the art is three simple things: a sender (someone who makes an announcement); an announcement; a recipient; what makes the art different from other kinds of communication? the recipient is unknown; the announcement is coded.* [L *ars, artis*]

art */ärt/ n* a kind of distillation and exploration of, or an abstraction from, the abilities we apply in everyday life to doing more immediately useful things; *like building roads and negotiating peace settlements.* [L *ars, artis*]

art */ärt/ n* a kind of language. [L *ars, artis*]

art */ärt/ n* a kind of making that adds something, whether positive or negative, that is new to the intellectual or emotional or formal repertoire of the community for which it is made. [L *ars, artis*]

art */ärt/ n* a kind of representation that is purposive in itself and, though without an end, nevertheless promotes the cultivation of the mental powers for sociable communication. [L *ars, artis*]

art */ärt/ n* a label that some people get really upset over. [L *ars, artis*]

art /*ärt*/ *n* a language. [L ***ars, artis***]

art /*ärt*/ *n* a language; *as P.A. Bastien, who is FAR more well-versed in this subject than I am, has already expressed* (P.A. Bastien, *ref not known*). [L ***ars, artis***]

art /*ärt*/ *n* a language; *or an exploration of unorthodox languages*. [L ***ars, artis***]

art /*ärt*/ *n* a language of emotion that can be communicated through various media; *books are an avenue, art is the way we package the content that travels through that avenue.* [L ***ars, artis***]

art /*ärt*/ *n* (*perh fig*) a large umbrella. [L ***ars, artis***]

art /*ärt*/ *n* (*pharmacol*) a legal drug; *arousing an atmospheric sensuality which adorns the recipient of the image*. [L ***ars, artis***]

art /*ärt*/ *n* a lie that makes us realise the truth. [L ***ars, artis***]

art /*ärt*/ *n* a lifestyle, not a job. [L ***ars, artis***]

art /*ärt*/ *n* a long con in the sense that the art community seems to have this crazy emperor's new clothes vibe to it; *case in point, the dead ladybug in a Styrofoam™ cup which sold at auction for nearly 30k back in 2001* (Styrofoam™, *closed-cell extruded polystyrene foam manufactured by The Dow® Chemical Company*). [L ***ars, artis***]

art /*ärt*/ *n (approx)* a loosely-based term for something that we do that tries to explain our inner human condition. [L ***ars, artis***]

art /*ärt*/ *n* a lot of fun; *and can be hilarious sometimes; I don't make it, but I like to look at it.* [L ***ars, artis***]

art /*ärt*/ *n (interrog)* a lot of people don't think art is physical, but why can't it be? *I mean, just look at the martial arts: they are a beautiful thing to watch in their own unique way (a bit like dance in fact), you can put so much emotion into the activity and it takes talent; I'm not talking about the fluttery flowery physical beauty either, because in the case of art, beauty is nearly synonymous with talent and emotion: if something takes enough emotion and enough passion and talent, it becomes beautiful (again, not necessarily physically).* [L ***ars, artis***]

art /*ärt*/ *n* a love. [L ***ars, artis***]

art /*ärt*/ *n (econ)* a lucrative and profitable field of economy; *and an important part of all of our lives, whether we are artistic ourselves or* *not.* [L *ars, artis*]

art */ärt/ n* a magic word which gives an object special significance. [L *ars, artis*]

art */ärt/ n* a majestic entity that will never get boring and will never be forgotten and replaced as an out of style thing; *due to its importance and popularity.* [L *ars, artis*]

art */ärt/ n* a making or doing of things that display form, beauty and unusual perception: *incl painting, sculpture, architecture, music, literature, drama, dance,* etc. [L *ars, artis*]

Art */ärt/ n (stat)* a male given name; *rare: 1 in 11111 males; popularity rank in the US: #710.* [Arthur]

art */ärt/ n* (*perh obs*) a manifestation of skill. [L *ars, artis*]

art */ärt/ n* a man-made representation of the world about us. [L *ars, artis*]

art */ärt/ n* a manual construct specifically designed as a token, a representation, a physical euphemism *etc etc.* [L *ars, artis*]

art */ärt/ n (econ)* a marker of wealth and social status. [L *ars, artis*]

art */ärt/ n (hist)* a marker of where we are today as a society; *artists are unpaid historians.* [L *ars, artis*]

art */ärt/ n* a marketing term. [L *ars, artis*]

art */ärt/ n (fig)* a marriage of eye and hand, that touches the soul. [L *ars, artis*]

art */ärt/ n* a matter of cultivating the soul and turning something perhaps 'normal' or mundane into something beautiful. [L *ars, artis*]

art */ärt/ n* a matter of hair-cut and neckties. [L *ars, artis*]

art */ärt/ n* a matter of opinion. [L *ars, artis*]

art */ärt/ n* a matter of opinion; *a person with a massive amount of tattoos may consider that art and someone else who sees those tattoos may as well, eg; we might also consider the ability to do something an 'art' as well perhaps such as the art of being able to hit a coin thrown into the air with a pistol; during the '60's many considered some of the designs on shirts art and then we can compare the art of say Whistler with the art of a Walt Disney animation so art really has to be up to the individual as to what he may consider art; some of* *what many consider graffiti on the side of a building in many cases can be considered art to someone else who sees that, including myself a time or two* (James Abbott McNeill Whistler *(1834–1903), Am painter;* Walter Elias Disney *(1901–66), Am business magnate, animator, cartoonist, producer, director, screenwriter, entrepreneur and voice actor).* [L *ars, artis*]

art */ärt/ n* a matter of taste; *and we will never concur on its purpose.* [L *ars, artis*]

art */ärt/ n (poss myth)* a meaning of communication with a transcendental power *ie* God. [L *ars, artis*]

art */ärt/ n* a meaningless concept. [L *ars, artis*]

art */ärt/ n* a means for exploring and appreciating formal elements for their own sake. [L *ars, artis*]

art */ärt/ n (econ)* a means for the maintenance of wealth in the hands of a few. [L *ars, artis*]

art */ärt/ n* a means of communicating or expressing emotions. [L *ars, artis*]

art */ärt/ n* a means of communication among people and a tool for enriching their knowledge of the world and of themselves. [L *ars, artis*]

art */ärt/ n* a means of communication; *and an important means of expressing any experience, or any aspect of the human condition.* [L *ars, artis*]

art */ärt/ n* a means of instilling in an individual a specific system of values; *and also provides great aesthetic enjoyment.* [L *ars, artis*]

art */ärt/ n (m)* a means of the integral social upbringing of an individual, assisting in his emotional and intellectual development. [L *ars, artis*]

art */ärt/ n (m)* a means of union among men, joining them together in the same feelings; *and indispensable for the life and progress toward well-being of individuals and of humanity.* [L *ars, artis*]

art */ärt/ n* a means to control one's real or fantasy universe through physical manipulation. [L *ars, artis*]

art */ärt/ n* a means to express the imagination in non-grammatical ways that are not tied to the formality of spoken or written language. [L *ars, artis*]

art */ärt/ n* a measure of high quality and high value. [L *ars, artis*]

art */ärt/ n* a medium which invokes emotion deliberately and/or meticulously. [L *ars, artis*]

art */ärt/ n* a medium of communication that is required in society. [L *ars, artis*]

art */ärt/ n* a medium of expression where the individual and culture come together. [L *ars, artis*]

art */ärt/ n* a medium of thought. [L *ars, artis*]

art */ärt/ n* a medium to reflect on despair. [L *ars, artis*]

art */ärt/ n* a mental concept; *the definition is subject to evolutional change, but at any given time there are: 1 standard definitions as are recorded by those who produce dictionaries; and there are: 2 non-standard definitions as produced by people with poorly based opinions that cannot survive using standard definitions*. [L *ars, artis*]

art */ärt/ n* a message conveyed through a medium with the maximum felicity afforded by said medium. [L *ars, artis*]

art */ärt/ n* a metamorphosis of the most common, ordinary things into something witty and worthwhile; *without the protracted toil so characteristic of nonmodern works.* [L *ars, artis*]

art */ärt/ n* a method of doing well some special work – often contradistinguished from science or speculative principles, *the art of building or engraving, the art of war, the art of navigation.* [L *ars, artis*]

art */ärt/ n* a method or knack of doing a thing. [L *ars, artis*]

art */ärt/ n* a million things; *including a painting on a wall and three minutes of sound; it's also the way a can of paint falls from a ladder or a six-year-old's drawing on the fridge or a photo in a museum.* [L *ars, artis*]

art */ärt/ n* (*meteorol*) a mirage. [L *ars, artis*]

art */ärt/ n* a mirror. [L *ars, artis*]

art */ärt/ n* a mirror; *one can create, or merely look at it and see their own thoughts hidden within; not only a mirror, but a very, very dirty mirror; it only lets you see a small portion of what it is and who you are, everything else we must piece together ourselves.* [L *ars, artis*]

art */ärt/ n (fig)* a mirror flipped by the breeze. [L *ars, artis*]

art */ärt/ n* a mirror of ourselves. [L *ars, artis*]

art */ärt/ n* a mirror reflecting reality as the artist sees it or wants it to be. [L *ars, artis*]

art */ärt/ n* a mirrored appearance of the world, lacking true reality; *while almost paradoxically retaining the ability to encourage irrational impulses in humans.* [L *ars, artis*]

art */ärt/ n* a mission, that of creating forms, sounds and movements which have not existed. [L *ars, artis*]

art */ärt/ n* a mix between a cognitive experience, as well as the aesthetic experience; *and sometimes solely one or the other.* [L *ars, artis*]

art */ärt/ n* a mixture of colour and design. [L *ars, artis*]

art */ärt/ n* a mode of practical and intellectual assimilation of reality; *which differs from purely intellectual assimilation (typical of theoretical knowledge) and from purely material assimilation.* [L *ars, artis*]

art */ärt/ n* a model of life created by man. [L *ars, artis*]

art */ärt/ n* a moral message we must capture. [L *ars, artis*]

art */ärt/ n* a most personal and subjective pursuit. [L *ars, artis*]

art */ärt/ n* a movement or rearrangement of physical qualities that stimulate the strength of one's mind through feeling and passion. [L *ars, artis*]

art */ärt/ n* a movement within. [L *ars, artis*]

art */ärt/ n* a mural painted on several walls of the gallery, erased at the end of the exhibition. [L *ars, artis*]

art */ärt/ n* a naked pirouette alone in the forest. [L *ars, artis*]

art */ärt/ n* a name not only for the power of doing something, but for the exercise of the power; *and not only for the exercise of the power, but for the rules according to which it is exercised; and not only for the rules, but for the result; painting, eg, is an art and the word connotes not only the power to paint, but the act of painting; and not only the act, but the laws for performing the act rightly; and not only all these, but the material consequences of the act or the thing painted; so of agriculture, navigation and the rest.* [L *ars, artis*]

art */ärt/ n* a natural gift. [L *ars, artis*]

art */ärt/ n* a necessary function in our world. [L *ars, artis*]

art */ärt/ n* a necessary human activity; *I need it when I am disconnected.* [L *ars, artis*]

art */ärt/ n* a need and not a want. [L *ars, artis*]

art */ärt/ n (neurol)* a neurally mediated activity by which the artist paints in a way that stimulates our central nervous system. [L *ars, artis*]

art */ärt/ n (perh mus)* a new kind of instrument, an instrument for modifying consciousness and organizing new modes of sensibility. [L *ars, artis*]

art */ärt/ n (inf)* a new way of communication; *it is never about exhibiting in museums or about hanging it on the wall; art should live in the heart of the people; ordinary people should have the same ability to understand art as anybody else; I don't think art is elite or mysterious; I don't think anybody can separate art from politics; the intention to separate art from politics is itself a very political intention; in China they treat art as some form of decoration, a self-indulgence; it is pretending to be art; it looks like art; it sells like art; but it is really a piece of shit.* [L *ars, artis*]

art */ärt/ n* a non-linguistic emotional communication; *it is a thing created to elicit an emotional response within the audience.* [L *ars, artis*]

art */ärt/ n* a non-scientific branch of learning. [L *ars, artis*]

art */ärt/ n* a one way street; *if a viewer interprets meaning from something that wasn't the artist's intent, it is only art in an instance: quantum art, if you must.* [L *ars, artis*]

Art */ärt/ n (appar joc)* a pain in the arse. [prob *Arthur*]

art */ärt/ n (interrog)* a painting done with such skill that it borders on photorealism? [L *ars, artis*]

art */ärt/ n* a painting, drawing, print or sculpture, existing in a single copy, in a limited edition of 200 copies or fewer that are signed and consecutively numbered by the author. [L *ars, artis*]

art */ärt/ n* a part of all aspects of life. [L *ars, artis*]

art */ärt/ n* a part of life. [L *ars, artis*]

art */ärt/ n* a part of our lives in

many ways; *and it remains an important ingredient to a complete and satisfying existence.* [L *ars, artis*]

art /*ärt*/ *n* a part of the process of communication. [L *ars, artis*]

art /*ärt*/ *n* a particular way of perceiving the world in both physical and spiritual terms. [L *ars, artis*]

art /*ärt*/ *n* a passive medium; *you sit there and look at/listen to somebody else's imaginings.* [L *ars, artis*]

art /*ärt*/ *n* a person's attempt to express an emotion or idea in a creative way; *typically using a non-analytical part of their mind.* [L *ars, artis*]

art /*ärt*/ *n* a person's ideas and feelings expressed through the elements and principles of design. [L *ars, artis*]

art /*ärt*/ *n* a person's intangible emotions and thoughts expressed or projected into a physical product. [L *ars, artis*]

art /*ärt*/ *n* a person's interpretation of the world and how they see it; *it can also reflect a wide range of emotions.* [L *ars, artis*]

art /*ärt*/ *n* a person's expression; *yet, my favourite kind of art strikes emotion in the onlooker; better still... makes the viewer think of something they never thought of before.* [L *ars, artis*]

art /*ärt*/ *n* a personal act of courage, something one human does that creates change in another. [L *ars, artis*]

art /*ärt*/ *n* a personal experience either expressed or impressed; *and when art is great the artist has touched on certain universal emotive truths that many people understand and appreciate.* [L *ars, artis*]

art /*ärt*/ *n* a personal expression. [L *ars, artis*]

art /*ärt*/ *n* a personal expression of emotion by way of symbolic representation. [L *ars, artis*]

art /*ärt*/ *n* a personal expression of the collective spirit. [L *ars, artis*]

art /*ärt*/ *n* a personal gift that changes the recipient; *the medium doesn't matter, the intent does.* [L *ars, artis*]

art /*ärt*/ *n* a phenomenon of indefinite duration and variable physical properties that expresses and embodies ideas, thoughts and/or emotions about life and existence. [L *ars, artis*]

art */ärt/ n* a phenomenon recognized solely in our unique capacity to view beauty; *and art is, by way of that recognition, a qualitative term to describe the bundling of various things that form an object of beauty.* [L *ars, artis*]

art */ärt/ n (interrog, photog)* a photograph in a tasteful frame, possibly in black-and-white, or at the very least some sort of sepia shade, making it look like it was taken in cowboy times? [L *ars, artis*]

art */ärt/ n* a physical thing which appeals directly to the senses and the emotions, created by someone with technical skill and emotional sensitivity and an ability to communicate this through their work; *the art may or may not contain a message, but art is not a message.* [L *ars, artis*]

art */ärt/ n* a picture. [L *ars, artis*]

art */ärt/ n* a picture of stairways and strange creatures. [L *ars, artis*]

art */ärt/ n (poss fig)* a picture of time. [L *ars, artis*]

art */ärt/ n* a picture or a sculpture; *it does not have to be beautiful, it can be anything you want.* [L *ars, artis*]

art */ärt/ n* a piece – both of form and with content – that aims to incite a reaction from its audience. [L *ars, artis*]

art */ärt/ n (pers)* a piece of chewing gum on my shoe is a piece of art if I say so. [L *ars, artis*]

art */ärt/ n* a piece of work completed by an artist that portrays a mood, feeling or tells a story. [L *ars, artis*]

art */ärt/ n* a piece of work that successfully inspires emotions and feelings in its chosen audience. [L *ars, artis*]

art */ärt/ n* a piece or work of some kind that represents *(perh symbolically)* an emotional or social-political point. [L *ars, artis*]

art */ärt/ n (interrog)* a pile of wrapped candies in the corner to represent a slow death from AIDS; *the disappearance of the candy pile, piece by piece, was supposed to represent his friend's body slowly falling apart, ultimately becoming nothing; it was visually stimulating and emotionally evocative, but didn't require much technical skill; is something like this art?* (AIDS, *acquired immunodeficiency syndrome; perh ref* Felix Gonzalez-Torres

(1957–96), Am artist). [L *ars, artis*]

art */ärt/ n* a play that makes us cry. [L *ars, artis*]

art */ärt/ n* a political means of productive relationships to achieve world harmony. [L *ars, artis*]

art */ärt/ n* a poor child born of poor parents. [L *ars, artis*]

art */ärt/ n* a portal into another world that was simultaneously soothing and scary. [L *ars, artis*]

art */ärt/ n* a portal to realities that can't be expressed any other way. [L *ars, artis*]

art */ärt/ n* a pose or gesture by a dancer, that makes one uncomfortable. [L *ars, artis*]

art */ärt/ n* a potential didactic tool for society. [L *ars, artis*]

art */ärt/ n* a powerful medium to make a social statement. [L *ars, artis*]

art */ärt/ n (relig)* a prayer; *there is nothing more discouraging for me than to hear a person who may be looking at a piece of art, particularly if it is something that I am working on and saying, 'Well, I don't know much about art so I cannot say anything about what you are doing.'* [L *ars, artis*]

art */ärt/ n* a privilege of the museums and the rich. [L *ars, artis*]

art */ärt/ n* a process of conscious transmittance of an artist's emotions to a certain audience. [L *ars, artis*]

art */ärt/ n* a process that is so personal that it becomes original. [L *ars, artis*]

art */ärt/ n* a process that occurs when a quality of emotion not experienced in our normal life is intentionally communicated to another through the medium of a work of art. [L *ars, artis*]

art */ärt/ n* a product created. [L *ars, artis*]

art */ärt/ n* a product of human creativity. [L *ars, artis*]

art */ärt/ n* a product of the human creative output, that exists in the same socio-economic limits as all other forms of human action; *while it can often be perceptive and far-fetched it still exists in the material restraints of the human existence.* [L *ars, artis*]

art */ärt/ n* a product or process of deliberately arranging symbolic elements in a way that influences and affects the senses, emotions and intellect. [L *ars, artis*]

art /ärt/ *n* a psychological focus or an emotional disposition that finds particular landing places in things that are only momentarily stable. [L *ars, artis*]

art /ärt/ *n* a purposeless mess; *without which life is a purposeless mess.* [L *ars, artis*]

art /ärt/ *n* a quality, not a medium; *not all video games are art, just like not all paintings are art.* [L *ars, artis*]

art /ärt/ *n* a quasi-public good; *and as such it will always have some inefficiency in its provision.* [L *ars, artis*]

art /ärt/ *n* a racket. [L *ars, artis*]

art /ärt/ *n* a range of forms, symbols and ideas with meanings that are malleable. [L *ars, artis*]

Art /ärt/ *n (derog, vulg)* a ratfucking bastard who owes me $800. [Arthur]

Art /ärt/ *n (inf, interrog)* a rather gorgeous male specimen leant forward to reveal his bronzed and toned builder's bum; is that art? *Just in case it is, we took a few pictures on our phone.* [Arthur]

art /ärt/ *n* a recreation of reality according to one's values; *it is not a creation out of a void, but a* re-creation, *a selective rearrangement of the elements of reality, guided by the artist's view of existence.* [L *ars, artis*]

art /ärt/ *n* a recreation of reality according to the artist's metaphysical value-judgments. [L *ars, artis*]

art /ärt/ *n* a recreation of reality according to the artist's values; *it is not a creation out of a void, but a* re-creation, *a selective rearrangement of the elements of reality, guided by the artist's view of existence.* [L *ars, artis*]

art /ärt/ *n* a reaction that I can't entirely explain. [L *ars, artis*]

art /ärt/ *n* a reaction to an action that in turn creates a fascinating reaction to a reactive force or object *(perh ref* Philosophiæ Naturalis Principia Mathematica *(1687) by Sir Isaac Newton PRS MP)*. [L *ars, artis*]

art /ärt/ *n* a real melting pot; *and I don't see why digital art can't be considered alongside traditional painting.* [L *ars, artis*]

ART /ärt/ *n (comput)* a real-time functional language; *it timestamps each data value when it was created.* [*Applicative Real-Time Programming*]

art */ärt/ n* a reality, not a definition; *inasmuch as it approaches a reality, it approaches perfection and inasmuch as it approaches a mere definition, it is imperfect and untrue.* [L *ars, artis*]

art */ärt/ n* a really broad category. [L *ars, artis*]

art */ärt/ n* a really powerful way of moving people; *and sometimes it takes something like art to really understand what mental illness is like.* [L *ars, artis*]

art */ärt/ n* a reflection of life and all it encompasses. [L *ars, artis*]

art */ärt/ n* a reflection of our own experiences in the modern world. [L *ars, artis*]

art */ärt/ n (relig)* a reflection of the splendour of God. [L *ars, artis*]

art */ärt/ n* a reflection of the subconscious, both individually and societally; *what you see is really what you get.* [L *ars, artis*]

art */ärt/ n* a reflection of truth according to the eye of the beholder. [L *ars, artis*]

art */ärt/ n* a reflection of what dwells deep in the realms of our imagination/psyche. [L *ars, artis*]

art */ärt/ n* a reflection on our own humanity, in every age, at every epoch. [L *ars, artis*]

art */ärt/ n* a reflective response. [L *ars, artis*]

art */ärt/ n* a reflective, responsive 'statement' manifesting focused observations about humankind and the world as seen through the eyes, experience and existential world/life view of the art maker. [L *ars, artis*]

art */ärt/ n (relig)* a relationship of persons; *and if there does not occur motions of love between the artist and the viewer and the art and God, then there is no beauty and therefore no art.* [L *ars, artis*]

art */ärt/ n* a relationship. [L *ars, artis*]

art */ärt/ n* a relative concept, defined, derived and conceived in the minds of each and every individual. [L *ars, artis*]

art */ärt/ n* a relative form of the absolute. [L *ars, artis*]

art */ärt/ n (prob joc)* a replacement for football. [L *ars, artis*]

art */ärt/ n* a representation of the creator; *it's one thing that all art throughout history has in common; whether it's the message behind it,* *the skills or just merely the style itself, there is always something about it that can represent the creator.* [L ***ars, artis***]

art */ärt/ n* a representation of us. [L ***ars, artis***]

art */ärt/ n* a residual word; *if an object, stripped of all functionality and necessity, still has some value left, the leftover is art.* [L ***ars, artis***]

art */ärt/ n* a revolt against fate. [L ***ars, artis***]

art */ärt/ n (prob fig)* a sandcastle, erected on a lonely beach, washed away by the tide. [L ***ars, artis***]

art */ärt/ n* a science with more than seven variables. [L ***ars, artis***]

art */ärt/ n (interrog)* a sculpture? *or a toilet masquerading as a sculpture? or a painting of a photograph of a toilet masquerading as a sculpture?* [L ***ars, artis***]

art */ärt/ n* a sculpture in the hands of the right person, an instrument in the hands of a novice or a lathe in the hands of a craftsman. [L ***ars, artis***]

art */ärt/ n* a search for a road and a search for freedom. [L ***ars, artis***]

art */ärt/ n* a search for form to effectively represent the abstract. [L ***ars, artis***]

art */ärt/ n* a selective re-creation of reality according to an artist's fundamental values. [L ***ars, artis***]

art */ärt/ n* a selective re-creation of reality according to an artist's fundamental view of life; *which includes his deepest values*. [L ***ars, artis***]

art */ärt/ n* a selective re-creation of reality according to an artist's metaphysical value-judgments. [L ***ars, artis***]

art */ärt/ n* a selective re-creation of reality according to the fundamental values of the artist. [L ***ars, artis***]

art */ärt/ n* a self-defining, broad-spectrum cultural force. [L ***ars, artis***]

art */ärt/ n* a self-conscious commentary on the philosophy of art. [L ***ars, artis***]

art */ärt/ n* a self-imposed interaction; *undaunted by the physical forces that wish to hinder a thought.* [L ***ars, artis***]

art */ärt/ n* a self-revelation or self-expression of the artist. [L ***ars, artis***]

art */ärt/ n* a self-rewarding activity. [L *ars, artis*]

art */ärt/ n (imit)* a sensation, we all do agree/ which earns proclamations of greatest beau-tee!/ yet martyr by silence each innocent saint/ who claims to see art where we say it ain't *(appar imit* Fr Gassalasca Jape, SJ*)*. [L *ars, artis*]

art */ärt/ n (m)* a sense of mankind; *what he perceives as 'art' is art.* [L *ars, artis*]

art */ärt/ n (m)* a sensibility of mankind; *what he perceives as 'art' is art.* [L *ars, artis*]

art */ärt/ n* a series of feelings and emotions one puts down on paper. [L *ars, artis*]

art */ärt/ n (perh joc)* a serious disease. [L *ars, artis*]

art */ärt/ n* a set of artefacts or images with symbolic meanings as a means of communication. [L *ars, artis*]

art */ärt/ n* a set of cultural and aesthetic practices that have many categories and cultural functions. [L *ars, artis*]

art */ärt/ n* a set of tools able to fix, tune, shape that broken machine human life is. [L *ars, artis*]

art */ärt/ n* a shared conversation. [L *ars, artis*]

art */ärt/ n* a shared emotion. [L *ars, artis*]

art */ärt/ n* a shifting, formless thing. [L *ars, artis*]

art */ärt/ n* a shocking display that leaves one feeling sick. [L *ars, artis*]

art */ärt/ n* a sight or sound that makes a person have provocative feelings or thoughts. [L *ars, artis*]

art */ärt/ n* a sign. [L *ars, artis*]

art */ärt/ n (derog)* a silly word made up by pompous people who want to make their hobbies sound more important than they actually are. [L *ars, artis*]

Art */ärt/ n (mus)* a singer – used to have a little duo with his buddy, Paul *(appar ref* Arthur Ira Garfunkel *(1941–), Grammy®-award winning Am singer, poet and Golden Globe®-nominated actor; and* Paul Frederic Simon *(1941–), Am musician and singer-songwriter)*. [Arthur]

art */ärt/ n* a single-minded attempt to render the highest kind of justice to the visible universe.

[L *ars, artis*]

art */ärt/ n* a sixth sense to us artists that allows us to connect with the world and even help humanity see a world of beauty. [L *ars, artis*]

art */ärt/ n* a skilful plan. [L *ars, artis*]

art */ärt/ n* a skilfully created form of expression of anything. [L *ars, artis*]

art */ärt/ n* a skill: *the art of conversation.* [L *ars, artis*]

art */ärt/ n* a skill applied to music, painting, poetry *etc.* [L *ars, artis*]

art */ärt/ n* a skill at doing a specified thing; *typically one acquired through practice.* [L *ars, artis*]

art */ärt/ n* a skill being used to express the artist's creativity; *or to engage the audience's aesthetic sensibilities; or to draw the audience towards consideration of the finer things.* [L *ars, artis*]

art */ärt/ n* a skill exercised for pure fancy or pleasure; *or for adding an element of fancy or pleasure to an element of utility.* [L *ars, artis*]

art */ärt/ n* a skill of designing something artistic in a way you can express yourself and the way you feel about art; *also, it is made the way you want it to look and there isn't anyone who's art isn't nice because it's their own.* [L *ars, artis*]

art */ärt/ n* a skill or ability. [L *ars, artis*]

art */ärt/ n* a skill or special ability. [L *ars, artis*]

art */ärt/ n* a skill that is attained by study, practice or observation: *the art of negotiation.* [L *ars, artis*]

art */ärt/ n* a skilled profession or trade, craft or branch of activity. [L *ars, artis*]

art */ärt/ n* a slippery, changing thing. [L *ars, artis*]

art */ärt/ n* a social construct. [L *ars, artis*]

art */ärt/ n* a social game played by professionals *(artists, critics, gallerists, curators* etc*)* and the public; *one that keeps changing as new rules emerge from interactions shaped by a previous version of the rules (including testing and breaking them).* [L *ars, artis*]

art */ärt/ n* a social luxury; *because most people don't have money or the time to try and create art and instead have to work for a living; but there are exceptions like the starving artists* *who seem destined to make art regardless of the personal cost to their own life; then we are really talking about art in terms of the natural-born geniuses.* [L *ars, artis*]

art */ärt/ n* a social matter that changes according to social changes; *and is therefore indefinable.* [L *ars, artis*]

art */ärt/ n (sociol)* a sociological construct; *and what is art is decided by the artists.* [L *ars, artis*]

art */ärt/ n (interrog)* a sock puppet? *a painting done by an elephant? a sculpture of an elephant with a sock puppet on its trunk, like the one you picked up at that yard sale only better because it's mounted on a marble plinth in a museum with a vaguely French name?* [L *ars, artis*]

art */ärt/ n (pharmacol)* a Soma of our conscience. [L *ars, artis*]

art */ärt/ n (mus)* a song. [L *ars, artis*]

art */ärt/ n (phys)* a sort of Heisenberg consideration, whereby it is possible to know either if something is art or not, or whether you like it or not, but not to know both at the same time *(*Werner Karl Heisenberg *(1901–76), Ger theoretical phys).* [L *ars, artis*]

art */ärt/ n* a soul put up on a pedestal. [L *ars, artis*]

art */ärt/ n (neg)* a soup can is not art; a toilet is not art; a pipe is not art; *these are things that exist for the primary purpose of holding soup, being urinated in, or being smoked (prob ref* Campbell's Soup Cans*, sometimes referred to as* 32 Campbell's Soup Cans*, a work of art produced in 1962 by Andy Warhol;* Fountain *(1917), a work by Marcel Duchamp (1887–1968);* The Treachery of Images *(Fr: La trahison des images), (1928–29), sometimes translated as* The Treason of Images*, a painting by Belgian surrealist painter René Magritte).* [L *ars, artis*]

art */ärt/ n* a source of joy and delight. [L *ars, artis*]

art */ärt/ n* a space where contemplation is given life to. [L *ars, artis*]

art */ärt/ n* a special artistic and figurative system of symbols, *or a specific artistic language (eg, the language of music, choreography, painting, architecture, or cinematography),* called upon to instil the artistic message that it contains in man's consciousness. [L *ars, artis*]

art */ärt/ n* a special faculty of the human mind; *to be classified with religion and science.* [L *ars, artis*]

art */ärt/ n (theol)* a special kind of game or prayer. [L *ars, artis*]

art */ärt/ n* a specific means of apprehending reality. [L *ars, artis*]

art */ärt/ n* a specific skill you've learned, *like the art of baking a delicious pie.* [L *ars, artis*]

art */ärt/ n (poss theol)* a spiritual reflection which is passing through the gate of perception. [L *ars, artis*]

art */ärt/ n* a spokesperson of the emotion of the artist. [L *ars, artis*]

art */ärt/ n* a spray-painted mural done by a kid. [L *ars, artis*]

art */ärt/ n* a statement; *literally every work that has ever been considered art throughout the entire history of humanity can be said to be a statement; it's the most commonly accepted academic definition of the term*. [L *ars, artis*]

art */ärt/ n* a story of all the best and most beautiful things in life and the most horrific and darkest parts of the world. [L *ars, artis*]

art */ärt/ n* a story of struggle of thought, actions and words. [L *ars, artis*]

art */ärt/ n* a stress reliever. [L *ars, artis*]

art */ärt/ n* a struggle; *the comfortable artist is no artist at all.* [L *ars, artis*]

art */ärt/ n* a struggle with the struggle erased. [L *ars, artis*]

art */ärt/ n* a stupid concept; *there is no consensus about what it means and the label is so often used to add false gravitas to banality.* [L *ars, artis*]

art */ärt/ n* a style of your own presentation. [L *ars, artis*]

art */ärt/ n* a subjective experience in the audience. [L *ars, artis*]

art */ärt/ n (theol)* a submission; *when an artist begins to work, they are not creating anything that could not have existed without their doing (*ie *creating something from nothing and therefore holding the eternal power of the Divine), rather they are taking a plunge into the imaginative realm for no reason other than they know it's a plunge to which they are being called; they don't know why they're being called, or (in most cases) what it is even that's calling them,* *they just know that they are and within their art they seek to explain something they could never explain otherwise.* [L *ars, artis*]

art */ärt/ n (philos)* a sufficient but not necessary condition for the identification of a candidate as a work of art is the construction of a true historical narrative according to which the candidate was created by an artist in an artistic context with a recognized and live artistic motivation and as a result of being so created, it resembles at least one acknowledged artwork. [L *ars, artis*]

art */ärt/ n* a superior skill that you can learn by study and practice and observation: *the art of conversation.* [L *ars, artis*]

Art */ärt/ n (stat)* a surname; *v rare; popularity rank in the US: #58705.* [origin unknown]

art */ärt/ n* a symbol of the free ranging spirit of our personalities. [L *ars, artis*]

art */ärt/ n* a symbolic representation of someone's ideas, emotions, or thoughts in general, intended to convey this, *or evoke a similar state in another.* [L *ars, artis*]

art */ärt/ n* a symbolical and harmonic superlanguage. [L *ars, artis*]

art */ärt/ n (mus)* a symphony. [L *ars, artis*]

art */ärt/ n (psychol)* a symptom of madness. [L *ars, artis*]

art */ärt/ n* a system of principles and rules for attaining a desired end. [L *ars, artis*]

art */ärt/ n* a system of rules serving to facilitate the performance of certain actions. [L *ars, artis*]

art */ärt/ n* a talent pursuing your ability of creation. [L *ars, artis*]

art */ärt/ n (vulg, perh joc)* a tampon in a teacup. [L *ars, artis*]

art */ärt/ n (prob fig)* a target looking for an arrow. [L *ars, artis*]

art */ärt/ n (philos)* a tautology. [L *ars, artis*]

art */ärt/ n (philos)* a tautology in that it is a presentation of the artist's intention; ie *he is saying that that particular work of art is art, which means, is a definition of art; thus, that it is art is true* a priori. [L *ars, artis*]

art */ärt/ n* a tearful poem, once written then burned by the poet. [L *ars, artis*]

art */ärt/ n* a technical skill rather than a manner of thinking. [L *ars, artis*]

art */ärt/ n* a tendency to unite dissimilar things. [L *ars, artis*]

art */ärt/ n* a term only non-artists feel they have to define. [L *ars, artis*]

art */ärt/ n* a term that describes a diverse range of human activities and the products of those activities, but is most often understood to refer to painting, film, photography, sculpture and other visual media; *music, theatre, dance, literature and interactive media are included in a broader definition of art or the arts.* [L *ars, artis*]

art */ärt/ n* a theoretical construct. [L *ars, artis*]

art */ärt/ n (psychol)* a therapy. [L *ars, artis*]

art */ärt/ n (psychol, pers)* a therapy; *since I'm neurotic and have no money to see a psychologist.* [L *ars, artis*]

art */ärt/ n (obs)* a thing of beauty. [L *ars, artis*]

art */ärt/ n* a thing or action done by a human being which changes the perceptions of the observer. [L *ars, artis*]

art */ärt/ n* a thing or experience created by a human being with some intention (not necessarily the sole intention) that it be experienced by some real or hypothetical other human being as beautiful; *and beautiful is, of course, a lot harder to define!* [L *ars, artis*]

art */ärt/ n* a thing that has been seriously intended for regard in any way pre-existing or prior artworks are or were correctly regarded. [L *ars, artis*]

art */ärt/ n* a thing understood not by the mind, but the heart. [L *ars, artis*]

art */ärt/ n* a thing which transcends its materiality. [L *ars, artis*]

art */ärt/ n* a thought-experiment; *and so I personally don't believe there are any rules when it comes to the act of conveying thoughts.* [L *ars, artis*]

art */ärt/ n* a thought-form that comes into being with the power to communicate through time. [L *ars, artis*]

art */ärt/ n* a three-letter word for disappointing your parents. [L *ars, artis*]

art */ärt/ n* a throwing out *(as in out there, into the space beyond our only* *selves)* of gratitude/announcement/recognition from the we within to the rest of what is because we are moved SO greatly we need to express – give it wings, movement from containment inside to its own glorious life. [L *ars, artis*]

art */ärt/ n* a tiny part of your soul that aims to express a mixture of every bit of person you are. [L *ars, artis*]

art */ärt/ n (interrog)* a toddler threw up some smarties that, if you squinted, looked a bit like Mickey Mouse™; is that art? (Michael Mouse *(1928–), official mascot of The Walt Disney™ Company).* [L *ars, artis*]

art */ärt/ n* a tool for examining, critiquing and generating change. [L *ars, artis*]

art */ärt/ n* a tool that is used to communicate emotion and feeling. [L *ars, artis*]

art */ärt/ n* a traditional statement of certain heroic and religious truths, *passed on from age to age, modified by individual genius, but never abandoned.* [L *ars, artis*]

art */ärt/ n (inf)* a train of thought wreck. [L *ars, artis*]

art */ärt/ n* a translation of stories and emotions. [L *ars, artis*]

art */ärt/ n* a tricky thing. [L *ars, artis*]

art */ärt/ n* a true idea plucked from the chaos of the mind. [L *ars, artis*]

art */ärt/ n* a true representation of your spirit. [L *ars, artis*]

art */ärt/ n* a tryst; *for in the joy of it maker and beholder meet.* [L *ars, artis*]

art */ärt/ n (inf)* a TYPE of expression; *it isn't a compliment you give to shit you enjoy!* [L *ars, artis*]

art */ärt/ n (prob photog)* a unique creative enterprise with a cadre of rules assembled, known or ascribed to by the shooter alone. [L *ars, artis*]

art */ärt/ n* a unique expression of oneself. [L *ars, artis*]

art */ärt/ n* a unique, well-designed creation. [L *ars, artis*]

art */ärt/ n* a uniquely human endeavour; *and act of genius.* [L *ars, artis*]

art */ärt/ n* a universal form of communication that touches on some sensibility in mankind. [L *ars, artis*]

art */ärt/ n* a universe we can participate in. [L *ars, artis*]

art */ärt/ n* a vehicle for altering perceptions. [L *ars, artis*]

art */ärt/ n* a vehicle for any expression. [L *ars, artis*]

art */ärt/ n* a vehicle for expressing ourselves. [L *ars, artis*]

art */ärt/ n* a vehicle for the expression or communication of emotions and ideas. [L *ars, artis*]

art */ärt/ n* a version of reality that means something to the artist and can only be experienced by others through their art. [L *ars, artis*]

art */ärt/ n* a very big moment in my heart. [L *ars, artis*]

art */ärt/ n* a very bizarre place to hide. [L *ars, artis*]

art */ärt/ n* a very fuzzy line; *and yet I feel fine placing some items within that category and some outside it.* [L *ars, artis*]

art */ärt/ n* a very personal thing. [L *ars, artis*]

art */ärt/ n* a very simple process: *half of it is based on honesty and the other half is just technique.* [L *ars, artis*]

Art */ärt/ n (appar joc)* a very small, off-duty Aust traffic cop; *or a banana.* [Arthur]

art */ärt/ n* a very useful word. [L *ars, artis*]

art */ärt/ n* a very vague word since it has so many different meanings; *however, most of the meanings go beyond the point that art is just the visual outcome of an artist's work; they go on a more inner emotional scale, as I like to say* 'in art you can release your emotions out in a way that would be impossible with anything other than art'; *people actually bond to what art you have created and I find that amazingly awesome.* [L *ars, artis*]

art */ärt/ n* a view of a landscape in the form of a painting. [L *ars, artis*]

art */ärt/ n* a visceral feeling. [L *ars, artis*]

art */ärt/ n* a vision of Truth; *opening a path that leads to recognition.* [L *ars, artis*]

art */ärt/ n* a visual art considered to have been created primarily for aesthetic purposes and judged for its beauty and meaningfulness, *specifically, painting,* *sculpture, drawing, watercolour, graphics and architecture.* [L *ars, artis*]

art /*ärt*/ *n* a visual documentation of the expression of ourselves historically, spiritually, mentally and physically; *the fulfilment is priceless for the creator who obsessively unravels the idea that haunts them.* [L *ars, artis*]

art /*ärt*/ *n* a visual expression of emotions and thoughts. [L *ars, artis*]

art /*ärt*/ *n* a visual expression, produced by humans, that represents or signifies emotion(s) and/or (an) idea(s). [L *ars, artis*]

art /*ärt*/ *n* a visual form of communication that touches on some universal sensibility in mankind. [L *ars, artis*]

art /*ärt*/ *n* a visual language that creates dialogue informing an intimate personal response of emotions. [L *ars, artis*]

art /*ärt*/ *n* a visual medium for self-expression. [L *ars, artis*]

art /*ärt*/ *n* a visual object or experience consciously created through an expression of skill, imagination and purpose. [L *ars, artis*]

art /*ärt*/ *n* a visual object or experience consciously created through an expression of skill or imagination; *the term art encompasses diverse media such as painting, sculpture, printmaking, drawing, decorative arts, photography and installation; the various visual arts exist within a continuum that ranges from purely aesthetic purposes at one end to purely utilitarian purposes at the other; this should by no means be taken as a rigid scheme, however, particularly in cultures in which everyday objects are painstakingly constructed and imbued with meaning.* [L *ars, artis*]

art /*ärt*/ *n* a visual provocation of emotion. [L *ars, artis*]

art /*ärt*/ *n* a visual puzzle that points to something else rather than actually participating in that Something Else. [L *ars, artis*]

art /*ärt*/ *n* a visual sign for a poetic or abstract thought. [L *ars, artis*]

art /*ärt*/ *n* a visualized form of expression; *therefore whether political, humorous, touching or creative, it is aiming to express something to another, with the existence of the 'another (=audience)' always in mind.* [L *ars, artis*]

art */ärt/ n* a visualized proposition that is complete in its meaning and intention. [L *ars, artis*]

art */ärt/ n* a vocation; *becoming an artist is a bit like entering the priesthood: it entails sacrifice for a calling that is irresistible; the true artist does not embark on his/her path with the prime motive of making money, or even making a living; their prime motive is to make art; if, in the process of producing work, they become wealthy it is by default rather than by design; Francis Bacon, Damien Hirst, J.K. Rowling and Julian Schnabel have all made fortunes through their artistic endeavours in their own lifetimes (***Francis Bacon*** *(1909–1992), Irish-born Brit fig painter;* **Damien Steven Hirst** *(1965–), Eng artist, entrepreneur and art collector;* **Joanne ('Jo', 'J.K.') Rowling, OBE FRSL** *(1965–), Brit novelist;* **Julian Schnabel** *(1951–), Am artist and filmmaker).* [L *ars, artis*]

art */ärt/ n (poss milit)* a war of attrition. [L *ars, artis*]

art */ärt/ n* a waste of space, resources and money; *nothing more.* [L *ars, artis*]

art */ärt/ n* a waste of time. [L *ars, artis*]

art */ärt/ n* a way. [L *ars, artis*]

art */ärt/ n* a way for a person to try and express how they feel to other people; *most of the time, it doesn't work because only few people will understand that person; eg their soulmates.* [L *ars, artis*]

art */ärt/ n* a way for me to vent and let out all the weirdness/crazy. [L *ars, artis*]

art */ärt/ n* a way for people to put something out there that cannot be said in words; *or in the case of poetry and writing, cannot be stated matter-of-factually.* [L *ars, artis*]

art */ärt/ n* a way for people to show their feelings and desires. [L *ars, artis*]

art */ärt/ n (theol)* a way of a communication and owns a realm unseen yet to be revealed in the hands made by God and for God. [L *ars, artis*]

art */ärt/ n* a way of achieving a pleasurable response. [L *ars, artis*]

art */ärt/ n* a way of communicating ideas to an audience in a way that the audience finds engaging. [L *ars, artis*]

art */ärt/ n* a way of communication that can do better than words. [L *ars, artis*]

art */ärt/ n* a way of denying emptiness. [L *ars, artis*]

art */ärt/ n* a way of expressing an artist's emotions. [L *ars, artis*]

art */ärt/ n* a way of expressing, and a way of perceiving, that is more than the concrete information produced or experienced. [L *ars, artis*]

art */ärt/ n* a way of expressing one's feelings or emotions through the means of a self-made object or work. [L *ars, artis*]

art */ärt/ n* a way of expressing the deepest corners of your innermost being. [L *ars, artis*]

art */ärt/ n* a way of expressing your feeling in a created way. [L *ars, artis*]

art */ärt/ n* a way of expressing your thoughts and showing the way you feel of something. [L *ars, artis*]

art */ärt/ n (interj)* a way of expressing yourself; *and at the same time brightening the day for other people!* [L *ars, artis*]

art */ärt/ n* a way of expressing yourself when there is nobody to listen or understand. [L *ars, artis*]

art */ärt/ n* a way of expressing yourself with pictures, plays/skits, songs, *etc.* [L *ars, artis*]

art */ärt/ n* a way of expression that connects the viewer and the artist via an object. [L *ars, artis*]

art */ärt/ n* a way of how to bestow our slumbering passions and emotions. [L *ars, artis*]

art */ärt/ n* a way of letting your feelings out. [L *ars, artis*]

art */ärt/ n* a way of making others happy by looking at your creations. [L *ars, artis*]

art */ärt/ n* a way of making reality more present. [L *ars, artis*]

art */ärt/ n* a way of moving people. [L *ars, artis*]

art */ärt/ n* a way of opening our own minds. [L *ars, artis*]

art */ärt/ n* a way of rearranging the world so that it provides a kind of satisfaction that reality fails to deliver. [L *ars, artis*]

art */ärt/ n* a way of saying *'there is part of my life, of life, that I can control, where I can edit out (or in) the mess and chaos'.* [L *ars, artis*]

art */ärt/ n* a way of taking control.

[L *ars, artis*]

art /*ärt*/ *n* a way of viewing life, reality and your imagination all in one. [L *ars, artis*]

art /*ärt*/ *n* a way that somebody can express themselves through a different way of telling people and a way that you can have your own imagination and a way that you control yourself and what you do. [L *ars, artis*]

art /*ärt*/ *n* a way that you let your emotion out of your heart and find a place to put it. [L *ars, artis*]

art /*ärt*/ *n* a way to be heard from the heart or mind. [L *ars, artis*]

art /*ärt*/ *n* a way to deal with the world. [L *ars, artis*]

art /*ärt*/ *n* a way to elicit emotions from the viewer. [L *ars, artis*]

art /*ärt*/ *n* a way to escape the actual world. [L *ars, artis*]

art /*ärt*/ *n* a way to escape your surroundings and to help you with your problems in life. [L *ars, artis*]

art /*ärt*/ *n* a way to experience ourselves in relation to the universe. [L *ars, artis*]

art /*ärt*/ *n* a way to express everything out; *even if someone thinks your art (like a dance piece) is horrible or ugly, expressing yourself through dance, singing, poetry, painting, or any of those 'arts', there's always beauty to it.* [L *ars, artis*]

art /*ärt*/ *n* a way to express feelings in a creative and positive way. [L *ars, artis*]

art /*ärt*/ *n* a way to express how you feel; *or express how you want to feel.* [L *ars, artis*]

art /*ärt*/ *n* a way to express how you or others feel to me. [L *ars, artis*]

art /*ärt*/ *n* a way to express what you feel, an idea, or to create something that will make the people react and feel what you intend them to feel. [L *ars, artis*]

art /*ärt*/ *n* a way to express what you feel using all kinds of colours. [L *ars, artis*]

art /*ärt*/ *n* a way to express your creativity and imagination any way you choose. [L *ars, artis*]

art /*ärt*/ *n* a way to express your limitless imagination through your creativity. [L *ars, artis*]

art /*ärt*/ *n* a way to express your thoughts. [L *ars, artis*]

art /*ärt*/ *n* a way to express yourself in your own way; *and you can do whatever you like to your art work.* [L *ars, artis*]

art */ärt/ n* a way to express yourself or your surroundings; *it can be completely off the wall, but as long as you understand it and you got the chance to express how you felt, then it shouldn't matter what anyone has to say about it or whether they like it or not.* [L *ars, artis*]

art */ärt/ n* a way to express yourself through colours and drawing. [L *ars, artis*]

art */ärt/ n* a way to live your life. [L *ars, artis*]

art */ärt/ n* a way to make the invisible, the intangible, visible. [L *ars, artis*]

art */ärt/ n* a way to pass time, create lasting beauty, please yourself and others and a way of synthesizing something timeless. [L *ars, artis*]

art */ärt/ n (poss relig)* a way to personify and justify the existence of the human race; *and ultimately serving only to glorify the creator.* [L *ars, artis*]

art */ärt/ n* a way to release all feelings, weak or strong. [L *ars, artis*]

art */ärt/ n* a way to see things; *but with more colour and a better view but from the view of the person that did the work.* [L *ars, artis*]

art */ärt/ n* a way to share; *and it can be spiritual and soulful and it can be public, but for a lot of people it's just personal.* [L *ars, artis*]

art */ärt/ n* a way to show people how you feel. [L *ars, artis*]

art */ärt/ n* a way to understand our time; *the time in which we live; a way to apprehend and influence it; everything that tries to do this counts as art for me.* [L *ars, artis*]

art */ärt/ n* a way to use your imagination and creativity. [L *ars, artis*]

art */ärt/ n (inf)* a way you can visually express your emotion at any given time; *it's better than chewing someone's head off.* [L *ars, artis*]

art */ärt/ n* a whole. [L *ars, artis*]

art */ärt/ n* a whore of a word. [L *ars, artis*]

art */ärt/ n* a wile, trick. [L *ars, artis*]

art */ärt/ n* a window in which to examine; *as in, a painting should be a way to understand the topic of the painting and whatever.* [L *ars, artis*]

art */ärt/ n* a window into a person's mind. [L *ars, artis*]

art */ärt/ n* a window into the time and place in which it was created. [L *ars, artis*]

art */ärt/ n* a window to my world. [L *ars, artis*]

art */ärt/ n* a wonderful part of life; *but it is wonderful in the same way that sports or hobbies are wonderful, as a form of entertainment and escapism, not as a philosophical activity.* [L *ars, artis*]

art */ärt/ n* a word; *like the words that make up this sentence.* [L *ars, artis*]

art */ärt/ n* a word for a heuristic which we may or may not find to be useful for describing and differentiating certain human activities and artefacts from other activities and artefacts. [L *ars, artis*]

art */ärt/ n* a word not a judgment. [L *ars, artis*]

art */ärt/ n* a word that denotes exclusivity, but in the current day its meaning can only ever be inclusive. [L *ars, artis*]

art */ärt/ n (econ)* a word to exploit the bourgeois class and take their money. [L *ars, artis*]

art */ärt/ n* a word used all the time. [L *ars, artis*]

art */ärt/ n (hist)* a word with a long history and many meanings. [L *ars, artis*]

art */ärt/ n* a word with the letters: A,R,T. [L *ars, artis*]

art */ärt/ n (appar joc)* a work full of sense by a senseless person ☺. [L *ars, artis*]

art */ärt/ n* a work has to have been planned by the artist from start to finish in order to qualify as art. [L *ars, artis*]

art */ärt/ n* a work of art. [L *ars, artis*]

art */ärt/ n* a work of art is re-created every time it is aesthetically experienced. [L *ars, artis*]

art */ärt/ n* a work of artistic craftsmanship. [L *ars, artis*]

art */ärt/ n* a work piece created by one or more people that is found to be either attractive or to have a hidden meaning; eg *a picture of a man throwing away perfectly good food with a homeless man outside.* [L *ars, artis*]

art */ärt/ n* about a fleeting moment; *or something*. [L *ars, artis*]

art */ärt/ n* about an artist suggesting or conveying a certain set of emotions in the viewer or viewing audience. [L *ars, artis*]

art */ärt/ n* about people; *by people; for people.* [L *ars, artis*]

art */ärt/ n (approx)* about the beauty; *it's maybe from you make or maybe from natural, but maybe from outside what you look or the inside of other, or just the moving of natural or stopping of animal at night…* etc. [L *ars, artis*]

art */ärt/ n* about the free flow of expression. [L *ars, artis*]

art */ärt/ n* about trying create something; *or capture a moment in an image to evoke certain ideas, emotions or objects or a combination of those in a manner that either captures one's attention or captures others' attention.* [L *ars, artis*]

art */ärt/ n* absorbing through our senses the work of an artist. [L *ars, artis*]

art */ärt/ n* abstract at times. [L *ars, artis*]

A.R.T. */ärt/ n* Academy of Realistic Taxidermy (A.R.T. Taxidermy School… *where you learn taxidermy from Champions).* [acronym]

art */ärt/ n* accusation, expression, passion. [L *ars, artis*]

art */ärt/ n* action into matter for those to whom it matters. [L *ars, artis*]

art */ärt/ n* activism. [L *ars, artis*]

art */ärt/ n* activity intended to make something special. [L *ars, artis*]

art */ärt/ n (econ, neg)* activity or production to no purpose; *certainly not to make a living*. [L *ars, artis*]

art */ärt/ n* adapts to and reflects the values of the time; *by speaking the language of the patron and by adjusting to the consensus of the most successful styles of the period.* [L *ars, artis*]

art */ärt/ n* adds depth to our existence. [L *ars, artis*]

art */ärt/ n* adds humanness to our life. [L *ars, artis*]

art */ärt/ n* adventure, freedom and wonder. [L *ars, artis*]

art */ärt/ n* aesthetic experience; *objects of art are designed to heighten awareness using aesthetic experience.* [L *ars, artis*]

ART */ärt/ n (inf, appar joc)* Aesthetic Retinal Titillation. [acronym]

art /ärt/ *n* aesthetic value. [L *ars, artis*]

art /ärt/ *n* aesthetic, creative representation. [L *ars, artis*]

art /ärt/ *n* aesthetics; *the science and theory of beauty in perception and expression.* [L *ars, artis*]

art /ärt/ *n (pers)* after studying art and its history for over two years I still have no idea. [L *ars, artis*]

ART /ärt/ *n* Albany Rapid Transit *(a part of multi-modal public transportation in the Capital District of New York State).* [acronym]

art /ärt/ *n (derog, vulg)* all a con; *and it was obviously incredibly effective since now they think that what is really instant gratification at heart is now pathetically to them art; I guess masturbation is the next step then as to what is to be called art (poss ref* Seedbed, *first performed by Vito Acconci 15–29 Jan 1972 at Sonnabend Gallery in New York).* [L *ars, artis*]

art /ärt/ *n* all about expression; *it's supposed to be done and felt, not said.* [L *ars, artis*]

art /ärt/ *n* all about getting the viewers/listeners to experience something; *some experiences only need crude techniques: shock, disgust; but subtle and long lasting experiences need to be crafted with great skill.* [L *ars, artis*]

art /ärt/ *n (econ, euphem)* all about money *and having to 'clean one's shoes' after treading in it.* [L *ars, artis*]

art /ärt/ *n* all about variety. [L *ars, artis*]

art /ärt/ *n* all around us. [L *ars, artis*]

art /ärt/ *n* all around us; *but it is undefined.* [L *ars, artis*]

art /ärt/ *n* all around us; *we just need to open our eyes wider to see it.* [L *ars, artis*]

art /ärt/ *n* all categories of art, idealistic or realistic, surrealistic or constructivist *(a new form of idealism)* must satisfy a simple test *(or they are in no sense works of art)*: they must persist as objects of contemplation. [L *ars, artis*]

art /ärt/ *n* all creative human endeavours; *excluding actions directly related to survival and reproduction.* [L *ars, artis*]

art /ärt/ *n (inf, zool)* all drawings could be called art; *especially in these empowered and egalitarian* *times, which I have no problem with: next door's cat can walk through spilt paint over my garden flags (the stone kind) and someone will call the result 'art' (and next door's cat is daft enough to do that BTW, unlike most).* [L *ars, artis*]

art */ärt/ n* all forms of art communicate something; *a feeling, an idea, a record of fact, another way of looking at something, a statement about something wrong in our society, an appreciation of something beautiful, a spiritual understanding.* [L *ars, artis*]

art */ärt/ n (pers)* all I've ever had. [L *ars, artis*]

art */ärt/ n (pers)* all I've got. [L *ars, artis*]

art */ärt/ n* all of the works that appear in a gallery or museum, *whether beautiful or ugly.* [L *ars, artis*]

art */ärt/ n (interrog)* all play; *isn't it?* [L *ars, artis*]

art */ärt/ n (appar joc)* all retards together. [acronym]

art */ärt/ n* all the enterprise of the mind made manifest through the soul. [L *ars, artis*]

art */ärt/ n* all the processes and products of human skill, imagination and invention. [L *ars, artis*]

art */ärt/ n* all things to all people. [L *ars, artis*]

art */ärt/ n* all views, all objects and approaches, all mediums, all visual, all audio. [L *ars, artis*]

art */ärt/ n* all we truly live for. [L *ars, artis*]

art */ärt/ n* all work created by man; *including carved wooden spoons, cave paintings and sculptures.* [L *ars, artis*]

art */ärt/ n* allows one to explore an idea further and in a different way, while opening doors to other people's interpretation; *this connects people and shares ideas, which in turn is sharing knowledge.* [L *ars, artis*]

art */ärt/ n* allows the individual to express things toward the world as a whole. [L *ars, artis*]

art */ärt/ n* allows the mind to soar to great heights and create an image that expresses, rather than states, the artist's product; *allowing the artist to describe, explain or even challenge the world through a different form of language.* [L *ars, artis*]

art */ärt/ n* allows us to represent, respond to and re-imagine our surroundings. [L *ars, artis*]

art */ärt/ n* almost anything; *it just has to be something that someone can find meaning in, something that inspires inspiration or conversation and/or something that expresses emotion (IMO).* [L *ars, artis*]

art */ärt/ n (inf)* almost anything that humans do; *and doesn't have to be the pompous crap that most people defining the term on this site say it is.* [L *ars, artis*]

art */ärt/ n* almost everything I see. [L *ars, artis*]

art */ärt/ n* almost everything you see. [L *ars, artis*]

art */ärt/ n* always about clarity; *no matter how abstract it may become.* [L *ars, artis*]

art */ärt/ n* always has been, and almost certainly always will be, a very personal appreciation; *it's why you may love Warhol and although I can appreciate what he did for the world, I just don't like it; and that's fine (*Andrew Warhola *(1928–87), Am artist).* [L *ars, artis*]

art */ärt/ n* always awakes our best side. [L *ars, artis*]

art */ärt/ n* always both a spiritual image of reality and a material structure; *constructed from sounds, forms, colours, or words.* [L *ars, artis*]

art */ärt/ n* always context and audience dependent. [L *ars, artis*]

art */ärt/ n* always difficult to understand; *and far away from my normal daily life.* [L *ars, artis*]

art */ärt/ n* always diverse. [L *ars, artis*]

art */ärt/ n* always evolving; *and its merits and meaning have been debated for centuries.* [L *ars, artis*]

art */ärt/ n* always focusing on the tiny details as well as the big picture; *you can see this quality in every art form.* [L *ars, artis*]

art */ärt/ n* always in constant change. [L *ars, artis*]

art */ärt/ n* always offers a perspective or point of view; *it is never simply a literal depiction or representation.* [L *ars, artis*]

art */ärt/ n* always on the move. [L *ars, artis*]

art */ärt/ n* always says *'Yes'*. [L *ars, artis*]

art */ärt/ n* always stems from the creative process. [L *ars, artis*]

art */ärt/ n* always technically evidence of an inspiration; *the better the work, the stronger it defies duplication.* [L *ars, artis*]

art */ärt/ n* always ticking down. [L *ars, artis*]

art */ärt/ n* an ability or skill. [L *ars, artis*]

art */ärt/ n* an ability that needs skill. [L *ars, artis*]

art */ärt/ n* an abstract concept we make up in our heads. [L *ars, artis*]

art */ärt/ n (derog)* an abstract idea that can easily be recreated by the average person who possesses no artistic ability. [L *ars, artis*]

art */ärt/ n* an abstract idea that people have conflicting ideas about. [L *ars, artis*]

art */ärt/ n (sociol)* an abstract idea which society attaches all meaning to, shaping and influencing it with the changing ideologies of our society. [L *ars, artis*]

art */ärt/ n (interrog)* an abstract rendition of emotions otherwise impossible to convey in mundane shapes and colours? [L *ars, artis*]

art */ärt/ n* an accolade and not just a medium. [L *ars, artis*]

art */ärt/ n* an act. [L *ars, artis*]

art */ärt/ n* an act of catharsis. [L *ars, artis*]

art */ärt/ n* an act of communication between two human beings that involves intentionality on the part of the creator and inference of that intentionality on the part of at least one impersonal experiencer; *by 'impersonal experiencer' I mean one who is not known to the artist, or who is deliberately focusing on the art as art, not as a personal communication by the artist; when I say 'Hi there' to my girlfriend it doesn't involve art; when I tell her I love her it doesn't involve art (where is the non-trivial inference?); when I write her a poem, it is art.* [L *ars, artis*]

art */ärt/ n* an act of courage. [L *ars, artis*]

art */ärt/ n* an act of creation out of the imagination. [L *ars, artis*]

art */ärt/ n* an act of defiance. [L *ars, artis*]

art */ärt/ n* an act of expressing our feelings, thoughts and observations. [L *ars, artis*]

art */ärt/ n* an act of making. [L *ars, artis*]

art */ärt/ n (relig)* an act of prayer. [L *ars, artis*]

art */ärt/ n (relig)* an act of prayer; *in fact art should come from the prayer of the artist and ought to call forth the prayer of the viewer: this prayer is immediate, intuitive and complete.* [L *ars, artis*]

art */ärt/ n* an activity designed to provoke a response; usu *an emotional one or a visceral gut reaction.* [L *ars, artis*]

art */ärt/ n* an activity requiring a fine skill. [L *ars, artis*]

art */ärt/ n* an activity through which people express particular ideas. [L *ars, artis*]

art */ärt/ n* an activity which creates an emotional link between the artist and the audience. [L *ars, artis*]

art */ärt/ n* (*poss derog*) an advanced form of onanism. [L *ars, artis*]

art */ärt/ n (geog)* an adventure into an unknown world; *which can only be explored by those willing to take the risks.* [L *ars, artis*]

art */ärt/ n* an aesthetic anaesthetic. [L *ars, artis*]

art */ärt/ n* an aesthetic given, presented to the viewer for contemplation and delight. [L *ars, artis*]

art */ärt/ n* an alternative word for 'being human'. [L *ars, artis*]

art */ärt/ n (philos)* analytic propositions; ie *if viewed within their context – as art – they provide no information whatsoever about any matter of fact.* [L *ars, artis*]

art */ärt/ n* an appeal to the aesthetic sensibilities. [L *ars, artis*]

art */ärt/ n* an application of certain principles to a specific medium. [L *ars, artis*]

art */ärt/ n* an apprenticeship that can be stretched into a lifelong education. [L *ars, artis*]

art */ärt/ n* an area of knowledge; *Picasso has said, 'art is a lie that brings us nearer to the truth'; according to his perspective art is a lie because it is expressing one's imagination and creativity;* eg *if one paints a scenery of mountain out of his own imagination, then it will be a lie because such a mountain doesn't exist but it brings the artist as well as the observers nearer to the truth that is the emotion underlying in the painting; hence art can be an area of knowledge because it shows the observers the knowledge of emotions* *via sense perception as a way of knowing* (Pablo Ruiz y Picasso *(1881–1973), Sp painter, sculptor, printmaker, ceramicist and stage designer).* [L *ars, artis*]

art */ärt/ n* an artefact discussed in such a way that information concerning the history of [its] production directs the viewer's attention to properties which are worth attending to. [L *ars, artis*]

art */ärt/ n* an artefact of a kind created to be presented to an artworld public. [L *ars, artis*]

art */ärt/ n* an artefact of any existing thing or pattern or idea. [L *ars, artis*]

art */ärt/ n* an artefact upon which society or some sub-group has conferred the status of candidate for appreciation. [L *ars, artis*]

art */ärt/ n* an artefact upon which some person(s) acting on behalf of the artworld has conferred the status of candidate for appreciation. [L *ars, artis*]

art */ärt/ n* an articulation of human imagination and creativity. [L *ars, artis*]

art */ärt/ n* an artist will create boundaries and everything within those boundaries is the art. [L *ars, artis*]

art */ärt/ n* an artistic way to express yourself in art. [L *ars, artis*]

art */ärt/ n* an assertion of ownership – for the artist and audience alike. [L *ars, artis*]

art */ärt/ n* an attempt at deciphering the wordless groans of my very being. [L *ars, artis*]

art */ärt/ n* an attempt to appropriate the world and make it yours. [L *ars, artis*]

art */ärt/ n* an attempt to better understand something that seemed magnificent and mysterious compared to ordinary human life. [L *ars, artis*]

art */ärt/ n* an attempt to communicate beyond words. [L *ars, artis*]

art */ärt/ n* an attempt to explain human existence; *whether it is to demonstrate perception or concepts or to evoke emotional sympathy or horror at the human condition or to express one's inner trials or social inequities, art allows us to communicate our being in some form of meaningful expression; it is a deep need, a communication with those who have lived before us and those that someday will follow and with* *our contemporaries that share our world.* [L *ars, artis*]

art */ärt/ n* an attempt to find in its forms, in its colours, in its light, in its shadows… *what of each is fundamental, what is enduring and essential – their one illuminating and convincing quality – the very truth of their existence.* [L *ars, artis*]

art */ärt/ n* an attitude; *culturally driven and available to anyone who chooses to adopt it.* [L *ars, artis*]

art */ärt/ n* an author conveying with all elements of craft emotions, ideas and sensations of value and of individualistic viewpoint. [L *ars, artis*]

art */ärt/ n* an avenue through which man attempts creation, to be a source, to produce that which has not previously existed. [L *ars, artis*]

art */ärt/ n* an early indicator of trends in culture. [L *ars, artis*]

art */ärt/ n* an eerie, ethereal notion that speaks more to individual minds and philosophies than to actual definitions. [L *ars, artis*]

art */ärt/ n* an effective tool to raise questions about the contemporary ubiquity of porn. [L *ars, artis*]

art */ärt/ n* an effort to contextualize our existence; *through an act of representation, it is hoped, the perceiver of that representation might, in fact, see the world and their relation to it, in an entirely new way.* [L *ars, artis*]

art */ärt/ n* an effort to express truth intuitively. [L *ars, artis*]

art */ärt/ n* an effort to make something more aesthetically valuable. [L *ars, artis*]

art */ärt/ n* an effort to rescue life from the arbitrary. [L *ars, artis*]

art */ärt/ n* an egg's idea of things that aren't eggs. [L *ars, artis*]

art */ärt/ n* an illusion of our limited mind. [L *ars, artis*]

art */ärt/ n* an emotional message conveyed via a medium to an audience. [L *ars, artis*]

art */ärt/ n* an encounter with the strange, the different, the unknown, the hidden, the not-yet-thought-of. [L *ars, artis*]

art */ärt/ n* an enigma wrapped in a riddle. [L *ars, artis*]

art */ärt/ n (educ)* an entertaining yet strongly educative experience. [L *ars, artis*]

art /*ärt*/ *n* an escape. [L *ars, artis*]

art /*ärt*/ *n* an escape from chaos. [L *ars, artis*]

art /*ärt*/ *n* an escape from reality. [L *ars, artis*]

art /*ärt*/ *n* an escape from the humdrum of life; *or, if you will, those long moments we wait between the times where we're truly living.* [L *ars, artis*]

art /*ärt*/ *n* an essentially contested and unstable category. [L *ars, artis*]

art /*ärt*/ *n* an eternal ring of keys. [L *ars, artis*]

art /*ärt*/ *n* an ever-changing, ever-growing cultural phenomenon. [L *ars, artis*]

art /*ärt*/ *n* an ever-changing, non-linear concept; *therefore, what might not be considered art now might become better understood in the future, the boundaries are ever-changing, you just need to look at history to see this*. [L *ars, artis*]

art /*ärt*/ *n* an evolutionary act; *the shape of art and its role in the society is constantly changing; at no point is art static; there are no rules.* [L *ars, artis*]

art /*ärt*/ *n* an evolving and global concept; *open to new interpretation, too fluid to be pinned down.* [L *ars, artis*]

art /*ärt*/ *n* an existence which allows you to express your emotions to an outside audience. [L *ars, artis*]

art /*ärt*/ *n* an experience in which meanings or values are expressed, or shown, rather than stated or said. [L *ars, artis*]

art /*ärt*/ *n* an experience that takes place inside the human mind and is not a thing. [L *ars, artis*]

art /*ärt*/ *n* an exploration of purpose that is taking the thinking and feeling process to new worldliness; *a qualitative leap.* [L *ars, artis*]

art /*ärt*/ *n* an explorative commentary, in visual terms, on what it means to be a human being. [L *ars, artis*]

art /*ärt*/ *n (interj)* an explosion! [L *ars, artis*]

art /*ärt*/ *n* an explosion in my soul. [L *ars, artis*]

art /*ärt*/ *n* an expression. [L *ars, artis*]

art /*ärt*/ *n* an expression and an

interpretation of our experience as humans. [L *ars, artis*]

art */ärt/ n* an expression and personal interpretation from the artist. [L *ars, artis*]

art */ärt/ n* an expression and release of SELF. [L *ars, artis*]

art */ärt/ n* an expression by the human hand rendering something measurably banal as something beautiful; *beauty being always a reward for our existence.* [L *ars, artis*]

art */ärt/ n* an expression of a feeling or experience in such a way that the audience to whom the art is directed can share that feeling or experience. [L *ars, artis*]

art */ärt/ n* an expression of an emotion. [L *ars, artis*]

art */ärt/ n* an expression of an idea. [L *ars, artis*]

art */ärt/ n* an expression of anything that creates a reaction. [L *ars, artis*]

art */ärt/ n* an expression of creativity. [L *ars, artis*]

art */ärt/ n* an expression of creativity visually powerful enough to give you a certain feeling without having to physically touch you; *it touches a certain part deep within you and that makes you feel good.* [L *ars, artis*]

art */ärt/ n* an expression of daily insights. [L *ars, artis*]

art */ärt/ n* an expression of emotion committed to a tangible format for others to interpret. [L *ars, artis*]

art */ärt/ n* an expression of emotion, creativity, *etc.* [L *ars, artis*]

art */ärt/ n* an expression of emotions and feelings. [L *ars, artis*]

art */ärt/ n* an expression of feeling that can be communicated through any or all of the senses. [L *ars, artis*]

art */ärt/ n* an expression of how one feels. [L *ars, artis*]

art */ärt/ n* an expression of human emotion of some form, put into a form that can be experienced by others in an aesthetic way; *poetry, literature, music, painting, sculpture and all these other forms of expression.* [L *ars, artis*]

art */ärt/ n* an expression of human thought that gets other people thinking about as well. [L *ars, artis*]

art */ärt/ n* an expression of intelligence. [L *ars, artis*]

art */ärt/ n* an expression of life; *which means it expresses emotions.* [L *ars, artis*]

art */ärt/ n* an expression of man's emotions or desires made visible. [L *ars, artis*]

art */ärt/ n* an expression of one's feelings or imagination. [L *ars, artis*]

art */ärt/ n* an expression of one's heart and what we love; *I suppose any individual expression is an attempt to influence others to some degree.* [L *ars, artis*]

art */ärt/ n* an expression of one's heart, soul, inner perspective. [L *ars, artis*]

art */ärt/ n* an expression of one's thoughts and desires. [L *ars, artis*]

art */ärt/ n* an expression of one's thoughts and feelings. [L *ars, artis*]

art */ärt/ n* an expression of oneself; *whether through painting, writing, making a game,* etc. [L *ars, artis*]

art */ärt/ n* an expression of our beliefs, our ways, our lives. [L *ars, artis*]

art */ärt/ n (theol)* an expression of our continuous longing to be closer to the eternal perfection of love that is God. [L *ars, artis*]

art */ärt/ n* an expression of our human spirit; *which enables us to create a visual image of our thoughts and emotions.* [L *ars, artis*]

art */ärt/ n* an expression of ourselves using a visual representation. [L *ars, artis*]

art */ärt/ n (philos)* an expression of philosophy. [L *ars, artis*]

art */ärt/ n* an expression of self; *mind, body or spirit.* [L *ars, artis*]

art */ärt/ n* an expression of someone's creativity; *whether it be painting, photography or garden sculptures.* [L *ars, artis*]

art */ärt/ n* an expression of the deepest inner you. [L *ars, artis*]

art */ärt/ n* an expression of the heart and soul. [L *ars, artis*]

art */ärt/ n* an expression of the inexpressible. [L *ars, artis*]

art */ärt/ n* an expression of the soul. [L *ars, artis*]

art */ärt/ n* an expression of the soul of the artist; *and it should have nothing to do with appealing to the masses.* [L *ars, artis*]

art */ärt/ n* an expression of the soul through a physical medium that comes in many forms – *traditional, contemporary, on canvas, paper and many other surfaces.* [L *ars, artis*]

art */ärt/ n* an expression of thoughts. [L *ars, artis*]

art */ärt/ n* an expression of what drives the soul; *for better or for worse.* [L *ars, artis*]

art */ärt/ n* an expression of what is and what could be. [L *ars, artis*]

art */ärt/ n* an expression of what it means to be human. [L *ars, artis*]

art */ärt/ n (inf, poss vulg)* an expression of what the artist is thinking/feeling, regardless of the medium; *it can be a song, a sewn pattern, or even a bunch of shit smeared on a cardboard box.* [L *ars, artis*]

art */ärt/ n* an expression of words, thoughts or emotion in a symbolic form. [L *ars, artis*]

art */ärt/ n* an expression of your connection with your inner self, your ideas, your emotions. [L *ars, artis*]

art */ärt/ n* an expression of your feelings on paper. [L *ars, artis*]

art */ärt/ n* an expression of your inner self. [L *ars, artis*]

art */ärt/ n* an expression of your viewpoint which can be 'written' in many ways. [L *ars, artis*]

art */ärt/ n* an expression on a medium or in sound, of what some person is feeling or thinking so strongly that they need to put it into something tangible, *so that another can maybe get a teeny tiny glimpse of the artist's state of mind.* [L *ars, artis*]

art */ärt/ n* an expression through sound, images, buildings, movies and more. [L *ars, artis*]

art */ärt/ n* an expression where the emphasis by its creator was more/greater on the medium rather than the message. [L *ars, artis*]

art */ärt/ n* an expression which is in the moment and ever-changing in one's imagination. [L *ars, artis*]

art */ärt/ n* an expression which we use to create something. [L *ars, artis*]

art */ärt/ n* an exquisite painting. [L *ars, artis*]

art */ärt/ n (comput)* an extremely

proficiently designed piece of software. [L *ars, artis*]

art */ärt/ n* an idea or concept that is not tangible that is conveyed by something that is tangible. [L *ars, artis*]

art */ärt/ n* an illusion. [L *ars, artis*]

art */ärt/ n* an image in which everything the artist has expressed is experienced in one moment as your brain reacts with its own emotional response to the work. [L *ars, artis*]

art */ärt/ n* an imaginary product; *since it is exhilarating nothingness for practical people with their feet on ground.* [L *ars, artis*]

art */ärt/ n* an imitation of nature. [L *ars, artis*]

art */ärt/ n* an imitation, 'Falsafi', or ideal and universal nature of the natural world and human world (**Falsafi**, *appar ref Aristotle (384–322 BCE), Gr philos b Stagirus).* [L *ars, artis*]

art */ärt/ n* an immediate realization of intent. [L *ars, artis*]

art */ärt/ n* an imposition of order on chaos. [L *ars, artis*]

art */ärt/ n (vulg, perh derog)* an inanimate object that makes animate objects do funny things; *(convulse with noise, destroy, masturbate).* [L *ars, artis*]

art */ärt/ n* an individual expression of creative thought. [L *ars, artis*]

art */ärt/ n* an individual's expression by which one reflects the society, culture and the environment in paintings, dance, music, sculpture, *etc etc.* [L *ars, artis*]

art */ärt/ n* an indulgence in fantasy. [L *ars, artis*]

art */ärt/ n* an indulgence in sensuousness. [L *ars, artis*]

art */ärt/ n* an infection. [L *ars, artis*]

art */ärt/ n* an infinite question; *and the way to capture a semblance of an answer.* [L *ars, artis*]

art */ärt/ n* an inherent universal trait of the human species; *as normal and natural as language, sex, sociability, aggression or any other characteristics of human nature.* [L *ars, artis*]

art */ärt/ n (biol)* an inherent universal (or biological) trait of the human species; *as normal or natural as language, sex, sociability, aggression or any of the other charac-*

teristics of human nature. [L *ars, artis*]

art */ärt/ n* an innate quality of something produced for the purposes of making the audience think, *or laugh, or cry, or get frustrated, or grin from ear to ear.* [L *ars, artis*]

art */ärt/ n (f)* an inner communication for the artist herself. [L *ars, artis*]

art */ärt/ n* an insight from one's mind. [L *ars, artis*]

art */ärt/ n* an instance of a conscious manipulation of a certain medium in order to communicate the artist's feelings to the audience; ie *to compel the audience to experience the same feeling that the artist has experienced.* [L *ars, artis*]

art */ärt/ n* an institutionalised status for appreciation; *but for those outside who have to look at it, it's nothing if it can't be laughed at.* [L *ars, artis*]

art */ärt/ n* an intangible attitude. [L *ars, artis*]

art */ärt/ n* an intellectual exercise or experiment. [L *ars, artis*]

art */ärt/ n* an intelligent endeavour to inspire original thought in a pleasing or provoking way. [L *ars, artis*]

art */ärt/ n* an intention; *not an elitist view of the present favourite.* [L *ars, artis*]

art */ärt/ n* an intentional human act, emotive in nature, created with craft and producing a transitory or enduring result; *the act itself needs to be intentional but not necessarily the artefact of the act if it reflects a creative decision; expressive acts and the products of those acts, not limited by logic and not subject to any subjective guidelines or restrictions; the act may be art while the product of the act may not, if craft is lacking; an act and/or artefact that is communicative and invested in some way with its creator's vision and purpose; commercial ends are not a concern if the other criterion is met.* [L *ars, artis*]

art */ärt/ n* an intentional, disciplined act. [L *ars, artis*]

art */ärt/ n* an intentionally created object. [L *ars, artis*]

art */ärt/ n (theol)* an interaction with the Holy Spirit. [L *ars, artis*]

art */ärt/ n* an internal appreciation of balance and harmony *(beauty).*

[L *ars, artis*]

art */ärt/ n* an internal dialogue of an artist, an attempt to make sense of his or her emotions through expressing them; *provided that expression of emotion, simply as expression, is not addressed to any particular audience: it is addressed primarily to the speaker himself and secondarily to any one who can understand.* [L *ars, artis*]

art */ärt/ n* an international language which is used through the world. [L *ars, artis*]

art */ärt/ n* an intimate part of preparing a person to meditate. [L *ars, artis*]

art */ärt/ n* an intuition of beauty. [L *ars, artis*]

art */ärt/ n* an inward dive. [L *ars, artis*]

art */ärt/ n (philos)* an item is an artwork at time t, where t is not earlier than the time at which the item is made, if and only if it is in one of the central art forms at t and is made with the intention of fulfilling a function art has at t or it is an artefact that achieves excellence in achieving such a function. [L *ars, artis*]

art */ärt/ n* an object on display that inspires contemplation, study and discovery as it presents complexities, challenge and joy. [L *ars, artis*]

art */ärt/ n* an object or experience. [L *ars, artis*]

art */ärt/ n* an object or idea to which someone has devoted time, thought and energy. [L *ars, artis*]

art */ärt/ n* an object that does not have any practical purpose. [L *ars, artis*]

art */ärt/ n* an observable attribute that persists to defy a normative definition. [L *ars, artis*]

art */ärt/ n* an occupation in which skill is employed to gratify taste or produce what is beautiful. [L *ars, artis*]

art */ärt/ n* an occupation requiring knowledge or skill: *the art of organ building*. [L *ars, artis*]

art */ärt/ n (milit)* an offensive weapon in the defense against the enemy. [L *ars, artis*]

art */ärt/ n* an ongoing practice that arises from what was done in the name of art last year or last decade or last century and which speaks to that history and heritage of creation, defining itself by and against those practices. [L *ars, artis*]

art */ärt/ n* an opportunity to see the world in a different way. [L *ars, artis*]

art */ärt/ n* an opportunity to view something differently. [L *ars, artis*]

art */ärt/ n* an Oreo™ box design; *and I would even dare to venture to say it had more cultural significance than many paintings out there because it's recognizable and incites a lot of emotions* (Oreo™ *(1912–), sandwich cookie consisting two chocolate disks with a sweet cream filling).* [L *ars, artis*]

art */ärt/ n (appar fig)* an orgasmic wail of ecstasy and, sometimes, agony. [L *ars, artis*]

art */ärt/ n* an original language developed by an artist to express their ideas to others. [L *ars, artis*]

art */ärt/ n* an original or unique item or an event that elicits a sensational response; *senses are aroused by this item or event; it doesn't have to be pretty… just memorable and stand out.* [L *ars, artis*]

art */ärt/ n* an outlet for inner human turmoil. [L *ars, artis*]

art */ärt/ n* an outlet for pain. [L *ars, artis*]

art */ärt/ n* an outlet for some people who really want to show their emotions. [L *ars, artis*]

art */ärt/ n* an outsider. [L *ars, artis*]

art */ärt/ n* an outward expression of a person's thoughts put on paper either through painting, drawing, writing or sculpture; *I don't feel there is any ugly art; there is beauty in art.* [L *ars, artis*]

art */ärt/ n* an outward expression of internal ideas and abstractions. [L *ars, artis*]

art */ärt/ n* an outward expression of your inner viewpoint or aspiration. [L *ars, artis*]

art */ärt/ n* an unstable category; *it lives or dies according to rules that cannot ever be systematised.* [L *ars, artis*]

art */ärt/ n (econ)* an upper-class activity associated with wealth; *the ability to purchase art; and the leisure required to pursue or enjoy it.* [L *ars, artis*]

art */ärt/ n (appar joc)* anchovies, raisins and toast. [acronym]

art */ärt/ n (fig)* another link in the

chain. [L *ars, artis*]

art */ärt/ n (econ)* another lucrative commodity to be bought and sold. [L *ars, artis*]

art */ärt/ n* another pointless definition. [L *ars, artis*]

art */ärt/ n (derog)* another word for crap. [L *ars, artis*]

art */ärt/ n* any act of creation for a purpose; *the same definition applies to magic.* [L *ars, artis*]

art */ärt/ n* any act of creation that extends one's understanding of the worlds around him/her and the extension of one's ego with a material result. [L *ars, artis*]

art */ärt/ n* any act or object created with the specific intention of evoking an emotional response. [L *ars, artis*]

art */ärt/ n (zool, interrog)* any act that expresses creativity and imagination; *elephants, when they paint, make choices to do paint strokes on the canvas and that's art; if elephant art shouldn't be considered 'art', then should a toddler's scribble be considered art? Also, I don't think elephants should be forced to produce art for the benefit of the zoo's wallets.* [L *ars, artis*]

art */ärt/ n* any act, or result of an act, which adds value. [L *ars, artis*]

art */ärt/ n* any activity or product done by people with a communicative or aesthetic purpose. [L *ars, artis*]

art */ärt/ n* any and everything that is pleasurable to your senses, such as what you see, hear, touch, smell and taste; *in most cases it would deal with your inner feelings not only what you can feel on the outside of your body.* [L *ars, artis*]

art */ärt/ n* any branch of creative work; *esp painting, drawing or work in any other graphic or plastic medium.* [L *ars, artis*]

art */ärt/ n* any brief definition of art would oversimplify the matter; *but we can say that all the definitions offered over the centuries include some notion of human agency, whether through manual skills (as in the art of sailing or painting or photography), intellectual manipulation (as in the art of politics), or public or personal expression (as in the art of conversation); recall that the word is etymologically related to artificial –* ie *produced by human beings; since this embraces many types of production that are not conventionally* *deemed to be art, perhaps a better term for them would be visual culture; this would explain why certain preindustrial cultures produce objects which Eurocentric interests characterize as art, even though the producing culture has no linguistic term to differentiate these objects from utilitarian artefacts; having said that, we are still left with a class of objects, ideas and activities that are held to be separate or special in some way; even those things which become art even though they are not altered in any material way – eg readymades – are accorded some special status in a describable way; because of this complexity, writers have developed a variety of ways to characterize the art impulse; Ellen Dissanayake's* What is Art For? *lists these as follows (in no particular order): the product of conscious intention, a self rewarding activity, a tendency to unite dissimilar things, a concern with change and variety, the aesthetic exploitation of familiarity vs. surprise, the aesthetic exploitation of tension vs. release, the imposition of order on disorder, the creation of illusions, an indulgence in sensuousness, the exhibition of skill, a desire to convey meanings, an indulgence in fantasy, the aggrandizement of self or others, illustration, the heightening of existence, revelation, personal adornment or embellishment, therapy, the giving of meaning to life, the generation of unselfconscious experience, the provision of paradigms of order and/or disorder, training in the perception of reality* (Ellen Dissanayake *(c1936–), independent scholar).* [L *ars, artis*]

art */ärt/ n* any communication that allows someone else to know what is inside my head. [L *ars, artis*]

art */ärt/ n* any craft touched with profound innovation; *where profundity does not imply aesthetic alone.* [L *ars, artis*]

art */ärt/ n* any craft, trade, or profession, or its principles: *the cobbler's art, the physician's art.* [L *ars, artis*]

art */ärt/ n* any craft with a political agenda; *as for instance in India, paintings of which the message is that the West is evil.* [L *ars, artis*]

art */ärt/ n* any creative interpretation of the world or some aspect of it. [L *ars, artis*]

art */ärt/ n* any creative output by a person. [L *ars, artis*]

art */ärt/ n (pers)* any creative work

that I can take pleasure in. [L *ars, artis*]

art */ärt/ n* any delivered experience. [L *ars, artis*]

art */ärt/ n* any effort that an individual performs to communicate an understanding *(of life, nature, the universe, order, disorder, beauty, truth, violence, or any conscious or non-conscious message)* to oneself or to others. [L *ars, artis*]

art */ärt/ n* any endeavour a person is inspired to perform that provokes an emotional reaction from an audience. [L *ars, artis*]

art */ärt/ n* any expression – created – which evokes a pleasant feeling within the observer. [L *ars, artis*]

art */ärt/ n* any expression of creativity and/or skill; *be it emotional or not in any media.* [L *ars, artis*]

art */ärt/ n* any expression of feeling that can be experienced by any of the five senses. [L *ars, artis*]

art */ärt/ n* any expression of thought. [L *ars, artis*]

art */ärt/ n* any expression of what it means to be human; *and that can be anything that relates to the human condition; it is representational, however; it can't be just anything, but something that most people know as art.* [L *ars, artis*]

art */ärt/ n* any field using the skills or techniques of art. [L *ars, artis*]

art */ärt/ n* any field using the techniques of art to display artistic qualities: *advertising art.* [L *ars, artis*]

art */ärt/ n* any form of creativity; *it can be a drawing, painting, sculpture, anything representative of a form or an idea; that said, I don't really think a pickled shark is art (perh ref Damien Hirst,* The Physical Impossibility of Death in the Mind of Someone Living, *1991).* [L *ars, artis*]

art */ärt/ n* any form of expression; *and can range from music, film, painting, video games, writing and more.* [L *ars, artis*]

art */ärt/ n* any form of expression that someone can create. [L *ars, artis*]

art */ärt/ n* any form of human self-expression, creatively in the attempt achieving reactions amongst the senses or feelings or emotions; *it can also be complex works of literature, music, paintings and sculptures* etc. [L *ars, artis*]

art */ärt/ n* any form that expresses one's personal creative capability *(whether in thought, music, writing, painting – or anything else)* that is NOT dependent on anyone else's criticism or stipulations as to the end-product. [L *ars, artis*]

art */ärt/ n* any human activity in which one emitter, by means of external signs, transmits previously experienced feelings; eg *a boy that has experienced fear after an encounter with a wolf later relates that experience, infecting the hearers and compelling them to feel the same fear that he had experienced – that is a perfect example of a work of art.* [L *ars, artis*]

art */ärt/ n* any human activity which doesn't grow out of either of our species' two basic instincts: *survival and reproduction.* [L *ars, artis*]

art */ärt/ n* any human endeavour that demonstrates passion in its creation; *you can love or hate whatever that endeavour produced, but if you can see the PASSION that went behind making it then, for me, that's art.* [L *ars, artis*]

art */ärt/ n* any image that elicits an emotional response (positive or negative) from the viewer; *that said what elicits emotional response from one person may not stir so much as a second glance from the next.* [L *ars, artis*]

art */ärt/ n* (*inf, joc*) any intentional modification of the environment that provokes one of the seven basic human expressions: *Yuk! OOO, Hmmmmm, Oi! Eh? MMMM, Ah!* [L *ars, artis*]

art */ärt/ n* any intentional visual display with the intent of self-expression *or in order to visually express a concept or theme.* [L *ars, artis*]

art */ärt/ n* any kind of expression about the place and times in which the artist lives. [L *ars, artis*]

art */ärt/ n* any man-made thing that increases either truth or beauty in the world; *it's important to note that this allows for art to be created that displays extreme aesthetic ugliness, as long as it contains an authentic experience.* [L *ars, artis*]

art */ärt/ n* any man-made creation. [L *ars, artis*]

art */ärt/ n* any man-made object that gives, or tries to give, aesthetic pleasure; *the latter being defined as either fundaceptual or an-*

throceptual (sensual or people-related) pleasure. [L *ars, artis*]

art */ärt/ n* any man-made object that gives, or tries to give, aesthetic pleasure; *the latter being defined as fundaceptual, anthroceptual or sagaceptual (sensual, people-related or narrative) pleasure.* [L *ars, artis*]

art */ärt/ n* any material, existing in the form of one or more senses, containing an artist(s)'s expressive thought(s) created, judged and given relative meaning by those who perceive it. [L *ars, artis*]

art */ärt/ n* any medium that has no purpose other than to be enjoyed. [L *ars, artis*]

art */ärt/ n* any medium that tantalizes our senses. [L *ars, artis*]

art */ärt/ n (sculpt)* any monumental statues in a church or cemetery. [L *ars, artis*]

art */ärt/ n* any object of which it catches the eye; *art has special meaning that everyone knows about; you just have to look for it and when you find, you will realize that that object you just saw was ART!* [L *ars, artis*]

art */ärt/ n* any object that brings a sense of understanding, appreciation and emotional completeness. [L *ars, artis*]

art */ärt/ n* any of various creative forms of expression: *painting, music, dancing, writing and the other arts.* [L *ars, artis*]

art */ärt/ n (poss theol)* any one of the Divine Languages, *including painting, sculpting, music, theatre, dance, poetry,* etc. [L *ars, artis*]

art */ärt/ n* any one thing we do which moves us forward. [L *ars, artis*]

art */ärt/ n* any original creation or presentation which was made with the main intent of appealing to and/or opposing someone's (anyone's) aesthetic; *where what is 'aesthetic' is determined by the viewer and is subjective, but generally can be thought of as a sense of beauty or elegance, including intellectual elegance.* [L *ars, artis*]

art */ärt/ n* any random picture of anything: *1 Shakespeare's plays are a work of art 2 van Gogh painted art 3 that picture of a stalk of broccoli is art* (William Shakespeare *(c1564–1616), Eng poet and playwright;* Vincent van Gogh

(1853–90), Du Post-Impressionist painter). [L *ars, artis*]

art */ärt/ n* any random splash of colour. [L *ars, artis*]

art */ärt/ n* any representation of expression that is portrayed in our world. [L *ars, artis*]

art */ärt/ n* any situation where you put your emotions out in a talented way that they can appeal to the senses of yourself and others. [L *ars, artis*]

art */ärt/ n* any skill or mastery. [L *ars, artis*]

art */ärt/ n* any specific skill or its application: *the art of making friends.* [L *ars, artis*]

art */ärt/ n* any time you bring your own vision, creativity and talent to the table. [L *ars, artis*]

art */ärt/ n* any type of creativity. [L *ars, artis*]

art */ärt/ n* any type of media that expresses your personal feelings, opinion or shows your thoughts on any subject. [L *ars, artis*]

art */ärt/ n* any useful activity that is performed skilfully; *not only in terms of technique but also in terms of aesthetic expression.* [L *ars, artis*]

art */ärt/ n* any visual, literary and/or auditory representation of an idea, with an intended message, which invokes emotion in an audience; *examples of art include, but are not limited to: poems, literature, music, dance, pottery, sculptures, painting/drawing,* etc. [L *ars, artis*]

art */ärt/ n (psychol)* any visual that tickles the mind. [L *ars, artis*]

art */ärt/ n (pers)* any work of art that touches, moves or inspires me. [L *ars, artis*]

art */ärt/ n* any work which artificially evokes a particular emotional reaction in the observer. [L *ars, artis*]

art */ärt/ n* anybody's; *by anybody, for anybody.* [L *ars, artis*]

art */ärt/ n* anything. [L *ars, artis*]

art */ärt/ n* anything; *anywhere, anytime, under any circumstances.* [L *ars, artis*]

art */ärt/ n (derog)* anything; *as long as someone else more pompous than you says it is.* [L *ars, artis*]

art */ärt/ n* anything; *as with the urinal, which is now defined as art because of the social 'consecration' (good word, Katja) which is given to it (prob ref* **Fountain** *(1917), a work by Marcel Duchamp (1887–1968);*

Katja, *ref not known*). [L ***ars, artis***]

art */ärt/ n* anything; *that is, if you believe it can; and if you label it that way; and if you persist in labelling it that way.* [L ***ars, artis***]

art */ärt/ n* anything – *a painting, a way of thinking, a response, a song,* etc – that provides a solution to a dilemma; *not a problem, a dilemma; a way out of these dilemmas so that we can gain a greater grasp on life.* [L ***ars, artis***]

art */ärt/ n* anything a curator says is art. [L ***ars, artis***]

art */ärt/ n* anything a person does that isn't exclusively for the purpose of survival or reproduction. [L ***ars, artis***]

art */ärt/ n* anything and everything. [L ***ars, artis***]

art */ärt/ n* anything and everything; *my poetry is art; JC and Ning's death-defying mind-boggling magic tricks are art; Kar's beautifully written works are art; my brother's drawings blu-taked onto the wardrobe are art; Adele, posed carefully against a green screen and photographed – that is art; Mona Lisa on toast could be, to some, a breakthrough and amazement in the history of art; to others, viewed with disinterest and only seen as simply toast to be eaten* (JC Sum, *Singaporean illusionist and illusion designer;* 'Magic Babe' Ning Cai, *Singaporean magician and entrepreneur;* Kar, *ref not known;* Adele Laurie Blue Adkins MBE *(1988–), Eng singer, songwriter, musician and multi-instrumentalist;* Mona Lisa, *half-length portrait of a woman by It artist Leonardo da Vinci (1452–1519)).* [L ***ars, artis***]

art */ärt/ n* anything and everything created, material and non-material. [L ***ars, artis***]

art */ärt/ n* anything and everything in the world that a person makes; *each piece of art means something different to everyone; some people don't define certain things as art; there's always someone who will though.* [L ***ars, artis***]

art */ärt/ n* anything artificial and above ordinary significance. [L ***ars, artis***]

art */ärt/ n* anything artificial at all. [L ***ars, artis***]

art */ärt/ n* anything by an artist who has undergone art training. [L ***ars, artis***]

art */ärt/ n (interj)* anything can be

a form of art or inspire art or become art! [L *ars, artis*]

art */ärt/ n* anything can be art as it can give inspiration; *the human body is art; Nature is art; so on and so forth.* [L *ars, artis*]

art */ärt/ n* anything can be art if the creator intended it to be such; *but art made for it's own sake becomes about aesthetics.* [L *ars, artis*]

art */ärt/ n* anything can be considered art if a few people *(eg an 'artist', an art gallery and an art reporter or critic)* proclaim something as 'art'; *and if someone fails to recognize that something is 'art', well, they must be closed-minded or maybe have some other cultural or even mental deficiency.* [L *ars, artis*]

art */ärt/ n* anything capable of changing or enhancing the way we look at the world. [L *ars, artis*]

art */ärt/ n* anything constructed for the purposes of art; ie *anything that is intended as art and as a bonus, if it is accepted as such.* [L *ars, artis*]

art */ärt/ n* anything created by one being which stirs emotion in another. [L *ars, artis*]

art */ärt/ n* anything created for its form rather than function. [L *ars, artis*]

art */ärt/ n* anything created that has the power to break one's heart. [L *ars, artis*]

art */ärt/ n* anything created which invokes response. [L *ars, artis*]

art */ärt/ n* anything created with the intention of it being art. [L *ars, artis*]

art */ärt/ n* anything designed for a purpose; *this purpose could be functional or expressive.* [L *ars, artis*]

art */ärt/ n* anything done by a man or a woman on paper, canvas, marble or a musical keyboard that people pretend to understand and sometimes buy. [L *ars, artis*]

art */ärt/ n* anything done by an artist. [L *ars, artis*]

art */ärt/ n* anything from an oil painting to a pile of rubble. [L *ars, artis*]

art */ärt/ n* anything from paintings, sculptures, poetry, music. [L *ars, artis*]

art */ärt/ n (interj)* ANYTHING GOES!! [L *ars, artis*]

art */ärt/ n* anything having a dual purpose, *a mundane one and a* *lofty one.* [L *ars, artis*]

art */ärt/ n* anything human beings do that is not directly associated with their survival. [L *ars, artis*]

art */ärt/ n (pers)* anything I say is art. [L *ars, artis*]

art */ärt/ n* anything intended to give a deeper insight into the human condition; *that insight, like some introspection, can be far from beautiful, although such insights can lead to beauty.* [L *ars, artis*]

art */ärt/ n* anything intentionally created to be ascetically [*perh* aesthetically] engaging. [L *ars, artis*]

art */ärt/ n* anything like I said can be art; *especially something that people can relate to and is creative.* [L *ars, artis*]

art */ärt/ n* anything made and not meant to be used to complete a task that is emotionally stimulating. [L *ars, artis*]

art */ärt/ n (comput)* anything made by a computer is computer art. [L *ars, artis*]

art */ärt/ n (zool)* anything made by an elephant is elephant art. [L *ars, artis*]

art */ärt/ n* anything made by human creativity; *it could be the ceiling of the Sistine Chapel or a hammer (***Sistine Chapel***, large and renowned chapel of the Apostolic Palace, official residence of the Pope in Vatican City).* [L *ars, artis*]

art */ärt/ n* anything made to give a deeper insight into the human condition. [L *ars, artis*]

art */ärt/ n* anything made with intent. [L *ars, artis*]

art */ärt/ n* anything more than Spartan necessity that has no practical purpose to keep one alive and breeding. [L *ars, artis*]

art */ärt/ n* anything not having to do with life. [L *ars, artis*]

art */ärt/ n* anything *(or object)* an individual *(or group)* creates on their own with meaning to themselve(s). [L *ars, artis*]

art */ärt/ n* anything other than designing; *like the painting of flowers or portraits or animals or even abstract art.* [L *ars, artis*]

art */ärt/ n* anything physical created by someone. [L *ars, artis*]

art */ärt/ n* anything presented as something created. [L *ars, artis*]

art */ärt/ n* anything produced by human creativity. [L *ars, artis*]

art */ärt/ n* anything produced through the human capacity to imagine; *dogs, for example, cannot produce art because their brains can only process what is; humans are able to process what might be*. [L *ars, artis*]

art */ärt/ n* anything someone does at least one thing to; *but then again, it may not be an object; it may simply be the thought, which can exist with or without the material object; wait, what about sound art…* [L *ars, artis*]

art */ärt/ n* anything someone does that isn't based in one of two basic instincts: *survival and reproduction.* [L *ars, artis*]

art */ärt/ n* anything that a person consciously creates with the intent of entertaining, impressing and/or invoking thought in a person. [L *ars, artis*]

art */ärt/ n* anything that a person does that expresses some sort of emotion. [L *ars, artis*]

art */ärt/ n* anything that came from the heart without the worry of *'is it good? bad? etc?'*. [L *ars, artis*]

art */ärt/ n* anything that can be appreciated by any single individual for purely its aesthetic value. [L *ars, artis*]

art */ärt/ n* anything that can help us gain our own perspectives about, well, anything. [L *ars, artis*]

art */ärt/ n* anything that can invoke emotions either in the creator or in the viewer. [L *ars, artis*]

art */ärt/ n* anything that causes an emotional reaction – *sadness, awe, happiness,* etc – and is created by a human. [L *ars, artis*]

art */ärt/ n* anything that causes emotion. [L *ars, artis*]

art */ärt/ n (pers)* anything that causes me to smile. [L *ars, artis*]

art */ärt/ n* anything that causes people to argue about whether or not it's art. [L *ars, artis*]

art */ärt/ n* anything that causes someone to believe it to be so. [L *ars, artis*]

art */ärt/ n* anything that challenges its medium. [L *ars, artis*]

art */ärt/ n* anything that could bring you joy. [L *ars, artis*]

art */ärt/ n* anything that delivers a powerful emotional experience; *books, music, paintings, nature; even a meal can be an expression of art in everyday life; the world is brimming* *with art to enjoy.* [L ***ars, artis***]

art */ärt/ n (inf)* anything that draws a reaction; **kiss*.* [L *ars, artis*]

art */ärt/ n (relig)* anything that evokes a deep enough emotion; *sometimes this is a decaying old car left in a deserted lot, sad as that may be; I can still see the beauty in the pit marks on the chrome; sometimes it's the way random elements line up together, the art being a joint effort of man and God.* [L ***ars, artis***]

art */ärt/ n* anything that evokes emotion. [L *ars, artis*]

art */ärt/ n (psychol)* anything that expresses a person's feelings or thoughts. [L *ars, artis*]

art */ärt/ n (opthalmol)* anything that gives you tunnel vision. [L *ars, artis*]

art */ärt/ n* anything that has been 'made special'. [L *ars, artis*]

art */ärt/ n* anything that has been created by an self-deciding entity. [L *ars, artis*]

art */ärt/ n* anything that has been created with the intention of satisfying the creative expression of the artist; *like a communication of the mind to the physical world, embodied in a form of some kind that can be shared and reflected upon.* [L *ars, artis*]

art */ärt/ n* anything that has been deliberately created and that elicits an emotional response; *any response – happiness, sadness, anger, fear, joy etc; I could go on.* [L *ars, artis*]

art */ärt/ n* anything that is a reflection of a thought, idea or feeling. [L *ars, artis*]

art */ärt/ n* anything that is an extension of the self which initially came up with its concept. [L *ars, artis*]

art */ärt/ n* anything that is beautiful in general. [L *ars, artis*]

art */ärt/ n* anything that is beautiful or makes me think. [L *ars, artis*]

art */ärt/ n* anything that is beautiful to the viewer and/or creates emotion in the viewer. [L *ars, artis*]

art */ärt/ n* anything that is created by people not solely for a utilitarian purpose; *something can have a utility and also be art, though.* [L *ars, artis*]

art */ärt/ n* anything that is designed to be aesthetically pleasing. [L *ars, artis*]

art */ärt/ n* anything that is done well. [L *ars, artis*]

art */ärt/ n* anything that is not purely functional. [L *ars, artis*]

art */ärt/ n* anything that is sensationalist. [L *ars, artis*]

art */ärt/ n* anything that is thoughtfully produced yet has no pragmatic purpose. [L *ars, artis*]

art */ärt/ n* anything that isn't self-destructive or degrading. [L *ars, artis*]

art */ärt/ n* anything that makes you squirm when you look at it, the opposite of good… in short, bad. [L *ars, artis*]

art */ärt/ n* anything that makes you stop and think and smile. [L *ars, artis*]

art */ärt/ n* anything that means something. [L *ars, artis*]

art */ärt/ n* anything that moves you. [L *ars, artis*]

art */ärt/ n* anything that people add to their 'output' which is not functionally necessary and is other than the default properties of that output. [L *ars, artis*]

art */ärt/ n* anything that people would still be willing to create even if they weren't getting paid. [L *ars, artis*]

art */ärt/ n* anything that pleases the eye. [L *ars, artis*]

art */ärt/ n* anything that provokes an emotional reaction. [L *ars, artis*]

art */ärt/ n* anything that seems to inspire particular feelings; *the bigger the feelings, the better the art; no feelings = no art.* [L *ars, artis*]

art */ärt/ n* anything that serves no practical function and could possibly appeal to somebody's sense of pleasure. [L *ars, artis*]

art */ärt/ n* anything that serves no purpose other than itself. [L *ars, artis*]

art */ärt/ n* anything that shows emotion in some way. [L *ars, artis*]

art */ärt/ n* anything that someone can express that enables someone to have an emotion. [L *ars, artis*]

art */ärt/ n (inf)* anything that someone finds aesthetically pleasing; *that can lead to some really sick shit, but that's why we have* *serial killers: the patterns and rituals that they follow in their murders is art to them.* [L *ars, artis*]

art */ärt/ n* anything that someone put time into creating. [L *ars, artis*]

art */ärt/ n (econ)* anything that someone puts money down for and calls 'art'. [L *ars, artis*]

art */ärt/ n* anything that someone spends many years working on, practising and refining. [L *ars, artis*]

art */ärt/ n* anything that stimulates people into 'thinking about their feelings and feeling about their thoughts'. [L *ars, artis*]

art */ärt/ n* anything that stirs an emotional response. [L *ars, artis*]

art */ärt/ n* anything that stirs your emotions, that makes you feel something, that creates a reaction in your thought processes on a level higher than base instinct. [L *ars, artis*]

art */ärt/ n* anything that you appreciate. [L *ars, artis*]

art */ärt/ n* anything that you call art that gives you some sort of feeling. [L *ars, artis*]

art */ärt/ n* anything that you feel expresses creativity. [L *ars, artis*]

art */ärt/ n* anything that you have an opinion on. [L *ars, artis*]

art */ärt/ n* anything that you make/do that expresses a statement or is for beauty or emotionally fulfilling. [L *ars, artis*]

art */ärt/ n* anything that's creative, passionate and personal. [L *ars, artis*]

art */ärt/ n (poss joc)* anything the artist says is art: *I am a work of art and everybody knows it.* [L *ars, artis*]

art */ärt/ n* anything valued that provokes feeling, thought or emotion. [L *ars, artis*]

art */ärt/ n* anything visual *(paintings, sculpture, dance, etc)* or audible *(music, spoken word, speeches, etc)*, that comes from the soul of one and speaks to the soul of another. [L *ars, artis*]

art */ärt/ n* anything we cannot do but admire, a work performed by someone to near-perfection in our eyes, regardless of opinions by others to the contrary. [L *ars, artis*]

art */ärt/ n* anything we do outside of our primal needs. [L *ars, artis*]

art */ärt/ n* anything we do that's not just needed for basic survival. [L *ars, artis*]

art */ärt/ n* anything where we do something 'unnecessary' to express a feeling or attitude – to express ourselves. [L *ars, artis*]

art */ärt/ n* anything where you put some sort of effort into it and give it a meaning. [L *ars, artis*]

art */ärt/ n* anything which anybody cares to apply the term to; *whether they were the originator or not.* [L *ars, artis*]

art */ärt/ n* anything with a true meaning; *I mean, a sculpture made out of rusted, twisted metal could be considered art, because it could show the artist's anguish and hate and how he feels forgotten about in his time of agony and left to rust and fade away.* [L *ars, artis*]

art */ärt/ n* anything with no apparent purpose other than aesthetics. [L *ars, artis*]

art */ärt/ n* anything you can get away with. [L *ars, artis*]

art */ärt/ n* anything you can have a good discussion about; *and the better/longer the discussion, the better the art (kind of).* [L *ars, artis*]

art */ärt/ n* anything you consider to be beautiful. [L *ars, artis*]

art */ärt/ n* anything you create. [L *ars, artis*]

art */ärt/ n* anything you create with the intention of creating art. [L *ars, artis*]

art */ärt/ n* anything you find in an art gallery. [L *ars, artis*]

art */ärt/ n* anything you put in a frame. [L *ars, artis*]

art */ärt/ n (inf, perh vulg)* anything you put your blood, sweat, tears, passion and effort into; *or um in this case your genitalia into* (ref not known). [L *ars, artis*]

art */ärt/ n* anywhere you find a conscious thought, you will find art. [L *ars, artis*]

art */ärt/ n* appeals to a low element in the mind. [L *ars, artis*]

art */ärt/ n* application of skill to production of beauty *(esp visible beauty)* and works of creative imagination, *as in the fine arts.* [L *ars, artis*]

art */ärt/ n* applied knowledge, science, or letters. [L *ars, artis*]

art */ärt/ n* applying pigment to a surface. [L *ars, artis*]

art */ärt/ n (interj)* archaic and classical Gr numismatics and ceramics! [L *ars, artis*]

art */ärt/ n* arithmetic, geometry, music, astronomy, rhetoric (liberal arts), logic, grammar. [L *ars, artis*]

art */ärt/ n* arouses profound emotions similar to those resulting from real experiences. [L *ars, artis*]

art */ärt/ n* arranging objects to provoke a reaction. [L *ars, artis*]

art */ärt/ n* art. [L *ars, artis*]

art */ärt/ n* art; *everything else is everything else.* [L *ars, artis*]

art */ärt/ n* art; *no matter what it makes you feel.* [L *ars, artis*]

art */ärt/ n* art; *regardless of the audience.* [L *ars, artis*]

art */ärt/ n* art deals with things forever incapable of definition. [L *ars, artis*]

art */ärt/ n (math)* art = highly professional skillset + deep confidence in the importance of the message. [L *ars, artis*]

art */ärt/ n* art is the definition of art. [L *ars, artis*]

art */ärt/ n* artefacts produced by people for the artworld. [L *ars, artis*]

art */ärt/ n* artfulness. [L *ars, artis*]

art. */ärt/ n (abbrev)* article.

art. */ärt/ n (abbrev)* artifice.

art */ärt/ n* artifice. [L *ars, artis*]

art */ärt/ n* artifice; *the organising of elements, perspective, choice of colour;* etc. [L *ars, artis*]

art */ärt/ n* artificial. [L *ars, artis*]

art */ärt/ n* artificial chocolate flavouring. [L *ars, artis*]

art. */ärt/ n (abbrev, milit)* artillery.

art. */ärt/ n (abbrev)* artist.

art */ärt/ n* artistic production as such. [L *ars, artis*]

art */ärt/ n* artistic works: 1 *'artistic work' means – (a) a graphic work, photograph, sculpture or collage, irrespective of artistic quality, (b) a work of architecture being a building or a model for a building, or (c) a work of artistic craftsmanship;* 2 *'building' includes any fixed structure and a part of a building or fixed structure; 'graphic work' includes (a) any painting, drawing, diagram, map, chart or plan and (b) any engraving, etching, lithograph, woodcut or similar work; 'photograph'* *means a recording of light or other radiation on any medium on which an image is produced or from which an image may by any means be produced and which is not part of a film; 'sculpture' includes a cast or model made for purposes of sculpture.* [L *ars, artis*]

art */ärt/ n* artistry, prowess. [L *ars, artis*]

ART */ärt/ n* Artists' Rights and Theft Prevention Act 2004. [acronym]

art */ärt/ n* artwork. [L *ars, artis*]

art */ärt/ n (theol)* as far as it is able, follows nature, as a pupil imitates his master; *thus your art must be, as it were, God's grandchild.* [L *ars, artis*]

art */ärt/ n* as impossible to define as porn; *which the SCOTUS famously declined to define objectively in 1964 (***SCOTUS***, Supreme Court Of The United States).* [L *ars, artis*]

art */ärt/ n* as individual as ourselves; *and it can be a collective of a fraction of time.* [L *ars, artis*]

art */ärt/ n* as long as at least one person in the world *(including yourself)* thinks you're making art, then it's art. [L *ars, artis*]

art */ärt/ n* as long as there is a picture frame *(actual or metaphorical)*, it is art. [L *ars, artis*]

art */ärt/ n* as often a product of accident as intent. [L *ars, artis*]

art */ärt/ n* as real as it is fake. [L *ars, artis*]

art */ärt/ n (myth)* as real as unicorns. [L *ars, artis*]

art */ärt/ n* as universal as any individual human experience, writ large. [L *ars, artis*]

art */ärt/ n* asking questions. [L *ars, artis*]

ART */ärt/ n* Assisted Reproductive Technology; *but that is besides the point lol.* [acronym]

ART */ärt/ n (euphem)* Assuming Room Temperature; ie *dead: 'reserve a place for him in the morgue: that dude is ART'.* [acronym]

art */ärt/ n* at once surface and symbol; *those who go beneath the surface do so at their peril; those who read the symbol do so at their peril; it is the spectator and not life, that art really mirrors.* [L *ars, artis*]

art */ärt/ n* at the heart and soul of what we do when we bring ourselves to our work. [L *ars, artis*]

art */ärt/ n* attempts to persuade us that the world is or is not a given way. [L *ars, artis*]

art */ärt/ n* autobiographical; *in the same sense that the pearl is the oyster's autobiography.* [L *ars, artis*]

ART */ärt/ n (joc, sl, vulg)* Awesome Rocking Tits. [acronym]

art */ärt/ n* babies; *it takes a lot of sweating, a bit of a mess and a lot of pushing to make either art or babies, sometime the art/baby is beautiful, sometimes it's not that pretty, so yeah, a baby is art.* [L *ars, artis*]

art */ärt/ n (mus)* baby don't Hirst me, don't Hirst me, no more (**Damian Hirst** *(1965–), Eng artist, entrepreneur and art collector; prob ref* **What Is Love**, *written by Dee Dee Halligan, Dee Halligan, Junior Torello, © Hanseatic Musikverlag Gmbh & Co. Kg, GEMA).* [L *ars, artis*]

art */ärt/ n (mus)* baby don't stroke me, don't stroke me, no more *(prob ref* **What Is Love**, *written by Dee Dee Halligan, Dee Halligan, Junior Torello, © Hanseatic Musikverlag Gmbh & Co. Kg, GEMA).* [L *ars, artis*]

art */ärt/ n (interrog)* balance? [L *ars, artis*]

art */ärt/ n* basically a damn fine opportunity to act outside the confines of our ever-present upstanding and down the straight and narrow society that we encounter day to day. [L *ars, artis*]

art */ärt/ n (obs)* beautiful. [L *ars, artis*]

art */ärt/ n* beautiful but useless. [L *ars, artis*]

art */ärt/ n* beautiful not agreeable. [L *ars, artis*]

art */ärt/ n* BEAUTIFUL TO THE EYES. [L *ars, artis*]

art */ärt/ n (obs)* beauty. [L *ars, artis*]

art */ärt/ n (obs)* beauty; *like the music of the spheres – timeless, transcendent, immutable.* [L *ars, artis*]

art */ärt/ n (obs)* beauty; *the beauty of nature, the beauty of the world, the beauty of life.* [L *ars, artis*]

art */ärt/ n* beauty and freedom. [L *ars, artis*]

art */ärt/ n* beauty of the human mind and hand. [L *ars, artis*]

art */ärt/ n* beauty, truth and something bigger than you. [L *ars, artis*]

art */ärt/ n* becomes a conduit to

the unexplainable feeling of the drunkenness of new love or the devastation of loneliness; *it brings that feeling to the viewer rather than attempting to describe it.* [L *ars, artis*]

art */ärt/ n* begets more art just by its nature; *because we need to try again, to express it a little better, a little more wildly; and once we open the expression gates, everything else starts welling up, clamouring for expression too.* [L *ars, artis*]

art */ärt/ n* being able to run away without ever leaving your room. [L *ars, artis*]

art */ärt/ n* being the verb. [L *ars, artis*]

art */ärt/ n* better judged in retrospect. [L *ars, artis*]

art */ärt/ n* beyond beauty and ugliness. [L *ars, artis*]

art */ärt/ n* beyond the ability of our language to describe. [L *ars, artis*]

art */ärt/ n* beyond the limits of spoken and written language; *it speaks in metaphor, in symbol and in spirit.* [L *ars, artis*]

art */ärt/ n* beyond utility. [L *ars, artis*]

art */ärt/ n* Bioshock™ (Bioshock™, *first-person shooter video game developed by Irrational Games).* [L *ars, artis*]

art */ärt/ n* Bioshock 2™; *it's a story* (Bioshock 2™, *first-person shooter video game developed by 2K Marin).* [L *ars, artis*]

art */ärt/ n (inf)* blah blah blah, blah blah, video games, sneakers blah; *WTF? You all are some EMO folks.* [L *ars, artis*]

art */ärt/ n* blasphemous. [L *ars, artis*]

art */ärt/ n* bloody. [L *ars, artis*]

art */ärt/ n (inf sl)* bollocks. [L *ars, artis*]

art */ärt/ n* born in the gut of the artist; *if there is a deep-seated need and that vision is allowed to manifest itself.* [L *ars, artis*]

art */ärt/ n* born out of an ill-designed world. [L *ars, artis*]

art */ärt/ n (inf)* born when the Art Establishment embraces something that is submitted as art and says it's art; *I can piss on the floor and call it art, but it's not art unless someone with the power to anoint it as such believes in me, buys into my vision and accepts my reasons for* *claiming it as art; then it acquires value as a commodity and is coveted; I paint; my paintings are not art until someone who is accepted by the illuminati as knowing what art is accepts my claim for my work as being art, says 'OK, I see that' and says it's art; sublimity in self-expression exists apart from this kind of recognition, certainly, but if you want to make a living or be recognized by those who have the power, petition the illuminati: the title Art is not claimed, it is bestowed.* [L *ars, artis*]

art */ärt/ n (psychol)* both communication and personal therapy; *but this does not mean that these two aspects are necessarily one thing or contain 'art' as some amorphous quality.* [L *ars, artis*]

art */ärt/ n* both similar to and different from real life; *this is the most important aspect of its dialectical nature.* [L *ars, artis*]

art */ärt/ n (econ)* bought all the time by everyone. [L *ars, artis*]

art */ärt/ n* bound only by its creator's imagination. [L *ars, artis*]

art */ärt/ n* bounded spaces containing symbols that evoke experiences. [L *ars, artis*]

art */ärt/ n* breathing. [L *ars, artis*]

art */ärt/ n* bringing a partner to orgasm. [L *ars, artis*]

art */ärt/ n* bringing fantasy into reality. [L *ars, artis*]

art */ärt/ n* bringing out that which is deep and divine; *and cheering people up to do the same.* [L *ars, artis*]

art */ärt/ n* bringing to life what we see and feel. [L *ars, artis*]

art */ärt/ n* brings a new perception into the world and something new to consider. [L *ars, artis*]

art */ärt/ n* brings about inspiration; *and in this way, more art; it is self-propagating.* [L *ars, artis*]

art */ärt/ n* brings forward the world we are in, *as if for the first time.* [L *ars, artis*]

art */ärt/ n* brings happiness *or pleasure* to the observers *or practitioners.* [L *ars, artis*]

art */ärt/ n* brings to life notions that exist beyond the scope of language. [L *ars, artis*]

art */ärt/ n (inf)* broad as shit. [L *ars, artis*]

art */ärt/ n* broadens our horizons. [L *ars, artis*]

art /ärt/ *n* broadens your universe; *and lets you get aware of dimensions you don't normally look for.* [L *ars, artis*]

art /ärt/ *n* Broken Sword™, Shenmue™ and Ico™ (**Broken Sword™**, *franchise centered on a series of adventure games;* **Shenmue™**, *1999 adventure video game developed by Sega AM2;* **Ico™**, *action-adventure game developed by Team Ico).* [L *ars, artis*]

art /ärt/ *n (vulg, derog)* bullshit. [L *ars, artis*]

art /ärt/ *n (vulg, derog)* bullshit and consumerism. [L *ars, artis*]

art /ärt/ *n* but a poor imitation of the real art found in Nature; *no music can ever sound better than the wind and no painting can ever contain more colour and depth than the sky.* [L *ars, artis*]

art /ärt/ *n (relig)* but a shadow of the divine perfection. [L *ars, artis*]

art /ärt/ *n* by its nature mysterious. [L *ars, artis*]

art /ärt/ *n* calls on human reason and human emotions. [L *ars, artis*]

art /ärt/ *n* can and should reflect parts of ourselves back to us. [L *ars, artis*]

art /ärt/ *n* can be any old tat these days. [L *ars, artis*]

art /ärt/ *n* can be anything. [L *ars, artis*]

art /ärt/ *n* can be anything; *as long as its beauty reaches the conscious part of the observer's perception.* [L *ars, artis*]

art /ärt/ *n* can be anything; *as long as those who witness it understand that it comes from your mind.* [L *ars, artis*]

art /ärt/ *n* can be anything we want to be; *you can make it your own as long as you put a name next to it and you own it.* [L *ars, artis*]

art /ärt/ *n* can be as simple as stepping outside, noticing a few sticks and arranging them in an eye-pleasing way. [L *ars, artis*]

art /ärt/ *n* can be colourful, black and white, or plain. [L *ars, artis*]

art /ärt/ *n* can be disturbing. [L *ars, artis*]

art /ärt/ *n* can be enjoyed by the superficial masses and felt and inspire those with the ears to hear the message underneath the thin layer of cool. [L *ars, artis*]

art /ärt/ *n* can be found in any object crafted and expressed both by hand and by thought. [L *ars, artis*]

art */ärt/ n (inf)* can be high-minded polemic and debate, pure escapist entertainment or lots of time-wasting jibber jabber. [L *ars, artis*]

art */ärt/ n* can be imagined and interpreted. [L *ars, artis*]

art */ärt/ n* can be in any form; *visual forms and intangible forms.* [L *ars, artis*]

art */ärt/ n* can be in any form conceivable by man. [L *ars, artis*]

art */ärt/ n* can be intimidating; *but every time you make the choice to create yourself, or take the moment to listen to or view another's art form, you're that much closer to bringing more art into your life.* [L *ars, artis*]

art */ärt/ n* can be made to entertain, please, express, or represent something. [L *ars, artis*]

art */ärt/ n* can be manipulative, engaging, or straightforward revolting. [L *ars, artis*]

art */ärt/ n* can be nothing but violence, cruelty and injustice. [L *ars, artis*]

art */ärt/ n* can be things that are 'ugly', too; *it just has to make you think.* [L *ars, artis*]

art */ärt/ n* can be ugly, beautiful, or symbolizing; *all unique in its own way.* [L *ars, artis*]

art */ärt/ n* can be used to express misery and pain. [L *ars, artis*]

art */ärt/ n* can cause people to feel something emotionally unique. [L *ars, artis*]

art */ärt/ n* can change the world and the way people think. [L *ars, artis*]

art */ärt/ n* can describe several things: *a study of creative skill, a process of using the creative skill, a product of the creative skill, or the audience's experience with the creative skill.* [L *ars, artis*]

art */ärt/ n* can encompass all materials and views; *which is why so many people do not understand some art as they have limited views.* [L *ars, artis*]

art */ärt/ n* can evoke sadness, depression, violence or any other 'ugly' emotions or behaviours; *pretty things, too, but way too often, pretty is pretty damn boring.* [L *ars, artis*]

art */ärt/ n* can heal, torture, kill,

save lives, inspire, build dreams or shatter them, educate or render ignorant, foster and a value or eradicate perceptions, serve as a means of colonization, resistance or liberation; *the list is limitless.* [L *ars, artis*]

art */ärt/ n* can influence change. [L *ars, artis*]

art */ärt/ n* can make us nervous. [L *ars, artis*]

art */ärt/ n* can make you angry. [L *ars, artis*]

art */ärt/ n* can make you cringe. [L *ars, artis*]

art */ärt/ n* can make you sad. [L *ars, artis*]

art */ärt/ n* can make you upset. [L *ars, artis*]

art */ärt/ n* can never be defined. [L *ars, artis*]

art */ärt/ n* can never be judged or justified. [L *ars, artis*]

art */ärt/ n* can paint or sculpt an artist naked. [L *ars, artis*]

art */ärt/ n* can perform a specific function; *like reflect a truth, work to unify us or in the very least decorate a room.* [L *ars, artis*]

art */ärt/ n* can provoke thought and/or emotions, address taboos, be a commentary on the time we live in. [L *ars, artis*]

art */ärt/ n (neg)* cannot be applied to just any subject. [L *ars, artis*]

art */ärt/ n (neg)* cannot be defined by a single person; *as every individual places different emphasis on different aspects due to their life experiences, values and personality.* [L *ars, artis*]

art */ärt/ n (neg)* cannot be fully appreciated if you are not experienced. [L *ars, artis*]

art */ärt/ n (neg)* cannot be incomprehensible to great masses of people just because it is very good. [L *ars, artis*]

art */ärt/ n (neg)* cannot be labelled. [L *ars, artis*]

art */ärt/ n (neg)* cannot be named; *and cannot, by that very potency, be 'applied'; and if you have indeed applied it and only changed the world, well, changing the world is easy… a gnat can do it.* [L *ars, artis*]

art */ärt/ n (neg)* cannot be objectively determined; *since I can't necessarily look at a piece and know the heart and soul that went into its creation.* [L *ars, artis*]

art */ärt/ n (neg)* can't be measured; *there is no bit of paper that turns purple in the presence of art.* [L *ars, artis*]

art */ärt/ n (neg)* can't really be pinned down; *just as taking a walk around the park can't be pinned to any single goal, really; sometimes you just want to walk in the park.* [L *ars, artis*]

art */ärt/ n (perh fig)* carrots tangled round hair. [L *ars, artis*]

art */ärt/ n* catharis and exploration. [L *ars, artis*]

art */ärt/ n* causes a pleasant reaction. [L *ars, artis*]

art */ärt/ n* causes the suspension of will. [L *ars, artis*]

art */ärt/ n* changing just as men are; *and to what ends we can't be sure.* [L *ars, artis*]

art */ärt/ n* channelling an expression of being through yourself. [L *ars, artis*]

art */ärt/ n* channelling creative energy in a productive way. [L *ars, artis*]

art */ärt/ n* chaotic. [L *ars, artis*]

art */ärt/ n (econ)* cheap. [L *ars, artis*]

art */ärt/ n* CHI YUNG SUNG TUNG *(ref not known)*. [L *ars, artis*]

art */ärt/ n* chooses the artist; *artists have no choice in making art.* [L *ars, artis*]

art */ärt/ n* clarifies itself as the artist clarifies his or her own story. [L *ars, artis*]

art */ärt/ n* clear, sincere and singular; *(focused on one emotion).* [L *ars, artis*]

art */ärt/ n* clearly describes different types of mental agitations; *like loneliness, uncertainty, happiness and restlessness.* [L *ars, artis*]

art */ärt/ n* clever notions wrapped in clever visuals. [L *ars, artis*]

art */ärt/ n* close observation. [L *ars, artis*]

art */ärt/ n (vulg)* cocksucking. [L *ars, artis*]

art */ärt/ n (derog)* cold, mechanical, conceptual [*censored*]; ps *the attempts at contextualisation are particularly pathetic and symptomatic of a lack of conviction.* [L *ars, artis*]

art */ärt/ n* colour. [L *ars, artis*]

art */ärt/ n* colourful; *yet can be black and white.* [L *ars, artis*]

art */ärt/ n* comes from a higher impulse; *from a desire to express beauty and transcendence.* [L *ars, artis*]

art */ärt/ n* comes from a human instinct to produce something beautiful; *to add meaning to something otherwise very literal.* [L *ars, artis*]

art */ärt/ n* comes from a person and it's heartfelt. [L *ars, artis*]

art */ärt/ n* comes from an honest inquiry. [L *ars, artis*]

art */ärt/ n* comes from emotions (happy and sad), from beauty, imagination, inspiration and from a connection to the world around us; *you can have a completely balanced mental state and be a wonderful artist.* [L *ars, artis*]

art */ärt/ n* comes from one's ability to visualize. [L *ars, artis*]

art */ärt/ n* comes from the soul. [L *ars, artis*]

art */ärt/ n* comes from within; *and so expects a 'within' answer from the viewer whatever the form of it is.* [L *ars, artis*]

art */ärt/ n* comes from within as an expression. [L *ars, artis*]

art */ärt/ n* comes in many forms – *clay, paint, metal, words, electronics and the list continues on and on.* [L *ars, artis*]

art */ärt/ n* comes in many many different forms: **1** drawing **2** painting **3** sewing **4** writing **5** cooking **6** sculpting **7** creating jobs **8** dance **9** socialising **10** singing. [L *ars, artis*]

art */ärt/ n (joc)* comes in so many forms these days; *I myself am working on a brutal postmodern performance piece called* 'A Trip to the Dentist' *and it involves a random graffiti artist, my baseball bat and a confrontation in my back lane.* [L *ars, artis*]

art */ärt/ n* comes when the artist is floating downstream. [L *ars, artis*]

art */ärt/ n* comes when the artist steps out of his or her own *(or old)* way. [L *ars, artis*]

art */ärt/ n* commands an audience, commands interpretation; *and exists, therefore, as something absolute.* [L *ars, artis*]

art */ärt/ n* communal ritual. [L *ars, artis*]

art */ärt/ n* communicates something deeply personal and yet archetypal as well. [L *ars, artis*]

art */ärt/ n* communicating an idea

or emotion; *and while it employs crafting ability – in drawing and painting, printing, sculpture – or indeed in ceramics, fibre or beads – its purpose is to express something to the viewer, not to provide something to wear, to sit on, or to eat with.* [L *ars, artis*]

art */ärt/ n (poss fig)* communicating your view of the world from your little window. [L *ars, artis*]

art */ärt/ n* communication. [L *ars, artis*]

art */ärt/ n* communication; *and communication is the act of transferring a thought from one brain to another.* [L *ars, artis*]

art */ärt/ n (neg)* communication; *but contemporary art fails to communicate because of a disjuncture between subject and beholder, form and purpose.* [L *ars, artis*]

art */ärt/ n* completely personal; *and should not be dictated by the masses.* [L *ars, artis*]

art */ärt/ n* completes our hunger for expression. [L *ars, artis*]

art */ärt/ n* complex. [L *ars, artis*]

art */ärt/ n* composition, technique, perception and concept. [L *ars, artis*]

art */ärt/ n* comprised of technique and skill, but also emotion. [L *ars, artis*]

art */ärt/ n* concept, ideas and the confrontation of convention. [L *ars, artis*]

art */ärt/ n* conflated with what Lady Gaga does (Stefani Joanne Angelina 'Lady Gaga' Germanotta *(1986–), Am pop-singer, songwriter, activist, record producer, businesswoman, fashion designer, philanthropist and actress).* [L *ars, artis*]

art */ärt/ n* connects us. [L *ars, artis*]

art */ärt/ n* conscious and unconscious thoughts come together in a nonverbal form of communication. [L *ars, artis*]

art */ärt/ n* considered a uniquely human ability; *but that may not be true.* [L *ars, artis*]

art */ärt/ n* constant expansion and evolution. [L *ars, artis*]

art */ärt/ n* constantly evolving. [L *ars, artis*]

art */ärt/ n* constantly in flux because we are constantly in flux; *or else we are dead.* [L *ars, artis*]

art */ärt/ n* contains a variety of elements configured in such a way that they sometimes contradict each other and sometimes align with each other; *the overall design of alignments and contradictions can begin to resemble, or suggest, the complexity of the human spirit.* [L *ars, artis*]

art */ärt/ n* contains meaning beyond its apparent content. [L *ars, artis*]

art */ärt/ n* contextual and subjective. [L *ars, artis*]

art */ärt/ n* contextualized in our society and culture; *and this is a process that involves serious criticism and not mere 'marketing'.* [L *ars, artis*]

art */ärt/ n* continuously redefines itself. [L *ars, artis*]

art */ärt/ n* controlled by the artist. [L *ars, artis*]

art */ärt/ n* conversation. [L *ars, artis*]

art */ärt/ n* conveys emotion. [L *ars, artis*]

art */ärt/ n* conveys meaning. [L *ars, artis*]

art */ärt/ n* conveys something of the sublime. [L *ars, artis*]

art */ärt/ n* conveys the deviant behaviour of an artist. [L *ars, artis*]

art */ärt/ n (neg)* copying things is not art; *there's a ceramic piece in my local museum that looks like a raggedy leather purse you would buy at the thrift store; if I wanted to see that, I would go to the thrift, not the museum.* [L *ars, artis*]

art */ärt/ n (psychol)* could be a good way to relieve stress; *you can do art if you're mad, sad, depressed and more.* [L *ars, artis*]

art */ärt/ n* could be made in a type of art factory where all the machines do the work. [L *ars, artis*]

art */ärt/ n* could be, or is already, a powerful way of purging people, of ridding them of all their insanity, sinfulness and hunger for violence; *what if all criminals now behind bars for committing acts of violence considered the act of creating something personal, something that nobody else could create because of the acutely distinctive specificities invested in it, something that could earn them people's respect and appreciation without having to pull triggers, break noses or elbows, smoke weed or drink alcohol? Wouldn't that make our prisons emptier than most streets at 4am?* [L *ars, artis*]

art */ärt/ n* craft. [L *ars, artis*]

art */ärt/ n (econ)* craft with a juicy markup. [L *ars, artis*]

art */ärt/ n* created at the whim of the artist. [L *ars, artis*]

art */ärt/ n* created by an artist, to be presented to an 'artworld' public. [L *ars, artis*]

art */ärt/ n* created for the purpose of pleasing the senses. [L *ars, artis*]

art */ärt/ n* created to show the beauty in life. [L *ars, artis*]

art */ärt/ n* created when an artist creates a beautiful object, *or produces a stimulating experience that is considered by his audience to have artistic merit.* [L *ars, artis*]

art */ärt/ n* created with the purpose to be art; *something can be considered art – the 'Gears of War™ is art' argument – but that doesn't make it art (*Gears of War™*, military science fiction third-person shooter video game developed by Epic Games).* [L *ars, artis*]

art */ärt/ n* creates a discontinuity between itself and the unsynthesised manifold. [L *ars, artis*]

art */ärt/ n* creates an upward spiral of growth. [L *ars, artis*]

art */ärt/ n* creates its own laws; *ones of revolution and change.* [L *ars, artis*]

art */ärt/ n* creates meaning which is then shared amongst us. [L *ars, artis*]

art */ärt/ n (relig)* creating… *and creating is to appreciate God and His work.* [L *ars, artis*]

art */ärt/ n* creating a new reality that helps us to finally understand the old one. [L *ars, artis*]

art */ärt/ n* creating a piece that speaks louder than words. [L *ars, artis*]

art */ärt/ n* creating a world out of our thoughts, our dreams, our memories and our eyes. [L *ars, artis*]

art */ärt/ n* creating an illusion that in turn creates a reality. [L *ars, artis*]

art */ärt/ n* creating emotion in people; *that emotion doesn't have to be positive.* [L *ars, artis*]

art */ärt/ n* creating our innermost desires. [L *ars, artis*]

art */ärt/ n* creating something average; *or worse yet still being able to convince others it's art and worth a lot of money.* [L *ars, artis*]

art /ärt/ *n* creating something like a drawing or painting. [L *ars, artis*]

art /ärt/ *n* creating something that hasn't been seen, heard, or felt before, but which projects the feeling of the artist in a unique way to the audience. [L *ars, artis*]

art /ärt/ *n* creating, expressing, progressing, frustrating and obsessing. [L *ars, artis*]

art /ärt/ *n* creation and expression of representations of beauty; *as painting, music, theatre, drawing, sculpting,* etc. [L *ars, artis*]

art /ärt/ *n* creation first and foremost and for its own sake. [L *ars, artis*]

art /ärt/ *n* creation, imagination, recording, investigation, arbitration and culmination. [L *ars, artis*]

art /ärt/ *n* creation made from tools that forms one thing into a greater or another thing which pleases the beholder who sees what he/she wants to see or feel at the time. [L *ars, artis*]

art /ärt/ *n* creation of a display out of inspiration and imagination. [L *ars, artis*]

art /ärt/ *n* creation that allows for interpretation of any kind. [L *ars, artis*]

art /ärt/ *n* creations meant to evoke a thoughtful or meaningful response from the viewer. [L *ars, artis*]

art /ärt/ *n* creations of the mind. [L *ars, artis*]

art /ärt/ *n* creations that can influence my emotions and paint a vivid picture in my mind. [L *ars, artis*]

art /ärt/ *n* creative activity resulting in the production of paintings, drawings or sculpture. [L *ars, artis*]

art /ärt/ *n* creative activity resulting in the production of paintings, drawings, or sculpture: *she's good at art.* [L *ars, artis*]

art /ärt/ *n* creative expression derived from our sensual/intelligible experiences. [L *ars, artis*]

art /ärt/ *n* creative expression, or creativity that expresses some aspect of the author or authors' life philosophy, intentionally or not; *this gives it purpose beyond the mere pleasure of experiencing its existence, thus giving it value; this is why we claim* Inception *is a work of art while*

Transformers™: Revenge of the Fallen, *despite also being a blockbuster action film, is often considered not: one has themes and meaning beyond the surface, the other is just robots beating on each other for entertainment's sake* (Inception, *2010 science fiction film;* Transformers™: Revenge of the Fallen, *2009 Am science fiction action film).* [L *ars, artis*]

art */ärt/ n* creative forms of entertainment. [L *ars, artis*]

art */ärt/ n* creative manipulation and innovation. [L *ars, artis*]

art */ärt/ n* creative skill-imagination-visual form *etc etc.* [L *ars, artis*]

art */ärt/ n* creative story-telling. [L *ars, artis*]

art */ärt/ n* creative, visual and conceptual problem solving. [L *ars, artis*]

art */ärt/ n* creative work or its principles. [L *ars, artis*]

art */ärt/ n* creativity; *in the sense that it requires planning in order to achieve.* [L *ars, artis*]

art */ärt/ n* creativity combined with talent and craftsmanship. [L *ars, artis*]

art */ärt/ n* creativity, emotions, feelings. [L *ars, artis*]

art */ärt/ n* creativity is allowing yourself to make mistakes; art is knowing which ones to keep. [L *ars, artis*]

art */ärt/ n* creativity made manifest. [L *ars, artis*]

art */ärt/ n* creativity of man; *as distinguished from the world of nature.* [L *ars, artis*]

art */ärt/ n* culturally significant meaning, skilfully encoded in an affecting, sensuous medium. [L *ars, artis*]

art */ärt/ n* culture. [L *ars, artis*]

art */ärt/ n* cunning. [L *ars, artis*]

art */ärt/ n* cunning and trickery. [L *ars, artis*]

art */ärt/ n* cunning, artifice, crafty conduct. [L *ars, artis*]

art */ärt/ n (vulg, derog)* cunts cashing in on stupid people's lack of taste and intelligence. [L *ars, artis*]

art */ärt/ n* curiosity. [L *ars, artis*]

art */ärt/ n (photog)* darkroom manipulation of imaging and photographs. [L *ars, artis*]

art */ärt/ n* Deadly Premonition™

(Deadly Premonition™, *psychological horror video game developed by Access Games).* [L *ars, artis*]

art */ärt/ n (interj)* deals with generosity, imagination… and action too! [L *ars, artis*]

art */ärt/ n (inf, vulg)* decided by the creator; *but then, you're just setting yourself up for a whole lot of wank.* [L *ars, artis*]

art */ärt/ n* decided by the galleries that host the art; *even though they have their own (elitist) agendas.* [L *ars, artis*]

art */ärt/ n* decided by the viewer; *even though some people have very stupid taste.* [L *ars, artis*]

art */ärt/ n* decorative or illustrative elements in printed matter. [L *ars, artis*]

art */ärt/ n* defined by its vicinity to the gallery; *heap of old tyres – trash; heap of old tyres in a gallery – art.* [L *ars, artis*]

art */ärt/ n* defined by the admirer. [L *ars, artis*]

art */ärt/ n* defined by the aesthetic pleasure it creates. [L *ars, artis*]

art */ärt/ n* defined by the individual that makes the arbitrary judgment as to whether it is art or not. [L *ars, artis*]

art */ärt/ n* definitely communication; *but it can be transitive or intransitive, just like non-artistic communication; you know how sometimes you stub your toe and curse? You aren't cursing to someone, you're just cursing, but it makes you feel better; sometimes art is a conversation, or a lecture, or a joke; sometimes you stub your soul's toe and you just have to paint a picture to ease the pain.* [L *ars, artis*]

art */ärt/ n* definitely important. [L *ars, artis*]

art */ärt/ n* definitely more than the traditional arts *(painting, sculpture, music).* [L *ars, artis*]

art */ärt/ n* deliberately setting out to make something special. [L *ars, artis*]

art */ärt/ n (derog)* delivered with a revoltingly arrogant smirk. [L *ars, artis*]

art */ärt/ n* demonstrates creativity on the part of the person/people who produced it, is able to elicit emotion from those who see/listen/hear/otherwise interact with it and inspires one to think about it in detail. [L *ars, artis*]

art */ärt/ n* denotes skill in doing or performing that which is attained from the exercise of intuitive faculties. [L *ars, artis*]

art */ärt/ n* depends entirely on the intent of the creator; *others may not like it or understand it and in fact it may be really bad, awful, amateurish, stupid and/or downright repulsive – but that doesn't change the intent.* [L *ars, artis*]

art */ärt/ n* depends heavily on the creative abilities of the creator to use narratives and symbolisms to depict a deeper meaning; *can also contain realistic elements but then in most cases relies on the creator's skills to retain its realism.* [L *ars, artis*]

art */ärt/ n (vulg, derog)* depends on when you were born and how much of a ponce you are; *for me its paintings, sculptures and such, not a red ladder with a blue rung or a person on a floor covered in cheese (perh ref* Cosimo Cavallaro*, It-Can artist, filmmaker and sculpt).* [L *ars, artis*]

art */ärt/ n (joc)* depends on which room in the house the buyer hangs the thing: *in the hallway – art; in the bedroom – porn; in the kitchen – art, but you didn't charge them enough for it; in the toilet – not good enough to be art, but not stimulating enough to be porn.* [L *ars, artis*]

art */ärt/ n* depth. [L *ars, artis*]

art */ärt/ n* designated or consecrated as such in a suitable social context; eg *a gallery.* [L *ars, artis*]

art */ärt/ n* designed to destroy our culture and traditions; *it is not like this by accident; they know what they are doing.* [L *ars, artis*]

art */ärt/ n* detaches from the artist and stands alone and self-sufficient in the world; *the artist calves [perh carves] off a piece of himself or herself and when I encounter that piece – the artwork – I'm able to glimpse or sense the unique human spirit or human intelligence that created it.* [L *ars, artis*]

art */ärt/ n* determined by the new social conditions of artistic development and by the spiritual needs of people on the path of communist construction. [L *ars, artis*]

art */ärt/ n* device. [L *ars, artis*]

art */ärt/ n* devoted to an idea or a feeling that transcends the maker. [L *ars, artis*]

art */ärt/ n* different, creative and imaginative. [L *ars, artis*]

art */ärt/ n* different things to different people. [L *ars, artis*]

art */ärt/ n* directed or at least overseen by one's personal conscious evolution. [L *ars, artis*]

art */ärt/ n (poss derog)* dirt. [L *ars, artis*]

art */ärt/ n* discerning of one's self and one's environment and thought processes into probabilities and possibilities made tangible through individual creative processes reflecting the individual's need to live in a world beyond the commonality of material existence. [L *ars, artis*]

art */ärt/ n* disclosure. [L *ars, artis*]

art */ärt/ n* discovering something about the way you interact with the world and the things in it. [L *ars, artis*]

art */ärt/ n* discovery and development of elementary principles of nature into beautiful forms suitable for human use. [L *ars, artis*]

art */ärt/ n* disinterested, without use or purpose; *and this is regarded, not as a vice, but as a virtue.* [L *ars, artis*]

art */ärt/ n* divided into what is known as art for the elite and art for the masses. [L *ars, artis*]

art */ärt/ n (interrog)* do most people find it to be beautiful, or creative, or inventive/clever, or a true display of skills and talents? *If so, it's art.* [L *ars, artis*]

art */ärt/ n (hist)* documentation of our history. [L *ars, artis*]

art */ärt/ n (neg)* does not care who invents it, who nurtures and cares for it and it really doesn't care who is successful and who is not. [L *ars, artis*]

art */ärt/ n (neg)* does not exist to make the world a better place. [L *ars, artis*]

art */ärt/ n (neg)* does not form without growth and movement. [L *ars, artis*]

art */ärt/ n (neg)* does not have to be man-made; *Nature is full of art; sometimes even just a situation is art.* [L *ars, artis*]

art */ärt/ n (comput)* does not have to evoke feelings; *a good piece of software documentation can be properly considered a work of art: it expresses the writer's intentionality in describing the system and readers can infer this intentionality from the* *experience of the work.* [L ***ars, artis***]

art */ärt/ n (neg)* **does not inspire.** [L ***ars, artis***]

art */ärt/ n (neg)* **does not make you think or colour your world.** [L ***ars, artis***]

art */ärt/ n* **does not need to break the mold;** *but when it does its presence is palpable as a synthesis of art and its artist.* [L ***ars, artis***]

art */ärt/ n (neg)* **does not reproduce what we see;** *rather, it makes us see.* [L ***ars, artis***]

art */ärt/ n (neg)* **does not require a meaning;** *but it does require some consideration and technique on the part of the doer.* [L ***ars, artis***]

art */ärt/ n (neg)* **does not solely exist within beauty;** *but within the aesthetic.* [L ***ars, artis***]

art */ärt/ n (neg)* **does not uplift.** [L ***ars, artis***]

art */ärt/ n (neg)* **doesn't always have to be good, creative, inspiring, thought-provoking, or make you uncomfortable:** *math is art; science is art; web designs, Twitter™ posts and monologues are art; I don't always understand what others are trying to say, but I do 'get' that they are trying to say something* (**Twitter™**, *online social networking and microblogging service).* [L ***ars, artis***]

art */ärt/ n (neg)* **doesn't come much bigger than Manet, Munch and Vermeer** (**Édouard Manet** *(1832–83), Fr painter;* **Edvard Munch** *(1863–1944), Nor painter and printmaker whose intensely evocative treatment of psychol themes built upon some of the main tenets of late c19th Symbolism and greatly influenced Ger Expressionism in the early c20th;* **Johannes, Jan** *or* **Johan Vermeer** *(1632–75), Du painter who specialized in domestic interior scenes of middle-class life).* [L ***ars, artis***]

art */ärt/ n (neg)* **doesn't exist.** [L ***ars, artis***]

art */ärt/ n (neg)* **doesn't fit neatly into compartments;** *it spills over, sloshes around and commingles; it contains ambiguities and ironies.* [L ***ars, artis***]

art */ärt/ n (neg)* **doesn't necessarily have to be beautiful, appealing, or even significant; it doesn't have to make a statement or be an expression of the artist;** *some of it is, some of it isn't; but one thing all art has in common is that it is* *meant to entertain and to be displayed – not necessarily widely displayed, but meant to be viewed nonetheless.* [L *ars, artis*]

art */ärt/ n (pos)* does something to people. [L *ars, artis*]

art */ärt/ n (vulg, poss joc)* done by people who are shit at drawing. [L *ars, artis*]

art */ärt/ n* DOOM® 3™, as well as Fallout® New Vegas™ and Final Fantasy® VIII™; *but not Fallout® 3™ and Skyrim® too, for that matter; it is too repetitive in game play for me to call either art (*DOOM® 3™*, science fiction survival horror first-person shooter video game developed by id Software;* Fallout® New Vegas™*, action role-playing video game developed by Obsidian Entertainment;* Final Fantasy® VIII™*, a role-playing video game released for the PlayStation® in 1999 and Windows™-based personal computers in 2000;* Fallout® 3™*, action role-playing open world video game developed by Bethesda Game Studios;* Skyrim®*, action role-playing game, playable from either a first- or third-person perspective).* [L *ars, artis*]

art */ärt/ n* drawings and paintings. [L *ars, artis*]

art */ärt/ n (inf)* dreams come alive; *take all that weird, beautiful, ugly stuff that happens in your head when you are sleeping and bring it out and give it life, baby!* [L *ars, artis*]

art */ärt/ n* driven by an intuitive need to reveal ourselves as part of humanity's evolving creative processes; *moving us collectively towards greater understanding of what we are and what we can yet become.* [L *ars, artis*]

art */ärt/ n* driven by position, context, history and community. [L *ars, artis*]

art */ärt/ n* driven by the heart and not by the marketplace. [L *ars, artis*]

art */ärt/ n* echoes our deepest wants and fears. [L *ars, artis*]

art */ärt/ n* ecstatic union. [L *ars, artis*]

art */ärt/ n (educ)* educational. [L *ars, artis*]

art */ärt/ n (poss philos)* either an arrangement of conditions intended to be capable of affording an experience with marked aesthetic character or (incidentally) an arrangement belonging to a class or type of arrangements that is typically intended to have this capacity. [L *ars, artis*]

art */ärt/ n* either everything is art, or nothing is art. [L *ars, artis*]

art */ärt/ n* either moves you or not. [L *ars, artis*]

art */ärt/ n* either plagiarism or revolution. [L *ars, artis*]

art */ärt/ n* either sacred or a high form of culture. [L *ars, artis*]

art */ärt/ n* eliciting responses from people. [L *ars, artis*]

art */ärt/ n* elicits an emotional response from the audience. [L *ars, artis*]

art */ärt/ n* elicits feeling beyond shallow guise; *for even if it depicts shallowness it means more and is felt more than its depiction.* [L **ars, artis**]

art */ärt/ n (perh relig)* elicits one's still, small voice within. [L *ars, artis*]

art */ärt/ n* elusive. [L *ars, artis*]

art */ärt/ n* embodied meaning. [L *ars, artis*]

art */ärt/ n* embodies the aesthetics; *but the idea of aesthetics is not a universal for every culture.* [L *ars, artis*]

art */ärt/ n* embodies the most profound paradoxes and conflicts of social development. [L *ars, artis*]

art */ärt/ n* embraces whim. [L *ars, artis*]

art */ärt/ n* emergence. [L *ars, artis*]

art */ärt/ n* emotion being thrown out of someone in a creative manor [perh *manner*]. [L *ars, artis*]

art */ärt/ n* emotion contained. [L *ars, artis*]

art */ärt/ n* emotion, imagination and its marriage with the intellect. [L *ars, artis*]

art */ärt/ n* emotional. [L *ars, artis*]

art */ärt/ n* emotional, intellectual, physical and spiritual. [L *ars, artis*]

art */ärt/ n* emotions and thoughts and feelings; *or maybe just a guy/gal you're crushing on.* [L **ars, artis**; or perh *Arthur* or *Artemis*]

art */ärt/ n* emotions in a physical, tangible, touchable state. [L *ars, artis*]

art */ärt/ n* emotions turned into a masterpiece. [L *ars, artis*]

art */ärt/ n (psychol)* enables the practical activity of which it is an integral part to have an emotional and psychological influence upon an individual. [L *ars, artis*]

art */ärt/ n* enables us to find ourselves and lose ourselves at the same time. [L *ars, artis*]

art */ärt/ n* encompasses a lot of expression and storytelling and communication. [L *ars, artis*]

art */ärt/ n* encompasses all human activity; *but is transcended by the subset of science which is applied art – the application of human activity to describing the universe; art is all other activity and consequently deals in metaphysical assertions.* [L *ars, artis*]

art */ärt/ n* encompasses everything in life that we create to add colour, texture, shading and flavour to our lives. [L *ars, artis*]

art */ärt/ n* encompasses the beautiful and the ugly, the ancient and the immediate, the naively utopian and the wantonly destructive, the mercenary and the altruistic, the introspective and the revolutionary; *it allows for all those things simultaneously and remains open to the possibility that it is occasionally none of them.* [L *ars, artis*]

art */ärt/ n* encourages humility in the human soul; *because it's so easy to do and yet so difficult to do well.* [L *ars, artis*]

art */ärt/ n* engaged in, and evidenced by, an individual human consciousness; *collective or collaborative efforts don't quite cut it.* [L *ars, artis*]

art */ärt/ n* engages both the maker and the viewer and creates dialogues of wonder. [L *ars, artis*]

art */ärt/ n* engages us, like a magician does, by showing us what we are seeing with devices that we don't see; ie *shapes in place of things, lines in place of boundaries and movement, spaces around as well as within things, colour instead of light.* [L *ars, artis*]

art */ärt/ n* engaging. [L *ars, artis*]

art */ärt/ n* engenders our respect. [L *ars, artis*]

art */ärt/ n* enlarges experience by admitting us to the inner life of others. [L *ars, artis*]

art */ärt/ n* enraptures the imagination. [L *ars, artis*]

art */ärt/ n* enriches our minds by confronting us with previously unconsidered perspectives. [L *ars, artis*]

art /ärt/ *n* entertainment; *saying* 'it's not art, it's entertainment' *is like saying* 'it's not a cloud, it's condensed water vapour' – *you just make yourself look foolish.* [L ***ars, artis***]

art /ärt/ *n* entertains and informs; *TV, music, theatre, movies, books, newspapers.* [L ***ars, artis***]

art /ärt/ *n* entirely a creation of the human species. [L ***ars, artis***]

art /ärt/ *n (perh urol)* entirely a result of the artist's creative 'fountain'. [L ***ars, artis***]

art /ärt/ *n* envelopes technical skill and creativity and the way a viewer feels when looking at a piece; *that's why people like iPhone® pictures of your kids more than they like my DSLR pictures of food* (**iPhone®**, *a line of smartphones designed and marketed by Apple™ Inc.;* **DSLR**, *Digital Single-Lens Reflex camera).* [L ***ars, artis***]

art /ärt/ *n* epistemologically obsolete. [L ***ars, artis***]

art /ärt/ *n* essentially, in the eye of the beholder; *but at the top level of art, aesthetics mixes with marketing.* [L ***ars, artis***]

art /ärt/ *n* establishes and makes tangible a time, a place, a thought and an idea. [L ***ars, artis***]

art /ärt/ *n (obs)* eternal beauty! [L ***ars, artis***]

art /ärt/ *n (math)* even mathematics *(which I dislike ☺)* can be artistic. [L ***ars, artis***]

art /ärt/ *n* even when nonrepresentational, has limbs to dance and mouths to sing but is silent until made and will not move its body until formed; *yet it is always seen, even by the blind; and is known even to those we would consider lost; maybe even more so as some of the autistic and those deemed insane have shown understanding of art that only masters are capable of.* [L ***ars, artis***]

art /ärt/ *n* ever-changing. [L ***ars, artis***]

art /ärt/ *n* ever-changing; *as the ever-changing artist tries to show the people the ever-evolving, changing and growing world.* [L ***ars, artis***]

art /ärt/ *n* every art has one first principle, *or general major premise,* not borrowed from science, that which enunciates the object aimed at and affirms it to be a desirable object: *the builder's art assumes that it is desirable to have buildings; architecture (as one of the* *fine arts) that it is desirable to have them beautiful and imposing; the hygienic and medical arts assume, the one that the preservation of health, the other that the cure of disease, are fitting and desirable ends; these are not propositions of science; propositions of science assert a matter of fact – an existence, a co-existence, a succession, or a resemblance; the propositions now spoken of do not assert that anything is, but enjoin or recommend that something should be; they are a class by themselves; a proposition of which the predicate is expressed by the words 'ought' or 'should be' is generically different from one which is expressed by 'is' or 'will be'.* [L *ars, artis*]

art */ärt/ n* every aspect of life; *and life itself is some form of art; this would even include paedophilia since it creates much (sadness, rage, trauma, inner obstacles to either be overcome or be devoured by,* etc*) and provokes many thoughts (can I overcome this pain? can he change his ways? can I forgive him? should I forgive him?* etc*).* [L *ars, artis*]

art */ärt/ n (theol)* every creation that God made. [L *ars, artis*]

art */ärt/ n* every piece that was created to express creativity and with the purpose to share the beauty with those who can admire the piece. [L *ars, artis*]

art */ärt/ n* every regulated operation or dexterity by which organized beings pursue ends which they know beforehand; *together with the rules and the result of every such operation or dexterity.* [L *ars, artis*]

art */ärt/ n* every thought, every mood, every desire and every sensation that says: I. [L *ars, artis*]

art */ärt/ n* everything. [L *ars, artis*]

art */ärt/ n* everything; *except abstract concepts and ideas.* [L *ars, artis*]

art */ärt/ n* everything and nothing. [L *ars, artis*]

art */ärt/ n* everything around us; *from the clothes we wear to the cars we drive.* [L *ars, artis*]

art */ärt/ n* everything ever created; *by man or by nature.* [L *ars, artis*]

art */ärt/ n* everything excessive. [L *ars, artis*]

art */ärt/ n* everything one *(the creator or the viewer)* feels to be art. [L *ars, artis*]

art */ärt/ n* everything that comes

out of you when trying to express feelings and emotions, when you feel the need to express those feelings; *and the good outcome is to be able to transmit that feeling to the watchers or know that the watchers enjoy what you have created out of your own needs.* [L *ars, artis*]

art */ärt/ n* everything that goes into building everything around it. [L *ars, artis*]

art */ärt/ n* everything that has been created for ears and eyes. [L *ars, artis*]

art */ärt/ n (pers, relig)* everything that I am; *I love art, God bless.* [L *ars, artis*]

art */ärt/ n* everything that is done with passion: *music, paintings, sex, pain, destruction, love, life, death, darkness, light, dreaming.* [L *ars, artis*]

art */ärt/ n* everything that is made with no effort to be necessarily liked. [L *ars, artis*]

art */ärt/ n* everything that makes you look twice. [L *ars, artis*]

art */ärt/ n* everything that TOUCHES any amount of humans in any way; *whether it's a picture or photography, something written, a music piece, a sculpture, a building, a garment, origami, garden sculpturing, flower binding; a movie, a game, whatever.* [L *ars, artis*]

art */ärt/ n* everything that's left after you've taken away science and mathematics. [L *ars, artis*]

art */ärt/ n* everything that's on this site and doesn't break the rules. [L *ars, artis*]

art */ärt/ n* everything they put on a wall, floor, everything they photograph, video tape, build then smash. [L *ars, artis*]

art */ärt/ n* everything to some and something to all. [L *ars, artis*]

art */ärt/ n* everything which we distinguish from Nature. [L *ars, artis*]

art */ärt/ n* everything with a meaning to it. [L *ars, artis*]

art */ärt/ n* everything you can take the time to appreciate. [L *ars, artis*]

art */ärt/ n* everything you don't have to do. [L *ars, artis*]

art */ärt/ n* everything you enjoy. [L *ars, artis*]

art */ärt/ n* everywhere. [L *ars, artis*]

art */ärt/ n* everywhere; *but undefinable.* [L *ars, artis*]

art */ärt/ n* evokes emotions; *and allows us to know that we are not alone in the universe in experiencing these sensations.* [L *ars, artis*]

art */ärt/ n* evokes feelings of love, pain, fear and all of the things that we have been conditioned to hide in this society. [L *ars, artis*]

art */ärt/ n* exacting extraction of well-imagined, gracefully executed passion for a medium and a subject. [L *ars, artis*]

art */ärt/ n* exactly what lautnerlove98 [*sic*] said *(prob ref* lautnerlover98, *Ask® member since 2012).* [L *ars, artis*]

art */ärt/ n* exaggeration. [L *ars, artis*]

art */ärt/ n* excellence or aesthetic merit of conception or execution as exemplified by such works. [L *ars, artis*]

art */ärt/ n* exists as a reflection of power. [L *ars, artis*]

art */ärt/ n* exists only when the art object 'affords continuously renewed delight' and is 'indefinitely instrumental to new satisfying events'. [L *ars, artis*]

art */ärt/ n* exists to create emotion. [L *ars, artis*]

art */ärt/ n* exists to enrich our minds. [L *ars, artis*]

art */ärt/ n* exists to inspire us. [L *ars, artis*]

art */ärt/ n* exists to transport. [L *ars, artis*]

art */ärt/ n* exists within the everyday. [L *ars, artis*]

art */ärt/ n* expertly using a medium to convey an idea, experience and thoughts and be perceived by our senses for interpretation. [L *ars, artis*]

art */ärt/ n* explores what is commonly termed as the human condition. [L *ars, artis*]

art */ärt/ n* exploring ideas and expressing them through dance, poetry, theatre, visual art, music *etc.* [L *ars, artis*]

art */ärt/ n* expresses and glorifies reality/life/the human condition; *and we are emotionally stirred by what it expresses.* [L *ars, artis*]

art */ärt/ n* expresses emotion and ignites a response; *sometimes more effectively than words do.* [L *ars, artis*]

art */ärt/ n* expresses the passion from within. [L *ars, artis*]

art */ärt/ n* expressing emotion through creative means. [L *ars, artis*]

art */ärt/ n* expressing emotions in the way that ennobles your soul. [L *ars, artis*]

art */ärt/ n (interj)* expressing one's feelings, thoughts, hopes, dreams, love, *etc* in some form outside of their mind! [L *ars, artis*]

art */ärt/ n (relig)* expressing your deepest, most sacred concerns and feelings about life in any form possible. [L *ars, artis*]

art */ärt/ n* expressing yourself. [L *ars, artis*]

art */ärt/ n* expressing yourself in many different ways; *like in paintings, drawings and sculptures.* [L *ars, artis*]

art */ärt/ n* expression. [L *ars, artis*]

art */ärt/ n* (m) expression; *and expression we may describe, for our own ends, as the putting forth of purpose, feeling, or thought into a sensuous medium, where they can be experienced again by the one who expresses himself and communicated to others.* [L *ars, artis*]

art */ärt/ n* expression; *there's no right or wrong way to do something.* [L *ars, artis*]

art */ärt/ n* expression according to aesthetic principles: *that piece of art is truly amazing!* [L *ars, artis*]

art */ärt/ n* expression and creation. [L *ars, artis*]

art */ärt/ n* expression, development, life, death, imagination, dreams. [L *ars, artis*]

art */ärt/ n* expression for human life. [L *ars, artis*]

art */ärt/ n* expression of deepened feelings. [L *ars, artis*]

art */ärt/ n* expression of talent. [L *ars, artis*]

art */ärt/ n (inf)* expression of the moment; *I'm mostly derpy.* [L *ars, artis*]

art */ärt/ n* expression of thought in an original fashion. [L *ars, artis*]

art */ärt/ n* expression through attractive symbolism. [L *ars, artis*]

art */ärt/ n* expression with purpose. [L *ars, artis*]

art */ärt/ n* expression without provocation. [L *ars, artis*]

art */ärt/ n* expressions from within, released onto canvas; *or what-*

ever you are painting on. [L *ars, artis*]

art */ärt/ n* expressions that show emotion and soul through music or the creation of physical objects. [L *ars, artis*]

art */ärt/ n* extends beyond the object *or performance or process.* [L *ars, artis*]

art */ärt/ n* familiar and yet unknown. [L *ars, artis*]

art */ärt/ n (inf, joc)* 'fart' but without the 'f'. [L *ars, artis*]

art */ärt/ n* fascinating. [L *ars, artis*]

art */ärt/ n (interrog)* fashion is art, fashion is not art; *but at the end, who cares?* [L *ars, artis*]

art */ärt/ n* fat, fluffy baby ducks flying around on jetpacks *(perh ref* Sebastien Millon, *world renowned artist).* [L *ars, artis*]

art */ärt/ n* feeling and emotion. [L *ars, artis*]

art */ärt/ n* fights against war and stupidity. [L *ars, artis*]

art */ärt/ n* fills the time. [L *ars, artis*]

art */ärt/ n* film making or chalk drawings. [L *ars, artis*]

art */ärt/ n* Final Fantasy® VII™ (Final Fantasy® VII™, *a role-playing video game developed by Square (now Square Enix)).* [L *ars, artis*]

art */ärt/ n* finding yourself in life. [L *ars, artis*]

art */ärt/ n* finding yourself in something that is not yourself. [L *ars, artis*]

art */ärt/ n* fire; *not the fire that consumes but spreads and grows.* [L *ars, artis*]

art */ärt/ n (interrog)* first related to human existence and as an executive in the arts for spiritual pursuits, why? *Because this is a being coerced globalization era, many of the issues and problems of social reality is need for common resolve and respond to human society, namely: as a social community of the world is a re-shaping of the world, this is a different area each one can escape from reality in this context, art gives us maximum convenience and possible to tell, to interpret, to propose, to the metaphor, to symbolize, to confront, to create the world and its problems while their art is not to escape the artistic significance of human existence, nor pursue the interests of the market digital art, is associated concern itself with the* *world of art and it can be a plus grief, you can pour the physical and mental dedication and can even be muttering to face the world do self-representation, but one thing, it is by no means pro fashion trend, but also cater to the interests of non-flashy or more non-shadowing the spirit of freedom which can be studied metaphysical world, but not metaphysical speculation in land interests, artistic reason called art, all that it is still somewhat spiritual significance in the world of human performance first, the human subconscious still did not give up the last idealistic a reservation.* [L *ars, artis*]

art */ärt/ n* flawless. [L *ars, artis*]

art */ärt/ n* flawless expression of subconscious forces; *and becomes more fluid with practice.* [L *ars, artis*]

art */ärt/ n* fleeting. [L *ars, artis*]

art */ärt/ n* flexible; *it can be a painting, a statue, a play, or a book.* [L *ars, artis*]

art */ärt/ n* flexible and free. [L *ars, artis*]

art */ärt/ n* flux. [L *ars, artis*]

art */ärt/ n (interrog)* fluxus… isn't it? (**Fluxus**, *an international and interdisciplinary group of artists, composers, designers and poets that took shape the 1960s and 1970s).* [L *ars, artis*]

art */ärt/ n* food; *you can't eat it but it feeds you.* [L *ars, artis*]

art */ärt/ n* food can always be art. [L *ars, artis*]

art */ärt/ n (interj)* FOOD FOR NONSENSE! [L *ars, artis*]

art */ärt/ n* food for the soul. [L *ars, artis*]

art */ärt/ n* food for thought, eye candy or an investment. [L *ars, artis*]

art */ärt/ n* for everyone who chooses it. [L *ars, artis*]

art */ärt/ n* for it to be art, the artist needs to create more of it than he steals/finds and that people need to be able to understand it *(at least on some level)* without the artist needing to explain to them and justify its existence as art. [L *ars, artis*]

art */ärt/ n* for lifting our hearts and minds and spirits to the sun. [L *ars, artis*]

art */ärt/ n (pers)* for me; *like you are for you.* [L *ars, artis*]

art */ärt/ n (perh photog)* for people that feel that recording their every experience is vital to the world. [L *ars, artis*]

art */ärt/ n* for people who desire to express their findings. [L *ars, artis*]

art */ärt/ n* for people who search their souls and desire to know themselves *(perh ref Ancient Gr Delphic maxim).* [L *ars, artis*]

art */ärt/ n* for the seeker's enjoyment. [L *ars, artis*]

art */ärt/ n* form and content. [L *ars, artis*]

art */ärt/ n* formed life; *life as the potential, art as an actualization, or realization, of the potential of life.* [L *ars, artis*]

art */ärt/ n* fosters discussion and emotion. [L *ars, artis*]

art */ärt/ n* found in the way you express yourself. [L *ars, artis*]

art */ärt/ n* found meaning. [L *ars, artis*]

art */ärt/ n* free. [L *ars, artis*]

art */ärt/ n* free, open to interpretation and completely based on personal ideas. [L *ars, artis*]

art */ärt/ n* free speech under the Constitution *(prob ref Am* Constitution, *supreme law of the United States of America).* [L *ars, artis*]

art */ärt/ n* freedom. [L *ars, artis*]

art */ärt/ n* freedom of expression. [L *ars, artis*]

art */ärt/ n* freedom of expression, freedom *by* expression. [L *ars, artis*]

art */ärt/ n* freedom to be the pure creator; *with no 'commission' or specific 'job' in mind.* [L *ars, artis*]

art */ärt/ n (derog)* frequently created in a few minutes; *and yet it is held up by some in the art establishment as being of great artistic merit and it sells for hundreds of millions; just as the man in the street is ignored when it comes to our desires regarding immigration and sentencing for criminals* etc, *our opinions on art are also a million miles from those of the establishment; I am aware that quoting Hitler may raise a few eyebrows and probably isn't everyone's cup of tea* (Adolf Hitler *(1889–1945), Austrian-born Ger politician).* [L *ars, artis*]

art */ärt/ n* from the imagination. [L *ars, artis*]

art */ärt/ n* from the world around us. [L *ars, artis*]

art */ärt/ n (derog, vulg)* fucking wank. [L *ars, artis*]

art */ärt/ n (derog, vulg)* fuck'n shit. [L *ars, artis*]

art */ärt/ n* fulfils or assuages some need we have within. [L *ars, artis*]

art */ärt/ n* fulfils three criteria: **1** intentions of the artist **2** the quality of work **3** response of spectators; *however according to me if something just expresses emotions, then it is an art.* [L *ars, artis*]

art */ärt/ n* fulfils three criteria: **1** involves an individualized emotion **2** the release of truth **3** the ability to connect with the spectator. [L *ars, artis*]

art */ärt/ n* function. [L *ars, artis*]

art */ärt/ n* functionless process and action. [L *ars, artis*]

art */ärt/ n* fundamental. [L *ars, artis*]

art */ärt/ n* fundamentally language. [L *ars, artis*]

art */ärt/ n* fundamentally passive. [L *ars, artis*]

art */ärt/ n* general social opinion. [L *ars, artis*]

art */ärt/ n* generated, modified, qualified and defined by the person of the artist in the deepest recesses of the artist's soul. [L *ars, artis*]

art */ärt/ n* gives a 'voice' to the feelings and thoughts that may be hard to actually speak. [L *ars, artis*]

art */ärt/ n* gives an opportunity to design your own world; *and, as in your children, create a significant immortality.* [L *ars, artis*]

art */ärt/ n* gives an opportunity to endow new life and new meaning into the ordinary. [L *ars, artis*]

art */ärt/ n* gives life to human emotion. [L *ars, artis*]

art */ärt/ n* gives us a glimpse into our next level of consciousness. [L *ars, artis*]

art */ärt/ n* gives us an avenue to explore and convey our inner desires of communication other than words. [L *ars, artis*]

art */ärt/ n* gives us humans the ability to be honest about our lives and surroundings; *which we normally are not allowed to be.* [L *ars, artis*]

art */ärt/ n* gives us new thought and hope. [L *ars, artis*]

art */ärt/ n* gives us security. [L *ars,*

artis]

art */ärt/ n* giving a profound meaning to an object. [L *ars, artis*]

art */ärt/ n* giving us roadmaps to living a life of meaning. [L *ars, artis*]

art */ärt/ n* glorifying. [L *ars, artis*]

art */ärt/ n* gnoseological, ideological, aesthetic, or inventive. [L *ars, artis*]

art */ärt/ n (theol)* God is art. [L *ars, artis*]

art */ärt/ n (theol)* God's way of allowing us to feel a little of his passion to create. [L *ars, artis*]

art */ärt/ n* goes beyond the perception of beauty in the piece; *but seeks to connect to the viewer's emotions and makes him or her interpret the piece.* [L *ars, artis*]

art */ärt/ n* goes so deep within in your heart and ideas. [L *ars, artis*]

art */ärt/ n (econ)* good business is the best art. [L *ars, artis*]

art */ärt/ n* good craftsmanship. [L *ars, artis*]

art */ärt/ n* graphics, nontextual matter. [L *ars, artis*]

art */ärt/ n* (*poss pharmacol*) grass. [L *ars, artis*]

art */ärt/ n* Grim Fandango® (Grim Fandango®, *dark comedy neo-noir Windows™ adventure game).* [L *ars, artis*]

art */ärt/ n* grows better the more it improves or alters nature through a passage through what we might call the artist's soul or vision. [L *ars, artis*]

art */ärt/ n* grows from joy and sorrow; *but mostly from sorrow.* [L *ars, artis*]

art */ärt/ n* hacking the human. [L *ars, artis*]

art */ärt/ n* happens in your own mind. [L *ars, artis*]

art */ärt/ n* happens when someone responds to their world by making a new world; *this may not be the action of a healthy mind – who looks around them and says, 'I think I should make my own version of this'? It's the world as they make it, drawing out what they find most beautiful, most hideous, most sublime.* [L *ars, artis*]

art */ärt/ n* hard-earned work that is its own reward and has a degree of permanence. [L *ars, artis*]

art */ärt/ n* hard to define. [L *ars,*

artis]

art /ärt/ *n* has a form and a function. [L *ars, artis*]

art /ärt/ *n (approx)* has a non-functional quality as well as possibly a functional quality; *though in what combination I have no idea.* [L *ars, artis*]

art /ärt/ *n* has a particular status; *this status is conferred by a member of the artworld, usu an artist, who has the authority to confer the status in question by virtue of occupying a role within the artworld to which that authority attaches.* [L *ars, artis*]

art /ärt/ *n* has a terrible power to corrupt even the best characters. [L *ars, artis*]

art /ärt/ *n* has a variety of uses or roles; *there is art for beauty's sake; art for laughter's sake; art with a comment; art which provokes; all are valid; all are art.* [L *ars, artis*]

art /ärt/ *n* has almost seven billion definitions. [L *ars, artis*]

art /ärt/ *n* has an artistic effect. [L *ars, artis*]

art /ärt/ *n* has an emotional context. [L *ars, artis*]

art /ärt/ *n* has an essential bond with love. [L *ars, artis*]

art /ärt/ *n* has become impossible; *due to artistic as much of the complexity of fashion, it seems to have become no principle, but a common problem in the world in front of us if you restore human nature and artistic sources, it is necessary to say called good art is called caring people in the world, known as the problem of people thinking about the world and they are a group of people displaced bumps inner world, is not immersed in the sense to give up the comfort of self, the more reason not to give up the ideal philistine who.* [L *ars, artis*]

art /ärt/ *n* has been completely levitate and no longer have practical significance. [L *ars, artis*]

art /ärt/ *n (interrog)* has it been called art by the so-called 'art system'? *In our century, that's all that makes it art.* [L *ars, artis*]

art /ärt/ *n* has many purposes: *to celebrate the human and/or the divine, to interrogate the status quo, to unsettle and enlighten, to encourage entropy, to provoke and prod us out of complacency, apathy and stasis; this requires an alchemical combination of anarchy and self-discipline plus that mysterious fuel that drives the engine of creativity.* [L *ars, artis*]

art /ärt/ *n* has never been false

even when it seems to lie; *for it tells the full story of its origins, relying on the mind of the viewer to see each side per view per individual; and the mind will lie but it is not in the fault of art but the fault is in perception; still, without others, even the maker will not know all it has to tell.* [L ***ars, artis***]

art */ärt/ n* has no boundaries; *it's in everything we see and read, from the architecture of our homes, the shape of our cars, the cut of our clothing, to the words, fonts and photographs used on this page.* [L ***ars, artis***]

art */ärt/ n (appar joc)* has no definition; *its origin is related as follows by the ingenious Father Gassalasca Jape SJ: One day a wag – what would the wretch be at?/Shifted a letter of the cipher RAT/And said it was a god's name! Straight arose/Fantastic priests and postulants (with shows/And mysteries and mummeries and hymns/And disputations dire that lamed their limbs)/To serve his temple and maintain the fires/Expound the law, manipulate the wires/Amazed, the populace that rites attend/Believe whate'er they cannot comprehend/And, inly edified to learn that two/Half-hairs joined so and so (as Art can do)/Have sweeter values and a grace more fit/Than Nature's hairs that never have been split/Bring cates and wines for sacrificial feasts/And sell their garments to support the priests* (Father Gassalasca Jape SJ, *appar 'learned and ingenious cleric').* [L ***ars, artis***]

art */ärt/ n* has no intrinsic worth; *its value must all be invested by the observer.* [L ***ars, artis***]

art */ärt/ n* has no opposite; *it is a self-defining act.* [L ***ars, artis***]

art */ärt/ n* has nothing to do with skill level or even purpose sometimes; *I find some great looking art in things that shouldn't be art like the geometry of slicing open a purple cabbage or something.* [L ***ars, artis***]

art */ärt/ n (neg)* hasn't existed for over a century now. [L ***ars, artis***]

art */ärt/ n* has set us all free; *except for those who willfully choose to stay imprisoned.* [L ***ars, artis***]

art */ärt/ n* has something to do with emotions. [L ***ars, artis***]

art */ärt/ n* has the ability to encompass business and politics, philosophy and war, sports, even science. [L ***ars, artis***]

art */ärt/ n* has the ability to make hard hitting commentaries on difficult social issues. [L *ars, artis*]

art */ärt/ n (m)* has the aesthetic ability to define a person; *perhaps even uplift him in his approach to life.* [L *ars, artis*]

art */ärt/ n* has to address art history. [L *ars, artis*]

art */ärt/ n* has to appeal to a majority of people. [L *ars, artis*]

art */ärt/ n* has to be an act of personal imagination. [L *ars, artis*]

art */ärt/ n* has to be controversial to be artistic. [L *ars, artis*]

art */ärt/ n* has to be more than just some straight lines. [L *ars, artis*]

art */ärt/ n* has to be some tangible product, an experience – whether visual, audio, abstract (*eg* literary), *etc; if no tangible product (or experience) is generated, then what you have is not art, but merely recreation/mental exercise.* [L *ars, artis*]

art */ärt/ n* has to connect to so many people and give them a message… *then the ad directors of Walmart™, McDonald's™ and similar companies are the most powerful artists in the world (Wal-Mart Stores, Inc., branded as* Walmart™, *Am multinational retail corporation;* The McDonald's™ Corporation, *the world's largest chain of hamburger fast food restaurants).* [L *ars, artis*]

art */ärt/ n* has to give us something. [L *ars, artis*]

art */ärt/ n (relig)* has to go beyond the visible; *it arrives from a higher source, you can call it soul or God or universe and the artist expresses this, in one or another way.* [L *ars, artis*]

art */ärt/ n* (*inf, interrog*) has to have a beauty to it; *if you try and sell me your vomit with a toothpick flag in it then I ain't buying nothang. Like you know?* [L *ars, artis*]

art */ärt/ n* has to have a meaning behind it. [L *ars, artis*]

art */ärt/ n* has to move us. [L *ars, artis*]

art */ärt/ n* has to say something and move people emotionally. [L *ars, artis*]

art */ärt/ n* has to show a sense of creativity, skilfulness and complexity. [L *ars, artis*]

art */ärt/ n* has to speak to the culture in a big picture sense; *the artist must have a particular point of view that is relatively coherent.* [L *ars, artis*]

art */ärt/ n* has to successfully

transfer an emotion or thought from the artist to the person observing the art. [L *ars, artis*]

art /ärt/ *n* has transformative power. [L *ars, artis*]

art /ärt/ *n* has two parts: the message and the frame; *yes, lots of things have messages and the messages can be perfectly individual depending on the person, too; but if you don't 'get' anything from it, I don't believe you can call it art; more importantly, though, is the frame; not a literal frame, but the idea that something is 'art'; yeah, you can say that the tree you're passing on the sidewalk is art, but you don't say that because it's not how you see the tree; you see the tree as a tree; or, more likely, you don't see the tree at all; because there's no frame; contrast this to going to a museum – you're expecting art and so it's both easier to get some kind of message from it and consider it in that frame; that said, you can still find things that give you that message and then give it the frame yourself; but I essentially disagree with the idea that 'anything' is art.* [L *ars, artis*]

art /ärt/ *n* has varied meanings that can be different based on a person's experiences and emotions. [L *ars, artis*]

art /ärt/ *n (interrog)* have you ever seen or heard something so beautiful it stuck with you for the rest of the day? [L *ars, artis*]

art /ärt/ *n* headache-causing strobe lights blinding us. [L *ars, artis*]

art /ärt/ *n* helps define our existence and makes us less alone and frees our frustrations. [L *ars, artis*]

art /ärt/ *n* helps in deciding what ideas are worth investing in. [L *ars, artis*]

art /ärt/ *n (sociol)* helps society to find direction and perspective in its movement toward freedom and toward forms of social life appropriate for man. [L *ars, artis*]

art /ärt/ *n* hidden. [L *ars, artis*]

art /ärt/ *n* hidden in the shadows. [L *ars, artis*]

art /ärt/ *n* high quality of conception or execution, *as found in works of beauty.* [L *ars, artis*]

art /ärt/ *n* highly individual, *in the creation, the interpretation and the appreciation.* [L *ars, artis*]

art /ärt/ *n (hist)* historical. [L *ars, artis*]

art */ärt/ n* how creativity manifests itself. [L *ars, artis*]

art */ärt/ n (pers)* how I show what's inside my head. [L *ars, artis*]

art */ärt/ n* how our hearts/souls/ whatever-you-call-them reflect the world as they perceive it and imagine the world as they wish it to become. [L *ars, artis*]

art */ärt/ n* how we decorate space; *music is how we decorate time.* [L *ars, artis*]

art */ärt/ n* how we voice ourselves to allow others to see what makes us unique. [L *ars, artis*]

art */ärt/ n* how well you can explain something. [L *ars, artis*]

art */ärt/ n* how you feel. [L *ars, artis*]

art */ärt/ n* however we find ways to take what we're feeling inside ourselves and paint it, write it, sing it or shred it on the streets for everyone else to see. [L *ars, artis*]

art */ärt/ n* http://i.imgur.com/2qx9O.jpg *(uniform resource locator).* [L *ars, artis*]

art */ärt/ n* http://www.washingtonpost.com/lifestyle/style/artist-cai-guo-qiang-explodes-tree-on-the-national-mall/2012/11/30/620a251c-3b33-11e2-a263-f0ebffed2f15_video.html?hpid=z1 *(uniform resource locator).* [L *ars, artis*]

art */ärt/ n* human; *and it's very subjective based on the audience at any one given point in time.* [L *ars, artis*]

art */ärt/ n* human ability to make things. [L *ars, artis*]

art */ärt/ n* human activities which create aesthetic experiences that can be shared; *abstract expressionism certainly meets that criterion.* [L *ars, artis*]

art */ärt/ n* human effort to imitate, supplement, alter, or counteract the work of nature. [L *ars, artis*]

art */ärt/ n* human endeavour thought to be aesthetic and have meaning beyond simple description; *includes music, dance, sculpture, painting, drawing, stitchery, weaving, poetry, writing, woodworking,* etc. [L *ars, artis*]

art */ärt/ n* human expression in a visual form; *traditionally, this has been quite narrowly defined as drawing and printmaking, painting, sculpture and architecture; more recently, photography was included* *and more recently still, aspects of theatre have crossed into sculpture as performance art, while sculpture itself has overlapped with architecture in installation art.* [L ***ars, artis***]

art */ärt/ n* human expression of self through some medium or form that is inspired by, or inspires, emotion. [L *ars, artis*]

art */ärt/ n* human skill and agency, *opp to nature.* [L ***ars, artis***]

art */ärt/ n* human workmanship. [L *ars, artis*]

art */ärt/ n* human works of beauty considered as a group. [L *ars, artis*]

art */ärt/ n* humanistic. [L *ars, artis*]

art */ärt/ n* humans' amazing way to show what's going on in their head. [L *ars, artis*]

art */ärt/ n (inf)* I agree with the Dadaists and Duchamp: 'Art is shit' *(excrement, secretion)* (**Dada**, *art movement of the Eur avant-garde in the early c20th;* **Marcel Duchamp** *(1887–1968) Fr-Am painter, sculptor, chess player and writer).* [L ***ars, artis***]

art */ärt/ n (hort, pers) I decided to go for a bike ride through the oldest and, in my opinion, the finest neighbourhood in the city, searching for the best flower garden; it was going to be a contest and I was the judge; I do not spend my weekends gardening, nor have I ever judged a garden contest before; I also have never sauntered casually on my bicycle, using it for exercise and mountainous speed ventures was for me the norm; It seemed a relaxing idea, so out the door I went; early in my mission I discovered a residential garden of such magnitude, that it set the bar or standard that all other gardens would be judged; the garden had everything beautiful. It had colour, shade or shadow, design and a place; it was clean and well manicured; it had meandering walks, with areas for contemplation; I stopped for a while and saw the garden and its diverse vegetation, as a piece or pieces of art; the rest of the day became an art show; I saw artistic gardens and flowers everywhere; I began to smell the art, it became intoxicating; I started to see art in the design of homes and how the gardens were meant to compliment each other; I saw it in entrance ways, stain glass windows and staircases; there was art in the majestic tree-lined streets; I made it downtown to the river, where everything drains, including meandering bicy-*

clists; someone had designed the most unbelievable fountain, with marble walkways and hanging baskets of flowers; I talked with a few bystanders in the art gallery I was traveling and noticed they had art all over them; it was in their jewelry, hair style, clothes and a smile that remains etched in my mind; I stopped in a café for some nourishment and also to come down a little bit; unbelievably, the food was artistic, made by artisans, in a dinning room that defined decor in an unusual way; when I came back outside, I looked up and saw cotton ball clouds on a turquoise canvas, oh please stop! I ended my trip, or art show, five hours later, buying the best garden in the city a first place award; I see art much more often today and in many more places; not like that special day, but much more than I had. Art to me can be everything; *thanks.* [L ***ars, artis***]

art */ärt/ n* I don't know; *I think there have to be boundaries, definitions; I hate how more and more things are just becoming generalized.* [L ***ars, artis***]

art */ärt/ n* I have no idea what fine art is *and no idea what makes an image fine art.* [L ***ars, artis***]

art */ärt/ n (pers)* I know it when I see it. [L ***ars, artis***]

art */ärt/ n (pers)* I'll know it when I see it. [L ***ars, artis***]

art */ärt/ n* I'm pretty sure it requires a little bit of subtlety. [L ***ars, artis***]

art */ärt/ n (interrog)* I'm wondering if we can think of the definition as a range of qualities existing as a continuum; *of course, they must possess most of the qualities and exhibit them to a significant degree – but the lines of demarcating art from non-art aren't precise at all; does that make sense?* [L ***ars, artis***]

art */ärt/ n (pers, neg)* I really don't care anymore; *I've had nothing but hatred for the 'art' community for a long, long time and don't care to join their ranks.* [L ***ars, artis***]

art */ärt/ n (prob joc)* I woke up this morning and my pipes burst, completely filling my basement with art; *I had such an emotional response to it, I didn't know whether to call the plumber or have an opening.* [L ***ars, artis***]

art */ärt/ n* Ico® (Ico®, *action-adventure game developed by Team Ico).* [L ***ars, artis***]

art */ärt/ n* idea, production *(skill/*

effort) and obliqueness. [L *ars, artis*]

art */ärt/ n* ideally selfless. [L *ars, artis*]

art */ärt/ n* ideas and feelings expressed creatively through a medium; *with the ideas and feelings infused (packaged? imbued?) with this aesthetic quality.* [L *ars, artis*]

art */ärt/ n* ideas given form, given shape, given substance. [L *ars, artis*]

art */ärt/ n* ideas put forth in varied ways and mediums. [L *ars, artis*]

art */ärt/ n* ideas realized. [L *ars, artis*]

art */ärt/ n* if a human made it, it's art. [L *ars, artis*]

art */ärt/ n (m)* if a man is infected by the author's condition of soul, if he feels this emotion and this union with others, then the object which has effected this is art. [L *ars, artis*]

art */ärt/ n (m, opthalmol)* if a man sees life as a blur and paints a blur – that is art. [L *ars, artis*]

art */ärt/ n (inf)* if a person likes something, its art; *and if they don't like it, it's crap.* [L *ars, artis*]

art */ärt/ n (interrog, photog)* if a photographer takes a family portrait, or even a nature shot that captures EXACTLY what the scene looks like to the naked eye, is that art? *Now if that same photographer slows down the shutter speed and blurs a rushing river, waterfall, tall whispering grass, or even traffic to create the IDEA of movement and energy, while keeping the rest of the image perfectly in focus, is that art?* [L *ars, artis*]

art */ärt/ n (inf, poss derog)* if an artist makes one thing that looks like it was drawn by a five year old in five minutes, but it's really more complicated than that, then it's legitimate art; *if an artist makes thirty things that look like they were all drawn by five-year-olds in five minutes and they really took about that long to make and none of it is much more complicated than that, then it's legitimate crap.* [L *ars, artis*]

art */ärt/ n* if an artist says it's art, it's art. [L *ars, artis*]

art */ärt/ n (interrog)* if an artist took a bucket, filled it with green paint and called it art, would it be art? [L *ars, artis*]

art */ärt/ n (pers)* if I admire it, it is art; *even if I don't want it or wouldn't* *buy it.* [L *ars, artis*]

art */ärt/ n (pers)* if I can examine the work of another, a creative work of another and understand their intent, while finding a personal connection, then for me then art has been achieved. [L *ars, artis*]

art */ärt/ n (interrog)* if I make a business presentation, using 'creative skill and imagination,' is it art? [L *ars, artis*]

art */ärt/ n (interrog)* if I print a picture of, say, a can of Vienna sausages repeatedly, in a spectrum of colour, on a canvas, is that art? [L *ars, artis*]

art */ärt/ n (interrog)* if in doubt, ask yourself: is this artist trying to make me think or feel something (whether or not they succeed) or are they just decorating something with a nice pattern? *if the former, it's art, if the latter, it's craft.* [L *ars, artis*]

art */ärt/ n* if it annoys people who work in commercial radio. [L *ars, artis*]

art */ärt/ n* if it causes me to pause. [L *ars, artis*]

art */ärt/ n* if it is black and white it is art; *if it is full on everything showing in graphic detail then it is porn.* [L *ars, artis*]

art */ärt/ n (interrog)* if it is not appealing to the masses, to those who have no clue what art should be – is it art? [L *ars, artis*]

art */ärt/ n (interrog)* if it isn't art, what the hell is it doing in an art gallery and why are people coming to look at it? [L *ars, artis*]

art */ärt/ n (econ)* if it sells for $1.9m it's art; *if it's $2.99/month it's porn.* [L *ars, artis*]

art */ärt/ n (interrog, philos)* if most people intuitively think that X is an artwork and if the proposed philosophical definition says that X is not an artwork, then X is not an artwork and people should revise the way they categorize things as art; if most people intuitively categorize X as an artwork, while the descriptive definition says that X is not an artwork *(or vice versa),* then the descriptive definition is wrong and must be revised to achieve a better fit with intuitions; *is X an artwork?* [L *ars, artis*]

art */ärt/ n (interrog, zool)* if my pet elephant accidently spills paint on canvas, that's art also? [L *ars,*

artis]

art /ärt/ *n* if one creates something 'unnecessary' with the intention of it being a piece of art by any reference point they choose, it's half art; *if some other people agree with them, then it's art.* [L *ars, artis*]

art /ärt/ *n (f, poss m)* if she evokes any kind of aesthetic experience in you; *if she doesn't, dismiss her and put her down as a poser; but whatever you do, give her credit for her balls.* [L *ars, artis*]

art /ärt/ *n* if someone is interested in seeing it, it's art. [L *ars, artis*]

art /ärt/ *n* if someone or a group of people makes something with the intention of it being art, it is then art. [L *ars, artis*]

art /ärt/ *n* if someone says it's art, it's art; *at least to the person saying it.* [L *ars, artis*]

art /ärt/ *n (econ)* if someone tells you to do it, it's work; if nobody told you to do it but someone will pay for it, it's art; *if you have to give it away or leave it out for the dustmen, it's craft.* [L *ars, artis*]

art /ärt/ *n* if something even looks a little bit like art, it's art. [L *ars, artis*]

art /ärt/ *n (interrog)* if the artist intends it to be art, how can we argue with them, the creator, the person that made it? [L *ars, artis*]

art /ärt/ *n* if the spectators and auditors are infected by the feelings which the author has felt. [L *ars, artis*]

art /ärt/ *n* if you can capture the viewer's attention for more than ten seconds you know it's art. [L *ars, artis*]

art /ärt/ *n* if you celebrate it, it's art; *if you don't, it isn't.* [L *ars, artis*]

art /ärt/ *n (photog)* if you close your eyes and snap a photo of something you will not be conveying your idea but when you look at the print you will see that an idea has indeed been conveyed; *even if it is the gravel under your feet; includes poetry, literature, dance, collage,* etc etc. [L *ars, artis*]

art /ärt/ *n (poss vulg)* if you continue watching/reading after you've had a w4nk [perh *wank*] then it's art; *if you stop looking then it's porn.* [L *ars, artis*]

art /ärt/ *n* if you don't understand it. [L *ars, artis*]

art */ärt/ n (neg)* if you have to ask *'is it art?'* then it's probably not, just as if you have to ask if it's music, then it probably isn't; *like that 3-minutes-of-silence piece – total (bleep).* [L *ars, artis*]

art */ärt/ n (neg)* if you have to write a paragraph or an essay to explain your art, then it's not art; *pieces should present themselves; that said, once I am moved by a piece, I do find it interesting to know about the artist or how they came to create.* [L *ars, artis*]

art */ärt/ n* if you made it, it's art; *if you're just playing with something somebody else made, it ain't.* [L *ars, artis*]

art */ärt/ n* if you put a frame around it, you can call anything art. [L *ars, artis*]

art */ärt/ n* if you say something is art, it is. [L *ars, artis*]

art */ärt/ n* ignoring the tears for that one moment. [L *ars, artis*]

art */ärt/ n* illuminates the shadows in our hearts and minds. [L *ars, artis*]

art */ärt/ n* illustration. [L *ars, artis*]

art */ärt/ n (m)* illustrations representing man's thought, actions and temptations. [L *ars, artis*]

art */ärt/ n* illustrative material. [L *ars, artis*]

art */ärt/ n* illustrative or decorative material. [L *ars, artis*]

art */ärt/ n (sociol, neurol)* imagery that perpetuates the predominant shared social consensus and satisfies the parts of the brain that connect image with knowledge. [L *ars, artis*]

art */ärt/ n (sociol)* images made for social, moral, or thought-provoking reasons. [L *ars, artis*]

art */ärt/ n (interj)* imagination; *take the thought out of it and you have nothing!* [L *ars, artis*]

art */ärt/ n* imagination and passion expressed by creating a visual feature. [L *ars, artis*]

art */ärt/ n* imaginative skill; *as applied to representations of the natural world or figments of the imagination.* [L *ars, artis*]

art */ärt/ n* imitates the growth and emergence, the movement and genesis of being; *that which is not readily accessible through senses or even common sense.* [L *ars, artis*]

art */ärt/ n* imitation; *whether its object is a tree, a building, a feeling or* *an idea; exactly what each piece of art is imitating can be hard to say, especially when it's imitating more than one thing; the movie 'Aliens™', for example, is imitating hundreds of things, from the way people sound when they talk to imaginary creatures and speculative technology; according to Aristotle, the most important imitation in 'Aliens™' is the plot, which is an attempt to imitate the successes or failures we experience in real life (many argue that character is more important than plot and they're wrong); none of us has ever led a team of future marines on a mission to LV-426 to rescue a bunch of colonial terraformers, so you might think 'Aliens™' is up a creek, but what the movie is actually imitating is Human Experience 101: being stranded, being afraid, seeing a scary animal that wants to hurt you, facing death, facing pain, overcoming fear, conquering past trauma; we have all experienced all of these and we can recognize James Cameron's success or failure in capturing their essence (he succeeded wildly, 'Aliens™' is a masterpiece)* (**Aliens™**, *1986 Am science fiction action film co-written and directed by* **James Cameron** *(1954–), Can filmmaker, director, producer, screenwriter, inventor, engineer, philanthropist, and deep-sea explorer;* **Aristotle** *(384–322BCE), Gk philos b Stagirus;* **LV-426**, *satellite orbiting the ringed planet Calpamos;* **Human Experience 101**, *perh ref Room 101, a torture chamber in the novel Nineteen Eighty-Four by George Orwell in which the Party attempts to subject a prisoner to his or her own worst nightmare, fear or phobia, with the object of breaking down their resistance).* [L ***ars, artis***]

art */ärt/ n* imitation with some kind of intellectual purpose. [L ***ars, artis***]

art */ärt/ n* imperfect. [L ***ars, artis***]

art */ärt/ n* important. [L ***ars, artis***]

art */ärt/ n* important and normal and should be encouraged and developed; *but I am not sure if I am entirely convinced that it is necessary.* [L ***ars, artis***]

art */ärt/ n* in a constant state of change; *so nobody can really pin down what it is.* [L ***ars, artis***]

art */ärt/ n* in a distant realm in which you don't intervene. [L ***ars, artis***]

art */ärt/ n* in a word, everything. [L ***ars, artis***]

art /ärt/ *n* in any media, the process by which one expresses an intangible message in a tangible form. [L *ars, artis*]

art /ärt/ *n* in control. [L *ars, artis*]

art /ärt/ *n* in essence poetry. [L *ars, artis*]

art /ärt/ *n* in fact objective; *and yes it 'follows rules'; the rules for what art is are easy to find by looking up the term in a dictionary; and no dictionary definition of 'art' includes that it must be 'good' according to any set of guidelines.* [L *ars, artis*]

art /ärt/ *n (interj)* in my mind's eye! [L *ars, artis*]

art /ärt/ *n* in order to be authentic it is obliged to contain an idea and not constitute an imitation. [L *ars, artis*]

art /ärt/ *n (econ)* in order to become accepted as art, something has to be sold – *and purchased* – as art. [L *ars, artis*]

art /ärt/ *n* in the breath of a newborn, the pan of a chef, the scissors of a hair stylist, the stillness of death. [L *ars, artis*]

art /ärt/ *n* in the eye of the beholder. [L *ars, artis*]

art /ärt/ *n (psychol)* in the eye of the beholder, as they say; *but some forms mean nothing except to the artist and I respect that, too: art as therapy.* [L *ars, artis*]

art /ärt/ *n* in the eye of the beholder; *but when I go to a museum and see a canvas painted in one colour with a single line in another colour painted down the middle, I have to wonder (perh ref* **Onement VI** *by Barnett Newman (1905–70), signed and dated 1953 in dark blue paint on lower right corner).* [L *ars, artis*]

art /ärt/ *n* in the eye of the beholder; *NOT the over-educated examiner.* [L *ars, artis*]

art /ärt/ *n (inf)* in the eye of the beholder; *what some think of as art others think is pure crap!* [L *ars, artis*]

art /ärt/ *n* in the mind of the artist; *and the piece is merely a window to the message they wished to communicate; sure, on the outside that's just a red square with yellow dots but look a little deeper and discover how a person poured their SOUL into that red square with yellow dots; the love, dates, sex, marriage, love, first kid, miscarriage, drinking, fights, the divorce! The art is in building a bridge from your mind to the artist's, on pil-*

lars of yellow dots and pavers of red square; hmph; anyway, back to cat pictures. [L *ars, artis*]

art */ärt/ n* in the moment; *simply according to what one perceives, without the play of passions and morals.* [L *ars, artis*]

art */ärt/ n* in the purpose of its creator, to inspire emotion, to communicate more than what is explicitly said or shown. [L *ars, artis*]

art */ärt/ n* indefinite exploration of self, resulting in genuine inspiration. [L *ars, artis*]

art */ärt/ n* indeterminate yet constantly seeking determination; *it vanishes if it reaches the goal.* [L *ars, artis*]

art */ärt/ n* indirectly communicating some quality of experience. [L *ars, artis*]

art */ärt/ n* indiscriminate giving of the self. [L *ars, artis*]

art */ärt/ n* individual vision of how someone perceives the world. [L *ars, artis*]

art */ärt/ n (math)* infinite; *just as maths is.* [L *ars, artis*]

art */ärt/ n* INNER EXPLORATION. [L *ars, artis*]

art */ärt/ n* inner human idea/belief/sensibility taking outer form. [L *ars, artis*]

art */ärt/ n* innovative. [L *ars, artis*]

art */ärt/ n* inquiry, observation, analysis and translation. [L *ars, artis*]

art */ärt/ n (psychol)* insanity. [L *ars, artis*]

art */ärt/ n* inseparable from practical activities, religion, games and other forms of human associations. [L *ars, artis*]

art */ärt/ n* insight into what the world is like. [L *ars, artis*]

art */ärt/ n* insouciance is art; *lack of concern is not.* [L *ars, artis*]

art */ärt/ n* inspiration and the deepest thought of your imagination. [L *ars, artis*]

art */ärt/ n* intelligent human modification and wondrous ornamentation, based on true veneration of nature's reality. [L *ars, artis*]

art */ärt/ n* intended to be artistic or decorative; *art needlework.* [L *ars, artis*]

art */ärt/ n* intention by artist interpreted by viewer; *they don't always match and the art is not always successful.* [L *ars, artis*]

art */ärt/ n* intentional, meaningful aesthetics; *both Caravaggio and Duchamp were intentional and the physical properties of their pieces were meaningful; it sounds dry, but I don't really think defining art is important (***Michelangelo Merisi** *or* **Amerighi da Caravaggio***, (1571–1610), It artist active in Rome, Naples, Malta and Sicily;* **Marcel Duchamp** *(1887–1968), Fr-Am painter, sculptor, chess player and writer).* [L *ars, artis*]

art */ärt/ n* interactivity; *it's the entire point of art: if art does not interact with you it may as well be shoved in a box and never seen ever again.* [L *ars, artis*]

art */ärt/ n* inventive and illusory; *like the play of the imagination.* [L *ars, artis*]

art */ärt/ n* inviting. [L *ars, artis*]

art */ärt/ n* involves the manipulation of human systems; *systems of perception, thought, emotion and so forth.* [L *ars, artis*]

art */ärt/ n* is. [L *ars, artis*]

art */ärt/ n (interrog)* is a paint-by-numbers painting art? [L *ars, artis*]

art */ärt/ n* is also science and can be studied and debated. [L *ars, artis*]

art */ärt/ n (interrog)* is eating an art? [L *ars, artis*]

art */ärt/ n (interrog)* is fashion art? [L *ars, artis*]

art */ärt/ n (interrog)* is makeup art? [L *ars, artis*]

art */ärt/ n (interrog)* is my coffee splashed on a blank piece of paper art? [L *ars, artis*]

art */ärt/ n (interrog)* is photography art? [L *ars, artis*]

art */ärt/ n (interrog)* is puking rainbow-coloured milk art? *(perh ref* **Millie Brown** *(1986–), Brit performance artist, best known as Lady Gaga's 'vomit artist' and a founding member of the !WOWOW! Collective).* [L *ars, artis*]

art */ärt/ n (interrog)* is teaching art? [L *ars, artis*]

art */ärt/ n (interrog)* is this blog art? [L *ars, artis*]

art */ärt/ n (neg)* isn't a category of noun so much as it is a verb; *art is a way of relating to things, not a thing itself.* [L *ars, artis*]

art */ärt/ n (neg)* isn't found in lofts; *'No Milton, that's not art, it's the water tank' (***Milton***, perh ref Anoth-*

er Case of Milton Jones, Brit ra-dio programme, series 3, 2008). [L *ars, artis*]

art */ärt/ n (neg, inf)* isn't in the act itself; *so, you shit on my doorstep, ring the bell and hide; you could be expressing a disdain for social norms, a disrespect for myself, my house, or more generally for society; a very primitive rebellion against modern society and life; how does a chimp express itself? it throws shit; you're the chimp throwing shit at my house;* 'This! This is what I think of your rules! This is what I think of your gilded cage! Of your talent – less modern art! Free yourself! Free yourself and free me! It's shit, all shit! It's rot and filth and you're blind to it!' *says the shitter at the step; but you are, in this moment of animal raging, expressing a more sophisticated human behaviour, as well; you hid, you ran away, perhaps egressing to a vantage from which you may watch and take pleasure in the angst the discovery of your shit will evoke in me; you're sending a message that will yield you no tangible rewards, at least certainly not on the night of your shitting; thus, you are honouring the same social constructs you are raging against; your shit, in its repulsive vileness, denigrates the dialogue we might have had and replaces it with the oxidized fruit of your excretory system; which is why, when my doorbell rings the next night and I discover your squatting form at the portal, the literal barbarians at the gate, exposing the softest, most vulnerable pieces of your anatomy to more explicitly inform me of your rejection of modernity, be it art or the way I choose to live, or even simply rejection of me as a person worthy of not having you shit on my doorstep, I will not engage you in discourse; perhaps the fact that this time you did not flee is an expression of growing confidence, or at least surging contempt for whatever it is that drives you to equate modern art with depositing faeces on the porch of a stranger, but I will seize the opportunity to respond and together we will discover the nature of art; I will kick you; I will kick you in your ass; I could tell you how I felt, discovering your shit on my step, my confusion, my revulsion, my rage; I don't understand why you would do such a thing; if I somehow did understand, then perhaps my kicks would be angry statements of my demand for respect, mutual valuation of human experience and rejection of the anti-social components and mes-*

sages of your composition; but that's not what's happening, because shitting on my step is not art, in any form; art is a dialectic; the art is the thesis, the response of the audience the antithesis, the following works, the convoluted twisting of the art world's zeitgeist the synthesis; shitting on my step is a gesture so full of other cultural messages that it really cannot have a useful or even very interesting output; it's an ugly gesture in an aesthetic and social sense and worse it's monstrously banal; there will be no moment of clarity where I comprehend the capacity for your actions to carry a deeper meaning; the roughness of the act wears away my patience or desire to perceive; usually, 'shock' performances are deeply couched in the warning that what you're about to see will be distressing; without preparation, an audience will not perceive the merits of their horror or disgust, they will dwell in them and react to them, like me, kicking you. [L *ars, artis*]

art */ärt/ n (neg)* isn't necessarily how beautiful can you make a thing; *but how aware can you be.* [L *ars, artis*]

art */ärt/ n (neg)* isn't something that can be nailed down and stuffed into a genre. [L *ars, artis*]

art */ärt/ n (neg)* isn't subjective; *it's a word and it doesn't have a capital; of course it has connotations, but that's irrelevant in my book: the actual meaning of the word, as handed down by our friends the Romans, is more akin to something created with skill – a product of some craft or other, effectively; so games are art – it's that simple; and no I don't need validation, I'm just a pedant with a Classics degree.* [L *ars, artis*]

art */ärt/ n* isomorphic to man's real experiences. [L *ars, artis*]

art */ärt/ n* it is enough for an artist to deem something 'art' and put it in a publicly accepted venue. [L *ars, artis*]

art */ärt/ n* it is; it is; it is. [L *ars, artis*]

art */ärt/ n (philos)* item x is a work of art if and only if x is a work in activity P and P is one of the artforms. [L *ars, artis*]

art */ärt/ n (comput)* Jet Set Willy™ (Jet Set Willy™, *comput game orig written by Matthew Smith for the ZX® Spectrum™ home comput).* [L *ars, artis*]

.art */dot ärt/ n (comput)* Johnson-Grace Compressed Image *(file* *extension).* [L *ars, artis*]

art */ärt/ n* joins us together. [L *ars, artis*]

art */ärt/ n* (*vulg*) just a form of masturbation – doing stuff which rubs one's own sweet spots; *often this happens to rub others' sweet spots in a similar way, which is not all that surprising given that we are all similar (and closely related) organisms; that's really all there is to it, I have difficulty seeing what's supposed to be so difficult about this.* [L *ars, artis*]

art */ärt/ n* just a human concept; *what some may regard as artistic, others may regard as trash.* [L *ars, artis*]

art */ärt/ n (econ)* just a scam to make money and make us regular folks look stupid. [L *ars, artis*]

art */ärt/ n* just about anything that requires some skill and produces something of some sort of value to others; *parenting a child, coaching a sports team, making new friends, building a relationship, maintaining a relationship, cooking a beautiful meal, the list is never ending.* [L *ars, artis*]

art */ärt/ n* just an excuse for rich people to have parties. [L *ars, artis*]

art */ärt/ n* just another place you can got lost in. [L *ars, artis*]

art */ärt/ n* just another puzzle to solve. [L *ars, artis*]

art */ärt/ n* just another thing. [L *ars, artis*]

art */ärt/ n* just another way of expressing our innermost thoughts onto concrete media. [L *ars, artis*]

art */ärt/ n* just by virtue of functioning as a symbol in a certain way does an object become, while so functioning, a work of art. [L *ars, artis*]

art */ärt/ n* just existing. [L *ars, artis*]

art */ärt/ n* just is. [L *ars, artis*]

art */ärt/ n* just living; *we make artistic decisions from the time we get up each morning, it's just that we're not always aware of what it is we are doing: what colour tie will I wear? how will I comb my hair? lipstick? argh! I don't have one to go with this outfit! I don't know what colour the new car should be, but I was thinking a green car might be nice.* [L *ars, artis*]

art */ärt/ n* just surface and symbol and setting. [L *ars, artis*]

art */ärt/ n* just to be clear, video

games are not art; *Bioshock™ is art, but Tetris™ is not, however, both Bioshock™ and Tetris™ are video games* (**Bioshock™**, *first-person shooter video game developed by Irrational Games;* **Tetris™**, *tile-matching puzzle video game orig designed and programmed by Alexey Pajitnov).* [L *ars, artis*]

art */ärt/ n* justification for free porn: *this isn't child pornography, its 'art'.* [L *ars, artis*]

art */ärt/ n* keeps giving. [L *ars, artis*]

art */ärt/ n* kind. [L *ars, artis*]

art */ärt/ n (inf)* kind of like fashion, or television, or music, or department store shopping, or humans for that matter: *there's a lot of crap out there to weed through.* [L *ars, artis*]

art */ärt/ n* knack; *as, a man has the art of managing his business to advantage.* [L *ars, artis*]

art */ärt/ n* knowing the right people and becoming part of the right social circle; *the same can be said for modern music; there is very little talent or genius involved.* [L *ars, artis*]

art */ärt/ n* knowledge made efficient by skill. [L *ars, artis*]

art */ärt/ n* Kobe Bryant's footwork on the basketball court (**Kobe Bean 'Black Mamba' Bryant** *(1978–), Am prof basketball player for the Los Angeles Lakers of the National Basketball Association).* [L *ars, artis*]

art */ärt/ n* lack of passion, critical thinking and insecurity; *which is admittedly a result of a unhealthy and dysfunctional society.* [L *ars, artis*]

art */ärt/ n* language. [L *ars, artis*]

art */ärt/ n (derog)* largely a load of old cobblers and a big sham. [L *ars, artis*]

art */ärt/ n* largely new. [L *ars, artis*]

art */ärt/ n* layered. [L *ars, artis*]

art */ärt/ n* learning. [L *ars, artis*]

art */ärt/ n* learning through someone else's expression. [L *ars, artis*]

art */ärt/ n (poss joc)* lemon drizzle cake; *Victoria sponge could be art or craft, not sure.* [L *ars, artis*]

art */ärt/ n* letting go. [L *ars, artis*]

art */ärt/ n* letting your emotions out in a beautiful way. [L *ars, artis*]

art */ärt/ n* liberating ourselves from the current existence. [L *ars,*

artis]

art /ärt/ *n* life. [L *ars, artis*]

art /ärt/ *n* LIFE!! [L *ars, artis*]

art /ärt/ *n* LIFE!!!!!; *and anyone who says art is meaningless is an utter MORON*. [L *ars, artis*]

art /ärt/ *n* life; *life is art; live artfully*. [L *ars, artis*]

art /ärt/ *n* life, deliberately rearranged. [L *ars, artis*]

art /ärt/ *n* life formed in a way that speaks to people and affects them. [L *ars, artis*]

art /ärt/ *n* life to me; *everything and every day of our existence inspires or triggers the movement of art, from emotions, thoughts, dreams and* etc. [L *ars, artis*]

art /ärt/ *n* life's speculation and imagination and, of course, its loss. [L *ars, artis*]

art /ärt/ *n (relig)* lifts the mind and the heart to God. [L *ars, artis*]

art /ärt/ *n (fig)* like a fire; *it's born from what it's burning*. [L *ars, artis*]

art /ärt/ *n (fig)* like a joke: *you can't just explain humour to someone who doesn't get it*. [L *ars, artis*]

art /ärt/ *n (fig)* like a life itself; *it is created, born and grows, so for every artist, art should be like its own child*. [L *ars, artis*]

art /ärt/ *n (fig)* like a mirror which reflects our inner selves. [L *ars, artis*]

art /ärt/ *n (fig)* like a morning cup of coffee. [L *ars, artis*]

art /ärt/ *n (fig)* like a Sasori puppet which never wears away and lasts for eternity (Sasori, *renown as* Sasori of the Red Sand, *was an S-rank missing-nin from Sunagakure's Puppet Brigade and a member of Akatsuki, where he was partnered with Orochimaru and later, Deidara)*. [L *ars, artis*]

art /ärt/ *n (fig)* like a storyteller; *when you create art you have a motive behind whatever you make; art tells a story to me like Vincent van Gogh: when he created art it told a story plus he wanted to make statement with his art; I'm poetic so when I write poetry it's a form of art that tells my story for me* (Vincent van Gogh *(1853–90), Du Post-Impressionist painter)*. [L *ars, artis*]

art /ärt/ *n (fig)* like a strawberry cake. [L *ars, artis*]

art /ärt/ *n (fig)* like beauty; *it is in the eye of the beholder*. [L *ars, artis*]

art /ärt/ *n (fig)* like beauty; *it is*

ONLY defined by the eye of the beholder. [L *ars, artis*]

art */ärt/ n (fig)* like driving a red Ferrari F12 Berlinetta™; *you know you don't need a V12 to get from point A to point B, but having one makes the travel, well, a bit more meaningful* (Ferrari F12 Berlinetta™, *a front mid-engine, rear wheel drive grand tourer).* [L *ars, artis*]

art */ärt/ n (fig)* like good bread. [L *ars, artis*]

art */ärt/ n (fig)* like green trees. [L *ars, artis*]

art */ärt/ n (fig)* like life itself; *has grown by its own impulse and man has taken his pleasure in it without definitely knowing what it is; and we could safely leave it there, in the subsoil of consciousness, where things that are of life are nourished in the dark.* [L *ars, artis*]

art */ärt/ n (fig)* like morality; *it consists in drawing the line somewhere.* [L *ars, artis*]

art */ärt/ n (fig)* like paper towels and a box of apple drink. [L *ars, artis*]

art */ärt/ n (fig)* like punk: *1% talent, 99% people who just don't know what the (bleep) they are doing.* [L *ars, artis*]

art */ärt/ n (fig)* like racism; *we are what we are and if you hate fine art and would rather look at pornography you are that sort of person.* [L *ars, artis*]

art */ärt/ n (fig)* like singing; *everyone can sing, some people you just don't want to hear.* [L *ars, artis*]

art */ärt/ n (fig)* like soup; *there will be some vegetables you don't like but as long as you get some soup down you it doesn't matter.* [L *ars, artis*]

art */ärt/ n (fig)* like the smell of fries: *you can't explain it.* [L *ars, artis*]

art */ärt/ n (fig)* like white clouds in blue sky. [L *ars, artis*]

art */ärt/ n (fig)* like your own mind; *it has the bases and structures of what you have learned from others, yet at the same time you are (as a good artist) putting in your own thought and expressions; in a way, it is to let people see your world but it's also to let others think and contemplate.* [L *ars, artis*]

art */ärt/ n* Limbo® (Limbo® *(stylized LIMBO), a puzzle-platform video game, the first title by independent Dan game developer Playdead).* [L *ars, artis*]

art */ärt/ n* limited by the interpretation of the observer. [L *ars, artis*]

art */ärt/ n* limitless; *and is everything that is not nature.* [L *ars, artis*]

art */ärt/ n* limitless; *as cosmos.* [L *ars, artis*]

art */ärt/ n* literally fills the empty space of the page, the canvas, the empty space of sound, of movement, speech. [L *ars, artis*]

art */ärt/ n (inf)* literally whatever the hell you want it to be. [L *ars, artis*]

art */ärt/ n* (*lit*) literature. [L *ars, artis*]

art */ärt/ n* living, breathing, moving; *as long as you put emotion in it and cherish it.* [L *ars, artis*]

art */ärt/ n* logic; *that being the principal study in the faculty of arts.* [L *ars, artis*]

art */ärt/ n* logical application of ambiguous emotional attachment or value. [L *ars, artis*]

art */ärt/ n* long hallways of grandiose canvases of paint and golden frames, men in monocles and women in cocktail dresses and feather hats, all sipping on wine while smiling and nodding at the pictures on the walls. [L *ars, artis*]

art */ärt/ n (poss relig)* longing, yearning, for the earthly unobtainable 'other'. [L *ars, artis*]

art */ärt/ n* loud. [L *ars, artis*]

art */ärt/ n* loud and furious. [L *ars, artis*]

art */ärt/ n* love. [L *ars, artis*]

art */ärt/ n* love; evol si tra *(palindrome).* [L *ars, artis*]

art */ärt/ n* love and attention; *things or objects are just a collection of materials; it remains just that, until it gets a special value; the added value is love and attention.* [L *ars, artis*]

art */ärt/ n* love's by-product. [L *ars, artis*]

art */ärt/ n* made by a mind; *the mind in question might be human and might be animal and might even be artificial, but a mind is what's required.* [L *ars, artis*]

art */ärt/ n* made by artists *(sometimes they have other names, like 'shamans', eg),* whose role has been to be the border scouts of the culture; *to step out into realms of the psyche, or into realms of relations to nature or god or culture or other humans that are too new or too scary for other people to venture* *into.* [L *ars, artis*]

art */ärt/ n* made by the alone for the alone. [L *ars, artis*]

art */ärt/ n* made from and about focused observations of ourselves, others and the realities of our world. [L *ars, artis*]

art */ärt/ n (stat)* made of 50% of naked girls, 48% of kittens and 2% of originality. [L *ars, artis*]

art */ärt/ n* magic or occult knowledge or influence. [L *ars, artis*]

art */ärt/ n* magical. [L *ars, artis*]

art */ärt/ n (joc, inf)* mah shyt [prob *my shit*] on a platter. [L *ars, artis*]

art */ärt/ n (relig)* makes comprehensible to some degree the Mystery that is God. [L *ars, artis*]

art */ärt/ n* makes life easier, interesting and enjoyable. [L *ars, artis*]

art */ärt/ n (pers)* makes me question things. [L *ars, artis*]

art */ärt/ n (pers)* makes me think. [L *ars, artis*]

art */ärt/ n* makes people think. [L *ars, artis*]

art */ärt/ n* makes some kind of point about life, nature, the world; *and so on.* [L *ars, artis*]

art */ärt/ n* makes them feel something. [L *ars, artis*]

art */ärt/ n* makes us happy. [L *ars, artis*]

art */ärt/ n (relig)* makes visible the Beauties of the Invisible God. [L *ars, artis*]

art */ärt/ n* makes you feel or think. [L *ars, artis*]

art */ärt/ n* makes you reconsider the world and your place within it. [L *ars, artis*]

art */ärt/ n* makes you stop and think after and even during the experience. [L *ars, artis*]

art */ärt/ n* makes you think. [L *ars, artis*]

art */ärt/ n* makes you think and feel something. [L *ars, artis*]

art */ärt/ n* makes you think, contradict, interrogate, problem solve, create, connect, communicate; *and the list can go on but most importantly it makes us feel.* [L *ars, artis*]

art */ärt/ n* makes you think of other things, maybe even inspire you and change your emotions; *a red canvas doesn't give you any ideas and it doesn't give you any thoughts – you just might as well stare at a wall and call it art; also a plain red* *canvas is not art because anyone can do it which doesn't make it unique.* [L *ars, artis*]

art */ärt/ n (econ)* making money. [L *ars, artis*]

art */ärt/ n* making or expressing of that which is beautiful: as *painting, sculpture, architecture, music, literature, drama, dance,* etc. [L *ars, artis*]

art */ärt/ n* making something out of nothing and selling it. [L *ars, artis*]

art */ärt/ n* making the modern world felt. [L *ars, artis*]

art */ärt/ n* making the ordinary seem extraordinary. [L *ars, artis*]

art */ärt/ n* manifestation of consciousness and/or consciousness of manifestation. [L *ars, artis*]

art */ärt/ n* manifests human experience. [L *ars, artis*]

art */ärt/ n* manipulated. [L *ars, artis*]

art */ärt/ n (m)* man's expression of his joy in labour. [L *ars, artis*]

art */ärt/ n* many risks that have been taken; *followed by a long pause.* [L *ars, artis*]

art */ärt/ n* many splendid things. [L *ars, artis*]

art */ärt/ n* material and visible. [L *ars, artis*]

art */ärt/ n* Matisse, Van Gogh, Gauguin, Degas, Cézanne, Rousseau, Renoir, Toulouse-Lautrec, Picasso, Brancusi, Munch, Duchamp, Braque, Kandinsky; *and many more (*Henri-Émile-Benoît Matisse *(1869–1954), Fr artist, known for his use of colour and fluid and original draughtsmanship;* Vincent Willem van Gogh *(1853–90), Du Post-Impressionist painter;* Eugène Henri Paul Gauguin *(1848–1903), leading Fr Post-Impressionist artist;* Hilaire-Germain-Edgar De Gas *(1834–1917), Fr artist famous for his paintings, sculptures, prints and drawings;* Paul Cézanne *(1839–1906), Fr artist and Post-Impressionist painter; perh* Henri Julien Félix Rousseau *(1844–1910), Fr Post-Impressionist painter;* Pierre-Auguste Renoir *(1841–1919), Fr artist;* Henri Marie Raymond de Toulouse-Lautrec-Monfa *(1864–1901), Fr painter, printmaker, draughtsman and illustrator;* Pablo Ruiz y Picasso *(1881–1973), Sp painter, sculptor, printmaker, ceramicist* *and stage designer;* **Constantin Brâncusi** *(1876–1957), Rom-born sculptor;* **Edvard Munch** *(1863–1944), Norwegian painter and printmaker;* **Marcel Duchamp** *(1887–1968) Fr-Am painter, sculptor, chess player and writer;* **Georges Braque** *(1882–1963), major c20th Fr painter and sculptor;* **Vassily Vassilyevich Kandinsky** *(1866–1944), influential Russ painter and art theorist).* [L *ars, artis*]

art */ärt/ n* may be considered an exploration of the human condition; *what it means to be human.* [L *ars, artis*]

art */ärt/ n* may be impossible to define in 25 words or less. [L *ars, artis*]

art */ärt/ n* may look like nothing more than paint splatters; *but even the amateur eye should be able to discern between a paint-splattered drop cloth (with no intention behind the splatters) and an intentional splattering.* [L *ars, artis*]

art */ärt/ n* meaningless; *except to the observer.* [L *ars, artis*]

art */ärt/ n (vulg, euphem)* means penis; *fuck art; suck art; lick art; rub art; touch art; tickle art; just don't kick art.* [L *ars, artis*]

art */ärt/ n* means something to a girl; *but I can't tell you only girls know!!!!!* [L *ars, artis*]

art */ärt/ n* meant to make the observer see something in a different way. [L *ars, artis*]

art */ärt/ n* memories. [L *ars, artis*]

art */ärt/ n (inf)* mental vomit. [L *ars, artis*]

art */ärt/ n* mere imitation; *which threatens the soul.* [L *ars, artis*]

art */ärt/ n* merely aesthetic and self-interested and powerless. [L *ars, artis*]

art */ärt/ n* method, facility, or knack; *the art of threading a needle.* [L *ars, artis*]

art */ärt/ n* mimesis or representation. [L *ars, artis*]

art */ärt/ n* misunderstood and controversial and deep; *but so, so necessary.* [L *ars, artis*]

art */ärt/ n* misunderstood, mishandled, exploited and underappreciated. [L *ars, artis*]

art */ärt/ n* modern art is an oxymoron. [L *ars, artis*]

art */ärt/ n* morally dangerous; *and the state should monitor how artists,* *writers and musicians influence citizens' lives.* [L *ars, artis*]

art */ärt/ n* morally invaluable. [L *ars, artis*]

art */ärt/ n* more about why you do something rather than what or how; *if you have to think a lot to paint on a canvas, or write a song, or compose music, it isn't art.* [L *ars, artis*]

art */ärt/ n* more or less an imitation of life, or the natural world; *there is an innately human pleasure in the imitation of a thing and the recognition of that imitation; our brains like to look a bunch of colours and say, 'It looks like a face!'; we like it so much we do it to objects that aren't even trying to imitate anything, like clouds or ink blots; and we're so good at it that we can make fine grain distinctions between imitations of various quality, even when we lack the skill to create those imitations ourselves.* [L *ars, artis*]

art */ärt/ n* more than a breath, but less than an orgasm. [L *ars, artis*]

art */ärt/ n (relig)* more than a physical piece; *it is an event whose purpose is to build Christian unity through the feelings transmitted by the criteria of individuality, clarity and sincerity.* [L *ars, artis*]

art */ärt/ n* more than any old imitation of something else. [L *ars, artis*]

art */ärt/ n* more than just a bunch of cubes, a splot of paint or a Campbell's® chicken noodle can *(prob ref* Campbell's Soup Cans, *sometimes referred to as* 32 Campbell's Soup Cans, *a work of art produced in 1962 by Andy Warhol).* [L *ars, artis*]

art */ärt/ n* more than just home decor. [L *ars, artis*]

art */ärt/ n* more the act than the final product; *perhaps it is the inspiration.* [L *ars, artis*]

art */ärt/ n (neg)* most assuredly not something that is ultimately dependent of the way the audience reacts to it; *it's still art, even if it bombs terribly.* [L *ars, artis*]

art */ärt/ n (pers)* moves me either in a spiritual or intellectual way. [L *ars, artis*]

art */ärt/ n* moves you. [L *ars, artis*]

art */ärt/ n* much more than pictures, paintings, prints: *it is also about music, dance, videos and much more.* [L *ars, artis*]

art */ärt/ n* mundane, duplicable

and found in our day-to-day life. [L *ars, artis*]

art /*ärt*/ *n* music. [L *ars, artis*]

art /*ärt*/ *n* music; *as long as the mind is in tune with its soul.* [L *ars, artis*]

art /*ärt*/ *n* music, literature and cinema, *as well as visual art.* [L *ars, artis*]

art /*ärt*/ *n* music on paper or on a canvas; *the only difference is we do not have a musician jumping around on stage revealing their emotions; all we have is the pictures and we must decide how much emotion the artists put in their work on our own.* [L *ars, artis*]

art /*ärt*/ *n* music, performance and a lot of other elements combined. [L *ars, artis*]

art /*ärt*/ *n* music, statues, paintings/drawings, photos and architecture. [L *ars, artis*]

art /*ärt*/ *n* must always have a theme. [L *ars, artis*]

art /*ärt*/ *n (approx)* must be as real as it is fantasy (50% / 50%?). [L *ars, artis*]

art /*ärt*/ *n* must be controversial. [L *ars, artis*]

art /*ärt*/ *n* must be creative and original. [L *ars, artis*]

art /*ärt*/ *n* must be discernible to everyone. [L *ars, artis*]

art /*ärt*/ *n* must be endlessly interpretable. [L *ars, artis*]

art /*ärt*/ *n* must be inspiring; *which to me means improves my conscience, gives me an* 'Aha!' *intuitive insight, lifts me onto a plane that transcends the mundane.* [L *ars, artis*]

art /*ärt*/ *n* must be intelligible as a continuation of our art history. [L *ars, artis*]

art /*ärt*/ *n* must be more than a conversation piece; *and not every piece that shocks for shock's sake is good, even if in a gallery or a museum.* [L *ars, artis*]

art /*ärt*/ *n* must be more than merely sensationalist. [L *ars, artis*]

art /*ärt*/ *n* must be of its time. [L *ars, artis*]

art /*ärt*/ *n* must be original; *(have an historical identifiable material and auctorial source).* [L *ars, artis*]

art /*ärt*/ *n* must be painted with soul and feeling. [L *ars, artis*]

art /*ärt*/ *n* must be something that is made or presented by a person with the intention of being regarded in a certain way; *how to cash out 'a certain way' non-circularly eludes me.* [L *ars, artis*]

art /*ärt*/ *n* must be spiritual, enchanting, elating and surprising; *and it must be dissociated from materialism which only reduces it to a mere tradable commodity.* [L *ars, artis*]

art /*ärt*/ *n (sociol)* must be used as an instrument for social change. [L *ars, artis*]

art /*ärt*/ *n* must be viewed as an inherent universal (or biological) trait of the human species. [L *ars, artis*]

art /*ärt*/ *n* must bear resemblance to earlier pieces of art. [L *ars, artis*]

art /*ärt*/ *n* must come from the heart. [L *ars, artis*]

art /*ärt*/ *n* must communicate; *art shouldn't just match the couch.* [L *ars, artis*]

art /*ärt*/ *n* must create a specific emotional link between artist and audience, one that 'affects' the viewer; *thus, real art requires the capacity to unite people via communication (clearness and genuineness are therefore crucial values).* [L *ars, artis*]

art /*ärt*/ *n* must duplicate the experience of man and serve as its imaginary continuation and supplement. [L *ars, artis*]

art /*ärt*/ *n* must generate 'the spark of inner life'. [L *ars, artis*]

art /*ärt*/ *n* must have a lasting relevance. [L *ars, artis*]

art /*ärt*/ *n* must have a life of its own; *its own depths and stories and contrast and composition.* [L *ars, artis*]

art /*ärt*/ *n* must have a positive effect upon the human psyche to be called art; *pornography, for example, is not art since it is deleterious to at least one human subject depicted; and, in any case, if any depiction of such 'art' results in money changing hands for any reason, it definitely is not art.* [L *ars, artis*]

art /*ärt*/ *n* must have a story behind it; *a story that is immediately apparent to the viewer.* [L *ars, artis*]

art /*ärt*/ *n* must have some secret ingredient that is hard to describe but is often labeled as 'Soul, Aura, Genius, Originality' *etc. ad. inf.*; *the higher the concentration of this secret ingredient the greater the status of the work of art.* [L *ars, artis*]

art */ärt/ n* must have the ability to change those who see it. [L *ars, artis*]

art */ärt/ n* must have the right to risk being bad. [L *ars, artis*]

art */ärt/ n* must lead beyond the arts, to an awareness and a share of mutuality. [L *ars, artis*]

art */ärt/ n* must make people think, evoke an emotional response and challenge the viewer. [L *ars, artis*]

art */ärt/ n* must manifest itself in the public arena; *alongside changes to the country's political and economic climate.* [L *ars, artis*]

art */ärt/ n* must mean something to be relevant; *there might be several scribblings in the sketch book, but if they do not lead to some finished work with germane attributes, there is no point.* [L *ars, artis*]

art */ärt/ n (neg)* must never be a copy. [L *ars, artis*]

art */ärt/ n (neg)* must not be confused with porn. [L *ars, artis*]

art */ärt/ n (neg)* must not copy life; *but reproduce life's structure.* [L *ars, artis*]

art */ärt/ n* must point to something beyond itself. [L *ars, artis*]

art */ärt/ n (educ)* must remain part of the curriculum to help feed the 'soul of the nation'. [L *ars, artis*]

art */ärt/ n* must resemble real life by re-creating *(modeling)* reality in all its integrity and structural complexity. [L *ars, artis*]

art */ärt/ n* must say something. [L *ars, artis*]

art */ärt/ n* must serve the state. [L *ars, artis*]

art */ärt/ n* must show the world as changeable. [L *ars, artis*]

art */ärt/ n* must touch a chord. [L *ars, artis*]

art */ärt/ n (poss relig)* must work with religion and science as a force for the advancement of mankind. [L *ars, artis*]

art */ärt/ n (joc, euphem, pers)* my boner on a cold day. [L *ars, artis*]

art */ärt/ n (comput, neg)* my C++™ textbook certainly isn't a work of art (C++™, *programming language that is general purpose, statically typed, free-form, multi-paradigm and compiled).* [L *ars, artis*]

art */ärt/ n (pers)* my career. [L *ars, artis*]

Art */ärt/ n (pers)* my dog's name. [Arthur]

art */ärt/ n (pers)* my escape when my house is stressful. [L *ars, artis*]

art */ärt/ n (pers)* my exclusive reason for breathing. [L *ars, artis*]

Art */ärt/ n (pers)* my former roommate's cousin twice removed. [Arthur]

art */ärt/ n (pers)* my life. [L *ars, artis*]

Art */ärt/ n (pers)* my uncle. [Arthur]

art */ärt/ n (inf)* naked-lady statues with the arms busted off. *(perh ref* Aphrodite of Milos *(Gr:* Αφροδίτη της Μήλου, *Aphroditi tis Milou), better known as the Venus de Milo, an ancient Gr statue and one of the most famous works of ancient Gr sculpt.)* [L *ars, artis*]

art */ärt/ n* narrative plus visuals plus audio. [L *ars, artis*]

art */ärt/ n* Nat Tate (Nat Tate *(1928–60), fictional abstract expressionist who destroyed 99% of his work and leapt to his death from the Staten Island ferry).* [L *ars, artis*]

art */ärt/ n* nature amplified and made universal in a few deft strokes. [L *ars, artis*]

art */ärt/ n* nature concentrated. [L *ars, artis*]

art */ärt/ n* nature made by man. [L *ars, artis*]

art */ärt/ n* necessary. [L *ars, artis*]

art */ärt/ n* necessary for positive life experience. [L *ars, artis*]

art */ärt/ n* need not be uplifting; *much of the art displayed by the Germans in the 'Entartete Kunst' exhibit would not be something any of us would want to display over our sofas, but it is art (*Die Ausstellung Entartete Kunst *(19 July–30 November 1937), art exhibition organized by Adolf Ziegler).* [L *ars, artis*]

art */ärt/ n (derog, vulg)* needs to be fucking deliberate; *people simply being able to masturbate together a thesis-length rationalisation for something does not automatically make it profound – and that doesn't just apply to crap you'd see in art museums, English majors.* [L *ars, artis*]

art */ärt/ n (interrog)* needs to be smart and make us think? like what? a complex maths problem? or the solution to Israeli-Arab conflict? to help people? *then* *let's see if a hungry/thirsty child in Africa would choose the Mona Lisa over a glass of water and a bowl of cereal* (**Mona Lisa**, *half-length portrait of a woman by It artist Leonardo da Vinci (1452–1519)).* [L *ars, artis*]

art */ärt/ n* negotiating symbolic resonance. [L *ars, artis*]

art */ärt/ n* neither ethically good nor bad. [L *ars, artis*]

art */ärt/ n* neither good nor bad; *just a reflection of duality.* [L *ars, artis*]

art */ärt/ n (neg)* never a passion. [L *ars, artis*]

art */ärt/ n (neg)* never chaste; *it ought to be forbidden to ignorant innocents, never allowed into contact with those not sufficiently prepared: yes, art is dangerous – where it is chaste, it is not art.* [L *ars, artis*]

art */ärt/ n (neg)* never finished; *only abandoned.* [L *ars, artis*]

art */ärt/ n (neg)* never for entertainment. [L *ars, artis*]

art */ärt/ n (neg)* never right or wrong; *though sometimes good and sometimes bad.* [L *ars, artis*]

art */ärt/ n (neg)* never serious. [L *ars, artis*]

art */ärt/ n (neg)* no creativity = not art; *BY DEFINITION.* [L *ars, artis*]

art */ärt/ n (neg)* no function, no pleasure, no joy…; *but THRILLING, yes.* [L *ars, artis*]

art */ärt/ n (neg)* no laws can define it. [L *ars, artis*]

art */ärt/ n (neg)* no medium can contain it. [L *ars, artis*]

art */ärt/ n* non-rivalrous up to a point; *because it is congestible.* [L *ars, artis*]

art */ärt/ n (neg)* not a career choice in the same way as banking or plumbing. [L *ars, artis*]

art */ärt/ n (neg)* not a compliment in itself. [L *ars, artis*]

art */ärt/ n (neg)* not a game in which man lets off his excess of stored-up energy. [L *ars, artis*]

art */ärt/ n (neg)* not a gene or a specific talent. [L *ars, artis*]

art */ärt/ n (neg)* not a matter of life and death; *it is more important than that (perh ref* **William 'Bill' Shankly OBE** *(1913–1981) Scottish footballer and manager, best known for his time as manager of Liverpool Football Club).* [L *ars, artis*]

art */ärt/ n (neg)* not a means to better understand the world; *but a metaphysical way of giving meaning to it.* [L *ars, artis*]

art */ärt/ n (neg)* not a mirror held up to reality; *but a hammer with which to shape it.* [L *ars, artis*]

art */ärt/ n (neg)* not a one-sided conversation; *and it doesn't help to continue acting like it is.* [L *ars, artis*]

art */ärt/ n (neg)* not a problem to be solved. [L *ars, artis*]

art */ärt/ n (neg)* not a study of positive reality. [L *ars, artis*]

art */ärt/ n (neg)* not a thing; *it is a reaction to a thing.* [L *ars, artis*]

art */ärt/ n (neg)* not a 'what'; *it is a when and a why.* [L *ars, artis*]

art */ärt/ n (neg)* not about beautiful things; *but about ideas and gimmicks and statements and politics.* [L *ars, artis*]

art */ärt/ n (neg)* not about drawn lines and molded shapes and painted colours that interpret creation in a beautiful way and therefore please us. [L *ars, artis*]

art */ärt/ n (neg)* not about enforcing nothing or everything; *unless it resonates in nothing and everything.* [L *ars, artis*]

art */ärt/ n (neg)* not about the audience. [L *ars, artis*]

art */ärt/ n (neg)* not always handmade. [L *ars, artis*]

art */ärt/ n (neg)* not an opinion. [L *ars, artis*]

art */ärt/ n (neg)* not anything until it is judged by the public. [L *ars, artis*]

art */ärt/ n (neg)* not assigned the goal of primarily awakening in the reader 'good feelings'. [L *ars, artis*]

art */ärt/ n (neg)* not complicated, *contradictory nature of art is also fine, because we are no longer tangled what is art or artistic purity, but we are not trying to re-affirm the value and significance of this is true certainly, not false or virtual certainty, because in reality, there are many known masters, not the case, however soiled secular birthright, just glue artistic aura of art is certain is that true self art, only in the inner secret world gained a freedom and fun.* [L *ars, artis*]

art */ärt/ n (neg)* not cornflakes. [L *ars, artis*]

art */ärt/ n (neg)* not created; *rather, something created becomes art.* [L *ars, artis*]

art */ärt/ n (neg)* not created by sophisticated machinery. [L *ars, artis*]

art */ärt/ n (neg)* not debatable; *the more empty words used to establish a foundation for art then the more empty of art the thing is.* [L *ars, artis*]

art */ärt/ n (neg)* not education. [L *ars, artis*]

art */ärt/ n (neg, inf)* not every art piece is meant to convey a message; *sometimes, you do it because it's fucking fun.* [L *ars, artis*]

art */ärt/ n (neg)* not for nothing; *and not for anything either.* [L *ars, artis*]

art */ärt/ n (neg)* not having a Plan B. [L *ars, artis*]

art */ärt/ n (neg)* not just a pretty picture to look at. [L *ars, artis*]

art */ärt/ n (neg)* not just a swatch of colour and a blank canvas. [L *ars, artis*]

art */ärt/ n (neg)* not just an aggregate of marble and bronze, pounded or poured into shape. [L *ars, artis*]

art */ärt/ n (neg)* not just the FINE arts as we think of; *movies, clothing, shoes – anything.* [L *ars, artis*]

art */ärt/ n (neg)* not limited by labels or definition. [L *ars, artis*]

art */ärt/ n (neg)* not merely an imitation of the reality of nature; *but in truth a metaphysical supplement to the reality of nature, placed alongside thereof for its conquest.* [L *ars, artis*]

art */ärt/ n (neg)* not necessarily science; *but science is always art.* [L *ars, artis*]

art */ärt/ n* not only a form of self expression and an attempt at emotional connection, *it is the showing of a country's culture and history.* [L *ars, artis*]

art */ärt/ n* not only about originality and sophistication. [L *ars, artis*]

art */ärt/ n (neurol)* not only captures the essence of something but also amplifies it in order to more powerfully activate the same neural mechanisms that would be activated by the original object. [L *ars, artis*]

art */ärt/ n* not only the imitation of reality but also that which reflects *or comments on* something in reality. [L *ars, artis*]

art */ärt/ n* not only what you see and touch, but all the different emotions it makes you feel. [L *ars, artis*]

art */ärt/ n (neg)* not perfection like many think; *art is not straight lines or even looking at circles all of the time; often the best art is the art that shows real life flaws that make life beautiful; if one can capture those flaws in their art without having to correct them so the art is 'perfect', only then will their art truly be perfect.* [L *ars, artis*]

art */ärt/ n (neg)* not pleasure. [L *ars, artis*]

art */ärt/ n (neg)* not political action. [L *ars, artis*]

art */ärt/ n (neg)* not real. [L *ars, artis*]

art */ärt/ n (neg)* not really about expression for the artist. [L *ars, artis*]

art */ärt/ n (neg)* not solely about who has the best technique. [L *ars, artis*]

art */ärt/ n (neg)* not subjective. [L *ars, artis*]

art */ärt/ n (neg)* not the application of a canon of beauty *but what the instinct and the brain can conceive beyond any canon.* [L *ars, artis*]

art */ärt/ n (fig, poss relig)* not the bread but the wine of life. [L *ars, artis*]

art */ärt/ n (neg)* not the emotional spewing of irrational impulses; *but the selective recreation of reality.* [L *ars, artis*]

art */ärt/ n (neg)* not the expression of man's emotions by external signs. [L *ars, artis*]

art */ärt/ n (neg)* not the expression of merely the subjective sensations and experiences of the poet. [L *ars, artis*]

art */ärt/ n (neg)* not the free play of fantasy, feelings and moods. [L *ars, artis*]

art */ärt/ n (neg)* not the illustration of symbols and ideas. [L *ars, artis*]

art */ärt/ n (neg)* not the manifestation of some mysterious idea of beauty or God. [L *ars, artis*]

art */ärt/ n (neg)* not the possession of the few who are recognized writers, painters, musicians. [L *ars, artis*]

art */ärt/ n (neg)* not the production of pleasing objects. [L *ars, artis*]

art */ärt/ n (neg)* not the same thing as journalism. [L *ars, artis*]

art */ärt/ n (neg)* not the silver bullet that can take a person from abject despair to jolly happiness. [L *ars, artis*]

art */ärt/ n (neg)* not to be figured like an equation; *but to be lived like a dance.* [L *ars, artis*]

art */ärt/ n (neg)* not totally magnificence; *because magnificence is a property.* [L *ars, artis*]

art */ärt/ n (neg)* not truth. [L *ars, artis*]

art */ärt/ n (neg)* not universal; *but conceptually constructed by individuals whose perceptions are necessarily limited and parochial.* [L *ars, artis*]

art */ärt/ n* (*neg, derog*) not whatever you call it; *I loathe that cop-out definition and wish more people would come forward and call it what it is, crap.* [L *ars, artis*]

art */ärt/ n (neg)* not worth much without the mystique that dealers and critics attach to it. [L *ars, artis*]

art */ärt/ n (neg)* not your day job. [L *ars, artis*]

art */ärt/ n (neg, philos, theol, physiol, m)* not, as the metaphysicians say, the manifestation of some mysterious idea of beauty or God; not, as the aesthetical physiologists say, a game in which man lets off his excess of stored-up energy; not the expression of man's emotions by external signs; not the production of pleasing objects; and, above all, not pleasure; *it is a means of union among men, joining them together in the same feelings.* [L *ars, artis*]

art */ärt/ n* nothing but the vehicle of thought. [L *ars, artis*]

art */ärt/ n (derog)* nothing more than a miserable little pile of whatever you want. [L *ars, artis*]

art */ärt/ n* nothing more than life; *and if I can't draw or do art I can't imagine myself living.* [L *ars, artis*]

art */ärt/ n (inf)* nothing more than notoriety of your hobby; *because if you do this shit in your basement someone would probably get you some help if they don't tip the police bout your crazy ass first; a hobby you would do for free or for enjoyment; if you can get paid or people appreciated it it's just a bonus; but that's when the best art, thoughts are created; out of pure enjoyment – not necessity or desperation of production.* [L *ars, artis*]

art */ärt/ n (interrog)* nothing more than the imitation of life itself? [L *ars, artis*]

art */ärt/ n* nourishes the soul. [L *ars, artis*]

art */ärt/ n* now collectively called 'creative science'. [L *ars, artis*]

art */ärt/ n* nowhere. [L *ars, artis*]

art */ärt/ n* nude painting. [L *ars, artis*]

art */ärt/ n* objective. [L *ars, artis*]

art */ärt/ n* objects of particular sensory value in our culture. [L *ars, artis*]

art */ärt/ n* obsession. [L *ars, artis*]

art */ärt/ n* obviously subjective. [L *ars, artis*]

art */ärt/ n* of some lasting value. [L *ars, artis*]

art */ärt/ n* offers a unique opportunity of reading the world from a different perspective to those who decide to focus on it; *this is particularly the case with contemporary art, which can be seen as an expression of the best energies and deep anxieties of our times; it is a space for meditation, for the articulation of doubts and questions that are capable of leading to change.* [L *ars, artis*]

art */ärt/ n* offers us a place to start. [L *ars, artis*]

art */ärt/ n* offers us an opportunity to feel and to think beyond the efforts of our daily routine. [L *ars, artis*]

art */ärt/ n* often a celebration; *a reminder of humanity's brilliance that it's easy to overlook when you're wallowing.* [L *ars, artis*]

art */ärt/ n* often an individual sport. [L *ars, artis*]

art */ärt/ n* often expresses the resolution of past pain. [L *ars, artis*]

art */ärt/ n* often intended to appeal to and connect with human emotion. [L *ars, artis*]

art */ärt/ n* often over-explained; *and, like a joke, it dies in the process.* [L *ars, artis*]

art */ärt/ n* often thought of as beautiful; *though it has no need to be beautiful.* [L *ars, artis*]

art */ärt/ n (interrog)* oh yeah, art supposed to make you feel something? a strong emotion perhaps? *next time I would be standing at the entrance of a museum and slap every visitor's face really hard –*

they would experience such a heightened level of emotion in them that none of those pieces on the walls and hallways could create – anger, surprise, revenge, pain, fear, self-righteousness, thirst for justice, maybe laughter or even sexual arousal & joy (if they are into it) – or a combination of few or all of them; show me a piece of art that has made you feel like that last time – and from zero to full effect in a blink of an eye too. [L *ars, artis*]

art */ärt/ n* on the rise but can be quickly torn down. [L *ars, artis*]

art */ärt/ n* on the whole is mostly serendipitous. [L *ars, artis*]

art */ärt/ n* once you use your talent to create the image. [L *ars, artis*]

art */ärt/ n (derog)* one must 'feel' the cosmic plateau the artist has reached; *blahhhh, blahhhh and* etc. [L *ars, artis*]

art */ärt/ n* one of a kind. [L *ars, artis*]

art */ärt/ n* one of the few fields where the people who study it, know it, do it – *often for a lifetime* – are given so little credibility as experts in their field. [L *ars, artis*]

art */ärt/ n* one of the few subjects that is academically organized according to technique. [L *ars, artis*]

art */ärt/ n* one of the fine arts. [L *ars, artis*]

art */ärt/ n* one of the fine arts; *as, he prefers art to literature.* [L *ars, artis*]

art */ärt/ n* one of the forms of social consciousness. [L *ars, artis*]

Art */ärt/ n* one of the guys in my office; *silly goose.* [Arthur]

art */ärt/ n* one of the least interesting things we can say about a cultural object. [L *ars, artis*]

art */ärt/ n* one of the liberal arts. [L *ars, artis*]

art */ärt/ n* one of the many paths by which we attempt to understand ourselves and the world in which we live. [L *ars, artis*]

art */ärt/ n* one of the means of effective communication between people. [L *ars, artis*]

art */ärt/ n* one of the most subjective things in the world: *what I might like or love might be what someone else just hates; it's very open to interpretation, yet I've found that if I really stop to think about it, I don't like the particular piece of art at all; most of the 'Masters' I wouldn't pay* *them one red cent; I like instead obscure neighbourhood artists and my husband and I have bought most of our household art from Art Fairs – where you can find anything and everything.* [L *ars, artis*]

art */ärt/ n (interj)* one of the ways that feelings can out! [L *ars, artis*]

art */ärt/ n* one of the ways we are different from animals; *no other creature uses energy to make art; and art only becomes a possibility when a culture has reached a stable enough point that its members can indulge in non-survival oriented tasks.* [L *ars, artis*]

art */ärt/ n* one of those places where religion, politics, gender roles, societal issues – it's a place where all those ideas intersect. [L *ars, artis*]

art */ärt/ n* one of those subjective things. [L *ars, artis*]

art */ärt/ n* one of those things about us we can't pin down; *because it is outside physical explanation; standards and tastes change a little on the edges and cultures have different techniques and instruments, but all have art that all can recognize as art.* [L *ars, artis*]

art */ärt/ n* one of those things you do because you have a burning passion for it *and you couldn't live with out it.* [L *ars, artis*]

art */ärt/ n* one person's reaction to life. [L *ars, artis*]

art */ärt/ n* one person's reaction to life; *any definition of art that robs it of this inner response by a human creator is a worthless definition.* [L *ars, artis*]

art */ärt/ n* one's emotions to life and the things surrounding that person. [L *ars, artis*]

art */ärt/ n* one's personal form of expressing feelings, thoughts or ideas, through many varying mediums; *be that through painting, sculpture, music, dance or acting.* [L *ars, artis*]

art */ärt/ n (pers)* only a small amount of the photography, painting, sculpture or any other genre produced today, or in any age, is art; *how do I differentiate between what is and is not art? I know it when I see it; also, I reserve the right to change my mind later.* [L *ars, artis*]

art */ärt/ n* only comes from misery. [L *ars, artis*]

art */ärt/ n* only exists in your head. [L *ars, artis*]

art */ärt/ n* only painting and sculpture. [L *ars, artis*]

art */ärt/ n* only truly found when the design of a thing, action or idea deeply resonates with one *or more* of the many complexities of the observer's mind, idea, or personality. [L *ars, artis*]

art */ärt/ n (philos)* ontologically dependent on, and inferior to, ordinary physical objects; *which in turn are ontologically dependent on, and inferior to, what is most real: the non-physical Forms.* [L *ars, artis*]

art */ärt/ n (joc, imit)* ooh… Doh! *(perh ref* Homer Jay Simpson, *fictional character who appears in the animated television series The Simpsons).* [L *ars, artis*]

art */ärt/ n* open. [L *ars, artis*]

art */ärt/ n* open; *and one does not actually have to be an artist.* [L *ars, artis*]

art */ärt/ n* opening up. [L *ars, artis*]

art */ärt/ n* OPENS OUR LIFE & TOUCHES OUR BLINDNESS WITH LIGHT. [L *ars, artis*]

art */ärt/ n* opens up a new world to me. [L *ars, artis*]

art */ärt/ n* opinion, *totally subjective and fully intuitive.* [L *ars, artis*]

art */ärt/ n (interrog)* order? [L *ars, artis*]

art */ärt/ n* order, proportion and radiance. [L *ars, artis*]

art */ärt/ n* original work in any medium that conveys some sort of image of people, places, things, or ideas. [L *ars, artis*]

art */ärt/ n (appar joc)* originality, invention, harmony, conciseness, complexity and splendid insincerity. [L *ars, artis*]

art */ärt/ n* our closest relative to magic; *well besides technology, but who is to say that isn't art as well.* [L *ars, artis*]

art */ärt/ n* our cultural shorthand for what is worthwhile. [L *ars, artis*]

art */ärt/ n* our humanness speaking in ways that convey or evoke how we see ourselves and our world. [L *ars, artis*]

art */ärt/ n* our only hope. [L *ars, artis*]

art */ärt/ n* out of control. [L *ars, artis*]

art */ärt/ n* outrages. [L *ars, artis*]

art */ärt/ n (poss fig)* overflows the ice-cube tray. [L *ars, artis*]

art */ärt/ n* pain. [L *ars, artis*]

art */ärt/ n* painting. [L *ars, artis*]

art */ärt/ n* painting and photography. [L *ars, artis*]

art */ärt/ n* painting and sculpture. [L *ars, artis*]

art */ärt/ n* painting, drawing and sculpture. [L *ars, artis*]

art */ärt/ n* painting, drawing and sculpture as subjects you study. [L *ars, artis*]

art */ärt/ n* painting, drawing and sculpture that are created to be beautiful or to express ideas. [L *ars, artis*]

art */ärt/ n* painting, drawing, sculpture, *etc*. [L *ars, artis*]

art */ärt/ n* painting, sculpture, performance *(wacky modern performance art, sitcoms, dramatic movies, musicians)* and yes, video games too; *I'll accept text and verbal storytelling as well.* [L *ars, artis*]

art */ärt/ n* paintings and stuff. [L *ars, artis*]

art */ärt/ n (interj)* PAINTINGS OF HORSES! [L *ars, artis*]

art */ärt/ n* paintings on a wall or a play. [L *ars, artis*]

art */ärt/ n* paintings, statues, *etc*. [L *ars, artis*]

art */ärt/ n* part of the struggle. [L *ars, artis*]

art */ärt/ n* passion; *passion is love, love is light, light is life, art is life.* [L *ars, artis*]

art */ärt/ n* passion flowing through the artist for all to see. [L *ars, artis*]

art */ärt/ n* pattern informed by sensibility. [L *ars, artis*]

art */ärt/ n* peaceful and calming. [L *ars, artis*]

art */ärt/ n* people communicating through a non-literal medium. [L *ars, artis*]

art */ärt/ n (m)* perceived by the creator who wishes to express himself in an artistic form; *whether you or I agree or not.* [L *ars, artis*]

art */ärt/ n* perceived not asserted. [L *ars, artis*]

art */ärt/ n* perception, reflection and personal interpretation. [L *ars, artis*]

art */ärt/ n* permanent. [L *ars, artis*]

art */ärt/ n* permits you to step out of the social labyrinth *and into a quiet corner of your own private and humble joy.* [L *ars, artis*]

art */ärt/ n* perplexing. [L *ars, artis*]

art */ärt/ n* personal. [L *ars, artis*]

art */ärt/ n* personal adornment or embellishment. [L *ars, artis*]

art */ärt/ n* personal, insightful and completely objective [perh *subjective*] to each person viewing it. [L *ars, artis*]

art */ärt/ n (philos)* philosophically speaking, *(and yes, I have training here)* art exists; *this assertion means that it has perimeters even if we don't agree on what they are; A is A; A cannot be B; therefore art cannot, by definition, be 'everything'.* [L *ars, artis*]

art */ärt/ n (photog)* photo manipulation. [L *ars, artis*]

art */ärt/ n (photog)* photographers that set up their shots just so, wait for the perfect time of day, sun/shade, composition and only have (or allow) one shot to get it right. [L *ars, artis*]

art */ärt/ n (photog)* photographing. [L *ars, artis*]

art */ärt/ n (photog)* photographs or other illustrations in a newspaper, *etc.* [L *ars, artis*]

art */ärt/ n (photog)* photographs or other visual representations in a printed publication. [L *ars, artis*]

art */ärt/ n (photog)* photography without Photoshop™ (Adobe Photoshop™, *graphics editing program developed and published by Adobe Systems).* [L *ars, artis*]

art */ärt/ n* photos of cats, a drawing of a dinosaur, weird takes on ponies or Pokemon® are all art (Pokémon®, *a media franchise managed by The Pokémon Company and centered on fictional creatures called "Pokémon" which humans, known as Pokémon Trainers, catch and train to battle each other for sport).* [L *ars, artis*]

art */ärt/ n* pictorial and decorative material accompanying the text in a newspaper, magazine, or advertising layout. [L *ars, artis*]

art */ärt/ n* pictures and sculpture brought about from nothing. [L *ars, artis*]

art */ärt/ n* pictures and sculptures; *and all the rest.* [L *ars, artis*]

art */ärt/ n* plain. [L *ars, artis*]

art */ärt/ n* playing with the perceiver's emotions, giving them another perspective on existence. [L *ars, artis*]

art */ärt/ n* pleases universally without a concept; *subjective uni-*

versality: people ought to feel the same way as I do; an aesthetic judgment is that which, without any concept, is cognized as the object of a necessary satisfaction; thanks to Immanuel Kant (**Immanuel Kant** *(1724–1804), Ger philosopher widely considered to be a central figure of modern philosophy).* [L *ars, artis*]

art */ärt/ n (pl, interrog)* plural; *arts?* [L *ars, artis*]

art */ärt/ n* political discourse. [L *ars, artis*]

art */ärt/ n* porn. [L *ars, artis*]

art */ärt/ n (interrog)* porn? *No.* [L *ars, artis*]

art */ärt/ n* porn can be art. [L *ars, artis*]

art */ärt/ n* portrays something; *and more than that, it portrays something meaningful.* [L *ars, artis*]

art */ärt/ n* possesses an essence that does not depend upon the receiving ear. [L *ars, artis*]

art */ärt/ n* potatoes. [L *ars, artis*]

art */ärt/ n* pottery. [L *ars, artis*]

art */ärt/ n* power. [L *ars, artis*]

art */ärt/ n* powerful. [L *ars, artis*]

art */ärt/ n* practical skill. [L *ars, artis*]

art */ärt/ n* practical skill; *or its application, guided by principles.* [L *ars, artis*]

art */ärt/ n* practice not theory; *and nothing can make Duchamp's 'readymades' art because they were made for a specific non-artistic purpose; theory does not change a pile of Brillo® cartons in a supermarket into art, yet Danto thought if it was put in a gallery a substantive transformation took place; Andy Warhol's pretentious Brillo® Boxes (a pile of Brillo® cartons, replicas actually, so they are doubly pretentious) remain a pile of Brillo boxes wherever they are put* (**Marcel Duchamp** *(1887–1968), Fr-Am painter, sculptor, chess player and writer;* **Brillo®**, *provides a wide variety of household cleaning products and remains dedicated to one ideal... helping people everywhere to enjoy clean, healthy lifestyles;* **Arthur Coleman Danto** *(1924–2013), Am art critic and philosopher;* **Andrew Warhola** *(1928–87), Am artist).* [L *ars, artis*]

art */ärt/ n* practices that, upon reflection, are more than function. [L *ars, artis*]

art */ärt/ n (theol)* prayer. [L *ars,*

artis]

art */ärt/ n* preferable to life; *because it is safe even when it is severe.* [L *ars, artis*]

art */ärt/ n* pretentious nonsense. [L *ars, artis*]

art */ärt/ n* pretty much anything that's either music or visually appealing. [L *ars, artis*]

art */ärt/ n* pretty much everything. [L *ars, artis*]

art */ärt/ n* pretty much the one thing that seems to matter to me. [L *ars, artis*]

art */ärt/ n* (*inf, interrog*) pretty shit which is a b*tch [perh *bitch*] to make, you feel me? [L *ars, artis*]

art */ärt/ n* (*abbrev*) prfct [prob *perfect*]. [L *ars, artis*]

art */ärt/ n* primal expression. [L *ars, artis*]

art */ärt/ n* primarily a reflection of culture *and a means to understand ourselves in relation to culture.* [L *ars, artis*]

art */ärt/ n* primarily symbolic, *made and appreciated with joy.* [L *ars, artis*]

art */ärt/ n* printmaking. [L *ars, artis*]

art */ärt/ n* problematically conflated with the art market. [L *ars, artis*]

art */ärt/ n* produced with conscious artistry. [L *ars, artis*]

art */ärt/ n* produces a disinterested feeling of pleasure *or pain* in an individual. [L *ars, artis*]

art */ärt/ n* product which is high-end, rare and expensive. [L *ars, artis*]

art */ärt/ n* production and expression of aesthetics. [L *ars, artis*]

art */ärt/ n (pl)* products of creative work. [L *ars, artis*]

art */ärt/ n* progressive. [L *ars, artis*]

art */ärt/ n* propaganda; *it has been, mostly, commissioned by the Church and it is intended to overawe people, make them feel small, grateful, fearful and all sorts of other things; take all those pictures of Christ on the cross, bleeding copiously and with his mother, Mary and others weeping at his feet; those are horrible pictures; I really do not want to see pictures of people being crucified – anymore than I want to see pictures of little children having had their skin burned off by napalm bombs, or people who are skeletal and are dying of starvation; this is all repugnant and poison-*

*ous; it is people trying to manipulate other people emotionally; if you let your emotions govern you then you expose yourself to all sorts of bad things: to advertisers, to teasing and bullying, to bosses getting you to do things you do not want, to salesmen – the list is endless (*Jesus Christ *(c2BC-c30AD), the central figure of Christianity;* Mary *(c1stBC-early c1stAD), Israelite Jewish woman of Nazareth in Galilee and mother of Jesus).* [L *ars, artis*]

art */ärt/ n* properly made, enhances and enriches the lives of others. [L *ars, artis*]

art */ärt/ n* properties in the action from which we infer, *whether justly or not,* that the agent voluntarily and designedly puts forth skill for known ends and by regular and uniform methods. [L *ars, artis*]

art */ärt/ n* property; *property is theft.* [L *ars, artis*]

art */ärt/ n* prostitution. [L *ars, artis*]

art */ärt/ n* protected; *because not everyone can view art in the same way; some people could see a piece of art as just a hunk of junk where as others could see it as a beautifully wicked item that is full of the unknown; we as people don't know what everyone else looks like under their clothes (not to sound creepy!) so what the artist or creator was originally going for when they set in on an art project will only be truly known by them.* [L *ars, artis*]

art */ärt/ n (psychol)* provides a form of therapy for people whose minds are disturbed in some way. [L *ars, artis*]

art */ärt/ n* provides an opportunity for us to explore the world around us as well as our own consciousness. [L *ars, artis*]

art */ärt/ n* provides sustenance, *spiritual or worldly,* for people. [L *ars, artis*]

art */ärt/ n (prob fig)* provokes a wide range of debate and comment; *often to the accompaniment of axes grinding in the background.* [L *ars, artis*]

art */ärt/ n* provokes reflections, criticisms and reactions that are more or less similar to one another, but never identical; *my reading of a painting or my reaction to a symphony may share common features with that of the person contemplating the painting right next to me in an art gallery, or with the person* *sitting next to me in a theatre; yet our ideas, the product of our thinking of what that piece of art could actually mean or intend to say, will never be identical to that of our fellow appreciators; interpretations of art are like fingerprints – you could swear that mine are identical to yours, but they never occur to be so.* [L *ars, artis*]

art */ärt/ n (psychol)* psychology experiments. [L *ars, artis*]

art */ärt/ n* publicity-driven, sensationalist, commercial. [L *ars, artis*]

art */ärt/ n* pure expression that comes from a person's heart. [L *ars, artis*]

art */ärt/ n* purely entertainment and escapism. [L *ars, artis*]

art */ärt/ n* purely exists just to exist. [L *ars, artis*]

art */ärt/ n* purpose rearranged. [L *ars, artis*]

art */ärt/ n* pushing forward, breaking and re-inventing the rules. [L *ars, artis*]

art */ärt/ n* putting a vision you have in your mind into a medium other people can experience and explore. [L *ars, artis*]

art */ärt/ n* putting out something that is in your inner world. [L *ars, artis*]

art */ärt/ n* putting the artist's thoughts and ideas into concreteness. [L *ars, artis*]

art */ärt/ n* putting your thoughts, emotions into a creation. [L *ars, artis*]

art */ärt/ n* questions. [L *ars, artis*]

art */ärt/ n* quickens nature. [L *ars, artis*]

art */ärt/ n* quintessential to human meaning. [L *ars, artis*]

art */ärt/ n (derog)* quite frankly, ugly and repellent. [L *ars, artis*]

art */ärt/ n* quite useless; *that would make my beautifully painted garden gnomes art, except if the one with the fishing rod ever caught a fish.* [L *ars, artis*]

art */ärt/ n* raises questions without words. [L *ars, artis*]

art */ärt/ n (mus)* raucous noises called 'music' deafening us. [L *ars, artis*]

art */ärt/ n* raw. [L *ars, artis*]

art */ärt/ n* raw emotion and passion and intellect expressed through a medium beyond words. [L *ars, artis*]

art */ärt/ n* reached when a state of

self-satisfaction is realized. [L *ars, artis*]

art */ärt/ n* reading between the lines. [L *ars, artis*]

art */ärt/ n* realistic. [L *ars, artis*]

art */ärt/ n* reality represented through another's expression. [L *ars, artis*]

art */ärt/ n* really complex; *only a true artist can understand that.* [L *ars, artis*]

art */ärt/ n* really just a person opening up a can of instant-mood. [L *ars, artis*]

art */ärt/ n (fig, inf)* really like expelling gas in a public forum; *some people get offended, while others like it or just tolerate it and hang around; no matter what it has gotten the attention of the room.* [L *ars, artis*]

art */ärt/ n* rearranging and re-purposing the hidebound or meaningless into something new, something never before seen, something true that has perhaps never before been true. [L *ars, artis*]

art */ärt/ n* reason applied without limits, *geared towards an ideal and guided by the practical.* [L *ars, artis*]

art */ärt/ n (photog)* recognizing a truly moving scene and photographing it; *such as the early work of Ansel Adams (*Ansel Easton Adams *(1902–84), Am photog and environmentalist).* [L *ars, artis*]

art */ärt/ n* records subjective human beliefs and emotions. [L *ars, artis*]

art */ärt/ n* recycled reality. [L *ars, artis*]

art */ärt/ n* refers to an institutionalised space or an institutionally recognised space in which the various iconographies of a culture/society are formed into discrete objects; *all paintings, music, movies etc are essentially composed of these iconographies and are part of an institution or a centralised practice; where iconography = 'the visual images, symbols, or modes of representation collectively associated with a person, cult, or movement.'* [L *ars, artis*]

art */ärt/ n* reflective of the human experience. [L *ars, artis*]

art */ärt/ n* reflects both the moment in which it is created and the continuum of human consciousness. [L *ars, artis*]

art */ärt/ n* reflects, expresses, invokes and describes the ambiguity of humanity. [L *ars, artis*]

art */ärt/ n* reflects the maker. [L *ars, artis*]

art */ärt/ n* relatable emotion. [L *ars, artis*]

art */ärt/ n* relative to time – ever-changing; *we interpret art with the many facets of our mind.* [L *ars, artis*]

art */ärt/ n* relatively well-defined in dictionaries. [L *ars, artis*]

art */ärt/ n* rendering, creative expression and pain. [L *ars, artis*]

art */ärt/ n* representational or mimetic. [L *ars, artis*]

art */ärt/ n* represents life and how we deal with life. [L *ars, artis*]

art */ärt/ n* represents something or goes against something. [L *ars, artis*]

art */ärt/ n* reproductions of reality. [L *ars, artis*]

art */ärt/ n* requires a certain amount of education. [L *ars, artis*]

art */ärt/ n* requires creativity *(spontaneity, flexibility and most importantly a conscious attempt to express something); also requires intent and not merely something reflexive; then there are the primary level elements of art, such as beauty, composition, colour coordination, etc which for the purposes of this discussion are totally irrelevant and whose role in art has been rightly diminished in the art scene*. [L *ars, artis*]

art */ärt/ n* requires no explanation. [L *ars, artis*]

art */ärt/ n* requires some exchange of meaning between the artist, art and viewer; *this exchange can occur in so many aspects of human creation – music, writing, science, math and even simple interaction; and the artist doesn't have to be human, either; a gorgeous sunset is art of the sky; the trickle of water is art of the earth; the solar system and its rotations is art of the gravitational force (wow that sounds pretentious, I swear I'm not trying to be overly artsy).* [L *ars, artis*]

art */ärt/ n* responds to questions yet to be asked. [L *ars, artis*]

art */ärt/ n* reveals itself in psychic understanding of the inner essence of things; *and gives form to the relation of man with nothing, with the nature of the absolute.* [L *ars, artis*]

art */ärt/ n* reveals the beauty and poetry of the world, of every day life. [L *ars, artis*]

art */ärt/ n (perh theol)* revelation. [L *ars, artis*]

art */ärt/ n* revelations in personal, visual and emotional balance according to one's inherited and prescribed aesthetic cultural language. [L *ars, artis*]

art */ärt/ n* reward for us. [L *ars, artis*]

art */ärt/ n (derog)* ridiculous junk placed in weird situations. [L *ars, artis*]

art */ärt/ n* rigid and ruled. [L *ars, artis*]

art */ärt/ n* risk, intention, practice, exposure. [L *ars, artis*]

art */ärt/ n* satisfies a means of reaching out and sharing our individuality; *through subject matter that is uniquely personal yet universal in its tangible presentation.* [L *ars, artis*]

art */ärt/ n (pers)* saves me everyday. [L *ars, artis*]

art */ärt/ n* says something; *even if we don't know what; it's art because of its uniqueness, its creativeness; most of all, it's art because someone said it was art.* [L *ars, artis*]

art */ärt/ n* scary. [L *ars, artis*]

art */ärt/ n* scenery, music, architecture, a beautiful person; *people just don't take the time to appreciate it; that's why I constantly ogle pretty women.* [L *ars, artis*]

art */ärt/ n* SCIENCE. [L *ars, artis*]

art */ärt/* second person singular present indicative of *be.* [*From Middle Eng, from OE eart ('(thou) art'), second-pers sing pres indicative of wesan, from Proto-Ger *ar-t ('(thou) art', originally, '(thou) becamest'), second-pers sing preterite indicative form of *iranq ('to rise, be quick, become active'), from Proto-Indo-Eur *er-, *or(w)- ('to lift, rise, set in motion'); cognate with Faroese ert ('art'), Icelandic ert ('art'), OE earon ('are'), from the same preterite-present Ger verb.*]

art */ärt/ n* seduction. [L *ars, artis*]

art */ärt/ n* seeing and sharing the beauty in everything and anything. [L *ars, artis*]

art */ärt/ n* seeing through the soul of the artist. [L *ars, artis*]

art */ärt/ n* seeks to enlighten and entertain. [L *ars, artis*]

art */ärt/ n* seems to be an industry; *a way to create digital value activities, continue to prosper and de-*

velop, but also about its contradictions and conflicting definitions repeated day after day – not [giving] us too little knowledge about art, but too much! [L ***ars, artis***]

art */ärt/ n* seems to be an interface between the rhythm and integrity created in the material world, which call down and attract those corresponding components of a higher realm, *such that the artwork is, for the beholder, a gateway to the sublime.* [L ***ars, artis***]

art */ärt/ n* seems to fall into the same uniquely subjective eye of the beholder kind of thing as 'red'; *you cannot describe 'red' as you perceive it; we could try with wavelength quotes and poetic references and metaphor and allegory and on and on and on and on and, ultimately, we cannot (*usu*) be sure that the other person is perceiving it as you intend; I'm suggesting that the word 'art' has outlived it's usefulness in philosophical discussion.* [L ***ars, artis***]

art */ärt/ n (econ)* seems to go up satisfyingly in price; *with sections of the market sky-rocketing even during the tough times in recent years.* [L ***ars, artis***]

art */ärt/ n* seen in expert mountain climbers, who 'deliberately set out to make something special' by traversing great peaks; *or an experienced yachtsman who is able to guide his vessel through a storm, or the masterful execution of a back door cut for a thunderous slam dunk.* [L ***ars, artis***]

art */ärt/ n* self-deception. [L ***ars, artis***]

art */ärt/ n* self-discovery. [L ***ars, artis***]

art */ärt/ n* self-expression; *meaning it doesn't always have to consist of paintings, drawings, pottery, music, acting, dancing, writing; if you took your deepest emotions and combined it with snowboarding and made it beautiful, that would make art.* [L ***ars, artis***]

art */ärt/ n* self-expression that somehow transcends mere self-expression and crosses over into the realm of the truly sublime; *sublimity may take an infinite variety of forms which may elicit an infinite number of responses.* [L ***ars, artis***]

art */ärt/ n (derog, vulg)* self-gratifying masturbation: *the essence of creativity is held in the seed.* [L ***ars, artis***]

art */ärt/ n* sensual. [L ***ars, artis***]

art */ärt/ n (m)* serves to preserve an individual's contact with man's accumulated collective experiences and age-old wisdom; *as well as with man's concrete social and historical interests, aspirations and ideals.* [L ***ars, artis***]

art */ärt/ n* several of those ingenuities in the lower animals which popular theory at the same time declares to be instinctive. [L ***ars, artis***]

art */ärt/ n* Shadow of the Colossus® (Shadow of the Colossus®, *action-adventure game published by Sony™ Computer Entertainment (SCEI) for the PlayStation™ 2).* [L ***ars, artis***]

art */ärt/ n* shall be committed through the greed of the architect, the lust of a woman and the eye of a child. [L ***ars, artis***]

art */ärt/ n* shaped by its audience's perceptions. [L ***ars, artis***]

art */ärt/ n* shaped by its creator. [L ***ars, artis***]

art */ärt/ n* shaped by the identity of the artist. [L ***ars, artis***]

art */ärt/ n* sheep. [L ***ars, artis***]

art */ärt/ n (inf)* shit. [L ***ars, artis***]

art */ärt/ n (inf)* shit. *Art galleries are toilets. Curators are toilet attendants. Artists are bullshitters.* [L ***ars, artis***]

art */ärt/ n (inf)* shit and everything. [L ***ars, artis***]

art */ärt/ n (inf)* shit that you dig; *end of story.* [L ***ars, artis***]

art */ärt/ n* shockingly refreshing. [L ***ars, artis***]

Art */ärt/ n (abbrev)* short for Arthur as: *'Hey, I was just over at Art's house, he is so cool'.* [Arthur]

art */ärt/ n (abbrev)* short for *artifice.* [L ***ars, artis***]

art */ärt/ n (joc)* should be a foray into the unknown; *or to kinkily say it… an 'artventure'.* [L ***ars, artis***]

art */ärt/ n (milit)* should be a weapon against oppression. [L ***ars, artis***]

art */ärt/ n* should be fundamentally useless in survival terms; *it's what we do to purify ourselves of 'work'.* [L ***ars, artis***]

art */ärt/ n* should be interesting; *but it should also be tasteful as well.* [L ***ars, artis***]

art */ärt/ n* should be what you want it to be; *NOT what Mrs Fleabag says it should be – my teacher forces me to do small intricate drawings but I prefer to make large models.* (Mrs

Fleabag *ref not known).* [L ***ars, artis***]

art */ärt/ n* should challenge us. [L ***ars, artis***]

art */ärt/ n* should comfort the disturbed and disturb the comfortable. [L ***ars, artis***]

art */ärt/ n* should elicit an honest emotional response; *something Thomas Kinkade couldn't do* (Thomas Kinkade, *Painter of Light™ (1958–2012), Am painter of popular realistic, bucolic and idyllic subjects).* [L ***ars, artis***]

art */ärt/ n* should force us to make a choice; *I hate looking at a painting and thinking* 'oh that's nice'*; landscapes bore me to death, I would much rather look at a Dali or an Escher than a Gainsborough* (Salvador Domingo Felipe Jacinto Dalí i Domènech, *1st Marqués de Dalí de Pubol (1904–89), prominent Sp surrealist painter;* Maurits Cornelis Escher *(1898–1972), Du graphic artist;* Thomas Gainsborough FRSA *(1727–88), Eng portrait and landscape painter).* [L ***ars, artis***]

art */ärt/ n* should have no purpose or function other than itself; *paintings and sculptures go with art almost as well as hipsters in independent coffee shops.* [L ***ars, artis***]

art */ärt/ n (neg)* should not be bewildering or impenetrable. [L ***ars, artis***]

art */ärt/ n (neg, econ)* should not be developed for the purpose of profit; *selling a piece of art is, however, different than producing a piece of art for it to be sold.* [L ***ars, artis***]

art */ärt/ n (neg)* should not be developed to perform a practical or biological function; *it shouldn't be created centrally for entertainment or cooking or something of that nature, even developed for purely aesthetic purposes is arguable (a pretty painting itself wouldn't be art in my eyes).* [L ***ars, artis***]

art */ärt/ n (neg)* should not ever require a written explanation of what it is the artist intends to get across, hanging on the wall next to it: *if the art is not appealing to the public, no amount of written description of the failed attempt is going to improve the appreciation to the people viewing it.* [L ***ars, artis***]

art */ärt/ n* should probably at least get a reaction and get people talking. [L ***ars, artis***]

art */ärt/ n (neg)* shouldn't be defined by any one person. [L *ars, artis*]

art */ärt/ n* showing the human body in a beautiful way; *that often means showing and highlighting the lines of the human body – the focus will be on the body, not on sexual areas;* eg *a piece of art might show off the slope of a woman's hip, the lines in her back, the curve of her thighs or shoulders; the breasts are secondary, in art, to the beforementioned lines; expression or emotional impact is another part of art; it gives the impression of* 'oh, beautiful' *(often done with lighting, positioning, colour choice and expression); there is very rarely a 'sexual' feeling to said art.* [L *ars, artis*]

art */ärt/ n* showing the public a glimpse of your own imagination/mind. [L *ars, artis*]

art */ärt/ n* shows our fears, expectations, sight of view, calmness or distraction of the artist and too many things; *but I think original art barely says anything about the artist and only shows the beauty of life and gives us a path to truth and light not darkness and despondency.* [L *ars, artis*]

art */ärt/ n* shows us or reminds us of who we are. [L *ars, artis*]

art */ärt/ n* shows what you are feeling *or what you're thinking about.* [L *ars, artis*]

art */ärt/ n* significant form. [L *ars, artis*]

art */ärt/ n* simple and easy. [L *ars, artis*]

art */ärt/ n* simple yet complex. [L *ars, artis*]

art */ärt/ n* simplifies. [L *ars, artis*]

art */ärt/ n* simply a distraction. [L *ars, artis*]

art */ärt/ n (relig)* simply a way of expressing one's self; *I've seen art so terrible I couldn't even look at it; I've seen art that has brought people to tears over it; I do believe you and I and every human being is divine art; we are God's greatest creations.* [L *ars, artis*]

art */ärt/ n* simply anything you want it to be; *as long as you put a thoughtful meaning behind it.* [L *ars, artis*]

art */ärt/ n* simply how well you can use the tools and techniques of any medium to get that medium to communicate a thought, person, action, feeling, you name it; *in the movie, you see the battlefield and right away you know this is* *going to be epic; the music starts slowly and your heart starts pounding; you see the ferocity on faces and feel the desperation these people had; the weapons shatter under steel and muscle; it was only then that I realized what it must have been like and what these people had to go through to win their freedom* – now that is art. [L *ars, artis*]

art */ärt/ n* simply means 'work'. [L *ars, artis*]

art */ärt/ n (relig)* sings hallelujah. [L *ars, artis*]

art */ärt/ n* situationally defined; ie *any given cultural milieu will define it differently.* [L *ars, artis*]

art */ärt/ n* skill acquired by experience, study or observation. [L *ars, artis*]

art */ärt/ n* skill acquired by experience, study, or observation: *the art of making friends.* [L *ars, artis*]

art */ärt/ n* skill arising from the exercise of intuitive faculties: *'self-criticism is an art not many are qualified to practice'.* [L *ars, artis*]

art */ärt/ n* skill as a result of learning or practice. [L *ars, artis*]

art */ärt/ n* skill, dexterity or the power of performing certain actions, *acquired by experience, study or observation.* [L *ars, artis*]

art */ärt/ n* skill in creative arts. [L *ars, artis*]

art */ärt/ n* skill in joining or fitting. [L *ars, artis*]

art */ärt/ n* skill in scholarship and learning. [L *ars, artis*]

art */ärt/ n* skill or knowledge in a particular department. [L *ars, artis*]

art */ärt/ n* skill that is attained by study, practice, or observation. [L *ars, artis*]

art */ärt/ n* skill used to produce an aesthetic result. [L *ars, artis*]

art */ärt/ n* so ambiguous as to be meaningless. [L *ars, artis*]

art */ärt/ n* so complicated, with so many different forms and variations and limitless possibilities, that you can't actually really make any sort of foundational values or definition. [L *ars, artis*]

art */ärt/ n* so here's what happened on the way home tonight: *long drive, listening to the radio. I kept flipping through until I stopped on a station… thought it was a station… and then said,* 'What the hell is this?'; *it was some very strange* *noises and to keep myself entertained, I copied some of the noises until I thought I'd better listen quietly and figure out what this was I was mimicking; finally I came to the conclusion that I had stopped between stations and this was the strange product of two stations coming through badly;* 'It's art!' *I thought.* [L *ars, artis*]

art */ärt/ n* so much more than a nice sculpture or a pretty picture. [L *ars, artis*]

art */ärt/ n* so often about misery; *because modern life is so often miserable.* [L *ars, artis*]

art */ärt/ n* soft. [L *ars, artis*]

art */ärt/ n* solace. [L *ars, artis*]

art */ärt/ n (perh joc)* some kind of cheese sauce that goes on certain fruits. [L *ars, artis*]

art */ärt/ n* some kind of thing that looks a certain way. [L *ars, artis*]

art */ärt/ n (joc)* some of it is cr@p [prob *crap*]; *but hey-ho, at least it's a level playing field as long as Daddy has enough money to support you while you work on your unmade bed or pickled equine* (**unmade bed**, *perh ref My Bed (1998), a work by Brit artist Tracey Emin (1963–);* **pickled equine**, *perh ref Mother and Child (Divided) or related work by Brit artist Damian Hirst (1965–)).* [L *ars, artis*]

art */ärt/ n* some special attribute or value; *objectively present in the work.* [L *ars, artis*]

art */ärt/ n (interj)* some way to express your thoughts, to express how your mind works! [L *ars, artis*]

art */ärt/ n* some way we have of trying to make sense of ourselves and the world around us; *and, like consciousness, largely confined to humans.* [L *ars, artis*]

art */ärt/ n* somehow an unequivocal expression of its creator. [L *ars, artis*]

Art */ärt/ n* (*vulg*) someone you will never be allowed to fuck, *as it would be social suicide.* [Arthur]

art */ärt/ n* someone's created vision that tells you a story *or something about yourself.* [L *ars, artis*]

art */ärt/ n* someone's invitation to stand where she or he stands and see what she or he sees; *great art is to stand and see in such a way that to add to or to subtract from that experience is to mar what I stand and see.* [L *ars, artis*]

art */ärt/ n* someone's mental, sexual, physical outbursts of their conceptions of anything and everything. [L *ars, artis*]

art */ärt/ n* someone's personality being expressed out loud. [L *ars, artis*]

art */ärt/ n* someone's vision shared with others. [L *ars, artis*]

art */ärt/ n* something a person does or makes in order to convey information; *ideas, stories, images, feelings,* etc. [L *ars, artis*]

art */ärt/ n* something aesthetic. [L *ars, artis*]

art */ärt/ n* something and everything; *and nothing.* [L *ars, artis*]

art */ärt/ n* something/anything that has been recognized by the professional art world; eg *through an exhibit/fair in a museum or gallery, through a review by a renowned art critic,* etc. [L *ars, artis*]

art */ärt/ n* something appreciated for its own value; ie *it has no actual use.* [L *ars, artis*]

art */ärt/ n* something artists do and what people enjoy doing. [L *ars, artis*]

art */ärt/ n* something beautiful. [L *ars, artis*]

art */ärt/ n* something captivating that envelopes the viewer for a moment of awe; *that not only elaborates an aspirational point of view, but also teems with a unique finest [perh finesse].* [L *ars, artis*]

art */ärt/ n* something completely from within, expressed outwardly. [L *ars, artis*]

art */ärt/ n* something created; *it doesn't have to always have a purpose, other than to entertain; it could simply be an expression; I get a kick out of my job title, 'sandwich artist', but it's true!* [L *ars, artis*]

art */ärt/ n* something created by an artist that makes you see the world in a new way. [L *ars, artis*]

art */ärt/ n* something created for the primary purpose of establishing an emotional response within its audience. [L *ars, artis*]

art */ärt/ n* something created that evokes a genuine emotional response; *or makes someone think in a way they hadn't quite thought before.* [L *ars, artis*]

art */ärt/ n* something created to be art. [L *ars, artis*]

art */ärt/ n* something created to express an emotion or idea in a way where words would not suffice. [L *ars, artis*]

art */ärt/ n* something created which is designed to evoke an intellectual or visceral response. [L *ars, artis*]

art */ärt/ n* something created with honesty and purity truly from the heart. [L *ars, artis*]

art */ärt/ n* something created with skill, creativity and passion. [L *ars, artis*]

art */ärt/ n* something creative that someone with an imagination created. [L *ars, artis*]

art */ärt/ n* something creative, unique and artistic. [L *ars, artis*]

art */ärt/ n* something drawn or painted to express emotion. [L *ars, artis*]

art */ärt/ n* something experienced and/or created with one's mind, heart and soul. [L *ars, artis*]

art */ärt/ n* something for your eyes to look at. [L *ars, artis*]

art */ärt/ n (pers)* something I like that I could not do. [L *ars, artis*]

art */ärt/ n* something in the eye of the beholder. [L *ars, artis*]

art */ärt/ n* something in which order and chaos are not mutually exclusive. [L *ars, artis*]

art */ärt/ n* something involving people doing stuff to convey an idea, an aesthetic, or a feeling. [L *ars, artis*]

art */ärt/ n (appar philos)* something is a work of art if and only if someone had an insight that certain aesthetic properties would be determined by certain nonaesthetic properties and for this reason the thing was intentionally endowed with the aesthetic properties in virtue of the nonaesthetic properties as envisaged in the insight. [L *ars, artis*]

art */ärt/ n* something is a work of art if it is intended as art, presented as such and judged to be art by those qualified in such matters. [L *ars, artis*]

art */ärt/ n* something is a work of art if it is made with the declared intention to be a work of art and placed in a context where it is seen as a work of art. [L *ars, artis*]

art */ärt/ n* something is an artwork when it is created or chosen to elicit exemplar representation from aesthetic attention of the receiver responding to what the features of the work are like as new form and content reconfiguring experience in a way that has intrinsic value. [L *ars, artis*]

art /ärt/ *n (inf)* something is art because it was designed with no other purpose in mind than expressing emotion, idea, *blabla* in a non-conventional manner. [L *ars, artis*]

art /ärt/ *n* something is, *or is identifiable as,* an artwork if it resembles, *in the right way,* certain paradigm artworks, which possess most *although not necessarily all* of art's typical features. [L *ars, artis*]

art /ärt/ *n* something lacking in today's generation. [L *ars, artis*]

art /ärt/ *n* something made by an artist. [L *ars, artis*]

art /ärt/ *n (inf)* something man-made *(unnatural, I suppose you could say)* that someone creates that manages to touch someone else emotionally or psychologically; *it can be bullshit on the part of the artist, it can be psychosis on the part of the viewer, but I think it needs to make a difference to someone other than its creator in order to be considered art.* [L *ars, artis*]

art /ärt/ *n* something man-made that expresses the author's feelings about something; *in a way that captures the attention of other people.* [L *ars, artis*]

art /ärt/ *n* something newly organized. [L *ars, artis*]

art /ärt/ *n* something no one person can describe; *as it can be beautiful, dangerous, splendid and amazing all at once through many different mediums.* [L *ars, artis*]

art /ärt/ *n* something outside our ability to really talk much about. [L *ars, artis*]

art /ärt/ *n* something people argue about all the time. [L *ars, artis*]

art /ärt/ *n* something people can see and touch. [L *ars, artis*]

art /ärt/ *n* something people make; *they can make it with their hands, pencil, paint, pretty much of anything.* [L *ars, artis*]

art /ärt/ *n* something pretty and nice. [L *ars, artis*]

art /ärt/ *n* something produced by one's hands and mind; *let it be a drawing, painting, photograph, sculpture.* [L *ars, artis*]

art /ärt/ *n* something secluded, singular, *sui generis.* [L *ars, artis*]

art /ärt/ *n (poss sculpt)* something

set in stone: *everyone has the same experience, we're all viewing exactly what the creator intended; now you could say that this doesn't happen with abstract art, but at least you're still getting the same thing as everybody else, you may just view it differently.* [L *ars, artis*]

art */ärt/ n* something skilfully constructed by human artists. [L *ars, artis*]

art */ärt/ n* something such as a painting or sculpture that is of very high quality. [L *ars, artis*]

art */ärt/ n* something superfluous but beautiful. [L *ars, artis*]

art */ärt/ n* something symbolic that affects the way people experience the world, their perceptions, emotions, sense of reality and/or belief systems. [L *ars, artis*]

art */ärt/ n* something that a person spends time, using various tools, to achieve a visually pleasing result, one way or another; *and doing so with our limited senses (eyes, ears, touch...) and tools.* [L *ars, artis*]

art */ärt/ n* something that almost everyone would somehow be able to recognize; *and even if it lacks formalistic sophistication it reaches out and engages the viewer on some level.* [L *ars, artis*]

art */ärt/ n* something that appeals to someone. [L *ars, artis*]

art */ärt/ n* something that can be applied to anything; *so long as the motivation is active inquisition.* [L *ars, artis*]

art */ärt/ n* something that can take the form of plausibly infinite aspects. [L *ars, artis*]

art */ärt/ n* something that can take us away from reality into a world of its own. [L *ars, artis*]

art */ärt/ n (interj)* something that captivates the mind, makes you think and wonder! [L *ars, artis*]

art */ärt/ n (relig)* something that captures and expresses the beauty of God's creation. [L *ars, artis*]

art */ärt/ n* something that captures beauty; *and preserves it eternally.* [L *ars, artis*]

art */ärt/ n* something that causes discussion and provokes thought. [L *ars, artis*]

art */ärt/ n* something that challenges your perceptions. [L *ars, artis*]

art */ärt/ n* something that communicates with me. [L *ars, artis*]

art */ärt/ n* something that connects emotionally to the viewer. [L *ars, artis*]

art */ärt/ n* something that conveys deep meaning; *and is consequently judged to possess a special value – both cultural and monetary.* [L *ars, artis*]

art */ärt/ n* something that escapes definition; *and probably only can be sensed by each of us very differently.* [L *ars, artis*]

art */ärt/ n* something that evokes feeling; *doesn't always have to be beautiful, art can disturb and touch in other ways.* [L *ars, artis*]

art */ärt/ n* something that expresses an idea, an emotion or, more generally, a world view. [L *ars, artis*]

art */ärt/ n* something that fantasizes the eye of the viewer. [L *ars, artis*]

art */ärt/ n* something that forces and compels you to think; *and that can be a mint condition copy of Raging Bull or it can be the Kardashians: the same questions will be asked and you will be forced to confront yourself and you will be forced to triangulate where you stand on everything from racist politics to haircuts* (Raging Bull *(1980), Am biog sports drama film directed by Martin Scorsese, produced by Robert Chartoff and Irwin Winkler and adapted by Paul Schrader and Mardik Martin from Jake LaMotta's memoir Raging Bull: My Story;* Kourtney, Kim and Khloé Kardashian *et al, stars of Keeping Up with the Kardashians, Am reality television series).* [L *ars, artis*]

art */ärt/ n* something that generates a feeling in me. [L *ars, artis*]

art */ärt/ n* something that gives me the inspiration to contemplate over it. [L *ars, artis*]

art */ärt/ n* something that gives the imagination an incentive to spread its flight over a whole host of kindred representations that provoke more thought than admits of expression in a concept determined by words. [L *ars, artis*]

art */ärt/ n* something that happens in your mind but people can see it. [L *ars, artis*]

art */ärt/ n* something that has been made by humans and has a form *(so no music).* [L *ars, artis*]

art /ärt/ *n* something that has intentional symbolic or inherent meaning. [L *ars, artis*]

art /ärt/ *n* something that has no practical purpose at all: *you can't lean on it, sit on it, etc.* [L *ars, artis*]

art /ärt/ *n (pers)* something that I pour my soul into; *and when others see it, they feel my soul.* [L *ars, artis*]

art /ärt/ *n (inf)* something that inspires emotion in people; *it can be any emotion, such as excitement in the Transformers™ movies (ugh, its only a example chill down); or sadness when a character dies, or puzzlement when a character says a phase that makes you think of some moral, value, or other thing (***Transformers™***, 2007 Am science fiction action film based on the Transformers™ toy line).* [L *ars, artis*]

art /ärt/ *n* something that intends to *and succeeds in* evoking an emotional response. [L *ars, artis*]

art /ärt/ *n* something that is both functional and *(hopefully)* aesthetically pleasing to our eyes. [L *ars, artis*]

art /ärt/ *n (derog)* something that is created by man to entertain, educate or otherwise instill feeling, emotion, pleasure, or awareness of one or more subjects in a viewer, listener or user; *stupid concept, even more stupid that the concept has a following.* [L *ars, artis*]

art /ärt/ *n* something that is either beautiful, amazing and emotionally evoking; *unless it's something made by someone with REALLY good persuasive skills and/or excuses.* [L *ars, artis*]

art /ärt/ *n* something that is made for no purpose other than aesthetics; *the exception is that art may be a part of something that is made for a functional purpose.* [L *ars, artis*]

art /ärt/ *n* something that is made or done in a skilful or attractive way. [L *ars, artis*]

art /ärt/ *n* something that is made rather than something that springs from itself. [L *ars, artis*]

art /ärt/ *n (pers)* something that is made to entertain and please the senses; *and actually has the desired effect on me personally.* [L *ars, artis*]

art /ärt/ *n* something that is not easily reproduced; *I could take a mason jar, urinate in it, put a crucifix in it and take a picture of it: believe* *me, if I can do it, it's not art (perh ref* **Immersion (Piss Christ)** *a 1987 photog by Am artist and photog Andres Serrano).* [L *ars, artis*]

art */ärt/ n* something that is not real and must be made by human beings. [L *ars, artis*]

art */ärt/ n* something that is one of a kind. [L *ars, artis*]

art */ärt/ n* something that is really really close to people's hearts; *as expressions or as appreciation of beauty.* [L *ars, artis*]

art */ärt/ n* something that is subjective in so many ways; *and almost impossible to define.* [L *ars, artis*]

art */ärt/ n* something that just looks interesting. [L *ars, artis*]

art */ärt/ n (educ)* something that looks good and done because you had to for class. [L *ars, artis*]

art */ärt/ n* something that makes us more thoughtful and well-rounded humans. [L *ars, artis*]

art */ärt/ n* something that makes you feel; *sensory feel like colours, or feeling like disdain, sadness, happiness.* [L *ars, artis*]

art */ärt/ n* something that makes you more 'yourself'. [L *ars, artis*]

art */ärt/ n* something that makes you see/feel/think in a new way. [L *ars, artis*]

art */ärt/ n (poss relig)* something that makes your soul rest. [L *ars, artis*]

art */ärt/ n* something that manages to express itself meaningfully in a way that is exclusive to its chosen medium. [L *ars, artis*]

art */ärt/ n* something that may catch the public's eyes which fascinates them with wonder that they take a liking to. [L *ars, artis*]

art */ärt/ n* something that moves or speaks to the person. [L *ars, artis*]

art */ärt/ n* something that people feel has value because it is beautiful or expresses ideas. [L *ars, artis*]

art */ärt/ n* something that poses [poss *possesses*] talent. [L *ars, artis*]

art */ärt/ n* something that profoundly affects whoever is receiving it; *the 'Mona Lisa' is art because just about everybody who sees it is affected in some way – we're either enthralled with the detail, the ideas behind the detail, or even the history of the painting itself, but it has* *a massive effect on just about everyone who has ever heard about it or gone to see it (*Mona Lisa*, half-length portrait of a woman by It artist Leonardo da Vinci (1452–1519)).* [L *ars, artis*]

art */ärt/ n* something that requires some kind of talent to produce. [L *ars, artis*]

art */ärt/ n* something that restores your faith in humanity. [L *ars, artis*]

art */ärt/ n* something that should evoke emotion and beauty. [L *ars, artis*]

art */ärt/ n* something that shows the thoughts and feelings of a certain person. [L *ars, artis*]

art */ärt/ n (pers)* something that speaks to me emotionally; *or has a story within the work itself; not to be confused with the story behind its production.* [L *ars, artis*]

art */ärt/ n* something that stimulates an individual's thoughts, emotions, beliefs or ideas through the senses. [L *ars, artis*]

art */ärt/ n (interrog)* something that stirs an emotion in the viewer; *if that emotion is disbelief, amazement and a sense of wonder then why can that not be art?* [L *ars, artis*]

art */ärt/ n* something that stops you from the everyday *and puts you in a place to think and feel.* [L *ars, artis*]

art */ärt/ n* something that strikes emotion in other people's *(and your)* hearts. [L *ars, artis*]

art */ärt/ n* something that tells us something in a way we can't say in words. [L *ars, artis*]

art */ärt/ n* something that the artist begins and the viewer finishes. [L *ars, artis*]

art */ärt/ n* something that the artist is trying to portray; *it may not be obvious, but I feel like you can kind of feel the artist's mindset through the art.* [L *ars, artis*]

art */ärt/ n* something that transforms the everyday. [L *ars, artis*]

art */ärt/ n* something that uses creativity to make some sort of statement or impression. [L *ars, artis*]

art */ärt/ n* something that was mostly man-made and looks fine and is artful. [L *ars, artis*]

art */ärt/ n* something that will last forever. [L *ars, artis*]

art */ärt/ n* something that, conversely, we use to rid ourselves of the burdens of our more bestial impulses. [L *ars, artis*]

art */ärt/ n* something that's meant to entertain and provoke thought. [L *ars, artis*]

art */ärt/ n* something to do with scarcity or the effort it takes to replicate it; *with perhaps computer-generated art being the exception.* [L *ars, artis*]

art */ärt/ n* something to do with the way humans manipulate and modify the world. [L *ars, artis*]

art */ärt/ n* something to look at; *good art is worth looking at, bad art isn't and great art keeps you coming back again and again.* [L *ars, artis*]

art */ärt/ n* something to make the world bright. [L *ars, artis*]

art */ärt/ n* something to talk about when you're drunk and/or stoned, generally. [L *ars, artis*]

art */ärt/ n* something tragic. [L *ars, artis*]

art */ärt/ n* something unique. [L *ars, artis*]

art */ärt/ n* something visual; *or music that gives a message; I don't like the art at the college, too violent or strange.* [L *ars, artis*]

art */ärt/ n* something we could appreciate for its relative (or extreme) difficulty and therefore rarity; *try painting a landscape and see if anything remotely resembling Kinkade's painting comes out; record yourself singing 'Thriller' and listen if it sounds anything like Michael Jackson; challenge Kobe Bryant to a basketball game and see what happens; you may not like Kinkade or pop-music or basketball, but many people do and appreciate the product of exceptional practitioners of those and numerous other pursuits* (Thomas Kinkade, *Painter of Light™ (1958–2012), Am painter of popular realistic, bucolic and idyllic subjects;* Thriller, *song recorded by* Michael Joseph Jackson *(1958–2009), Am singer-songwriter, dancer, businessman and philanthropist;* Kobe Bean 'Black Mamba' Bryant *(1978–), Am prof basketball player for the Los Angeles Lakers of the National Basketball Association).* [L *ars, artis*]

art */ärt/ n* something which comes from one's imagination, inside the thoughts and the way of looking and feeling things. [L *ars, artis*]

art */ärt/ n* something which humans must do by their very nature. [L *ars, artis*]

art */ärt/ n* something which is functional and pleasing to your eyes. [L *ars, artis*]

art */ärt/ n* something which is *(primarily)* susceptible to art criticism; *(rather than other kinds of criticism).* [L *ars, artis*]

art */ärt/ n* something which only talent and creativity is able to create. [L *ars, artis*]

art */ärt/ n* something with intention. [L *ars, artis*]

art */ärt/ n* something with meaning. [L *ars, artis*]

art */ärt/ n* something wonderful that's left long into the future. [L *ars, artis*]

art */ärt/ n* something you believe in and have a passion for. [L *ars, artis*]

art */ärt/ n* something you can deal with. [L *ars, artis*]

art */ärt/ n* something you can display somewhere and it looks good. [L *ars, artis*]

art */ärt/ n* something you can hang on the wall. [L *ars, artis*]

art */ärt/ n* something you can keep your whole life and pass it down after you're gone; *and it can become even more valuable to the ones you pass it down to.* [L *ars, artis*]

art */ärt/ n* something you can pose next to. [L *ars, artis*]

art */ärt/ n* something you can see that was designed and grew. [L *ars, artis*]

art */ärt/ n* something you create that exhibits one's feelings or emotions. [L *ars, artis*]

art */ärt/ n* something you do to soothe the demons of the brain. [L *ars, artis*]

art */ärt/ n* something you like and don't like. [L *ars, artis*]

art */ärt/ n* something you look at. [L *ars, artis*]

art */ärt/ n* something you look at, enjoy and might be inspired by. [L *ars, artis*]

art */ärt/ n* something you not only hear but also feel. [L *ars, artis*]

art */ärt/ n* sometimes good, sometimes not so good; *but it lets them know they are alive.* [L *ars, artis*]

art */ärt/ n* sometimes strange. [L

ars, artis]

art */ärt/ n* soothes pain. [L *ars, artis*]

art */ärt/ n* sophisticated, unique, or whose duplication and reproduction by someone else is almost impossible. [L *ars, artis*]

art */ärt/ n* soul. [L *ars, artis*]

art */ärt/ n (poss fig)* sound construction of special ideas or materials that serves the purpose of expressing the deepest and direst and greatest and grandest of our dynamic feelings; *ones that simply must be vented or the supernatural will bilge from a holy cow, or worse.* [L *ars, artis*]

art */ärt/ n* sparks questions *(sometimes without answers)* in those who look at it. [L *ars, artis*]

art */ärt/ n* speaks before the artist knows what is being said. [L *ars, artis*]

art */ärt/ n* speaks loudest when there are no words to express it. [L *ars, artis*]

art */ärt/ n* speaks to each of us in its own way. [L *ars, artis*]

art */ärt/ n (psychol)* speaks to the needs of our daily lives; *which is really our psychological needs; and this opens up opportunities for art galleries to engage with audiences in a more emotional and intimate way.* [L *ars, artis*]

art */ärt/ n* special. [L *ars, artis*]

art */ärt/ n (m)* specifically a creation of man to show what is beyond himself; *to have him reflect, to console him in such a way that, at the depths of tragedy and the further depths of comedy, one is never brought out of a state of tremendous laughter, no matter how muted.* [L *ars, artis*]

art */ärt/ n* splotches of paint spilled on a canvas. [L *ars, artis*]

art */ärt/ n* spontaneity after the struggle. [L *ars, artis*]

art */ärt/ n (neg)* stagnancy is not art; *but stagnancy can be depicted through art in times when growth is scarce for understanding and, surprisingly, leads to growth.* [L *ars, artis*]

art */ärt/ n* status of mind. [L *ars, artis*]

art */ärt/ n* stems from the concept of craft; *but includes an added element of innovation or originality.* [L *ars, artis*]

art */ärt/ n* stillness; *which creates*

peace. [L *ars, artis*]

art /*ärt*/ *n* stimulates our aesthetic gland. [L *ars, artis*]

art /*ärt*/ *n* stimulates the senses. [L *ars, artis*]

art /*ärt*/ *n* stirs the soul. [L *ars, artis*]

art /*ärt*/ *n* stored humanity. [L *ars, artis*]

art /*ärt*/ *n* striking. [L *ars, artis*]

art /*ärt*/ *n (math)* structure + surface + subconscious + surprise. [L *ars, artis*]

art /*ärt*/ *n* study. [L *ars, artis*]

art /*ärt*/ *n* study, forethought and exertion. [L *ars, artis*]

art /*ärt*/ *n* stuff that you call art. [L *ars, artis*]

art /*ärt*/ *n* stuff that you don't ruin. [L *ars, artis*]

art /*ärt*/ *n* subject to an internally consistent set of rules that allow it to make sense; *the layers of paint applied to a painting form a system of their own; they are not laid down randomly, but they bend to an order that allows them to create meaning.* [L *ars, artis*]

art /*ärt*/ *n* subjective; *and means something different to every single person on earth.* [L *ars, artis*]

art /*ärt*/ *n* subjective; *because of that it's perfectly possible for something to both be art and not art at the same time depending on who's doing the defining; and that's what I love about it.* [L *ars, artis*]

art /*ärt*/ *n (inf)* subjective; *blah blah blah.* [L *ars, artis*]

art /*ärt*/ *n* subjective; *I find certain bits of 'art' not to be as such, a blank canvas with one stroke of a singular colour for instance, but if that's art to someone else however, my opinion doesn't supersede theirs.* [L *ars, artis*]

art /*ärt*/ *n* subjective and stimulating. [L *ars, artis*]

art /*ärt*/ *n (inf)* subjective as shit. [L *ars, artis*]

art /*ärt*/ *n* supposed to be a reflection of the society we live in; *and the life that traps us.* [L *ars, artis*]

art /*ärt*/ *n* supposed to make life better; *or at least more interesting.* [L *ars, artis*]

art /*ärt*/ *n* synthetic and constructive. [L *ars, artis*]

art /*ärt*/ *n* take an object; do something to it; do something else to it. [L *ars, artis*]

art /*ärt*/ *n* takes courage. [L *ars,*

artis]

art */ärt/ n* takes skill, practice and training. [L *ars, artis*]

art */ärt/ n* takes the world or even the universe and makes a singular expression framed by the time it took to make, the time it takes to view and the time it leaves a lasting imprint on the maker and the viewer; *the frame is not always the value of the work though, but it can be.* [L *ars, artis*]

art */ärt/ n* takes you outside your usual perception. [L *ars, artis*]

art */ärt/ n* taking your thoughts, feelings, ideas and forming them into something tangible; *whether abstract or straightforward.* [L *ars, artis*]

art */ärt/ n* tangible products of an artist's skill in the craft; *such as paintings, sculptures, some gardens, buildings etc; I do not view blank canvases or piles of dirt and such as art and if I'm honest with you it annoys me slightly that they are claimed as such.* [L *ars, artis*]

art */ärt/ n* taps into unspoken knowledge, numberless measure and a categorical intelligence. [L *ars, artis*]

art */ärt/ n* teaches us something; *but only insofar as it makes us think about the past or consider the future.* [L *ars, artis*]

art */ärt/ n techne, or having a correct understanding of the principles involved* (**techne**, *a term etymologically derived from the Gr word* **τέχνη**, *often translated as 'craftsmanship', 'craft', or 'art').* [L *ars, artis*]

art */ärt/ n* Tetris™ is art; *even when you take away all the colours and music, it is still art; the gameplay mechanics, the control scheme and the purposefully chosen shapes make it art; even with colours and music gone, it is still a compelling puzzle game* (**Tetris™**, *tile-matching puzzle video game orig designed and programmed by Alexey Pajitnov).* [L *ars, artis*]

art */ärt/ n* Tetris™ is art; *it's a work of someone's creativity, passion and emotions* (**Tetris™**, *tile-matching puzzle video game orig designed and programmed by Alexey Pajitnov).* [L *ars, artis*]

art */ärt/ n (neg)* Tetris™ is not art; *it's a game, an activity* (**Tetris™**, *tile-matching puzzle video game orig designed and programmed by Alexey Pajitnov).* [L *ars, artis*]

art */ärt/ n* texture, pattern, movement and colour. [L *ars, artis*]

art */ärt/ n* that human, creative endeavour that sublimes *(goes beyond)* our ability to describe it; *this obviously means that art is a 'feeling', that is a 'concept' that can be communicated only in terms of a feeling; should you try and say 'why?' some particular thing is art, you immediately bring yourself into the realm of language with all its limits (limits mostly defined by our scientific phrasings and the uses of such language).* [L *ars, artis*]

art */ärt/ n* that human endeavour which illuminates the contiguous nature of reality. [L *ars, artis*]

art */ärt/ n* that human endeavour which illuminates the contiguous nature of reality; *momentarily breaking us free from our illusion that the universe has a dual nature.* [L *ars, artis*]

art */ärt/ n* that in which the hand, the head and the heart of man go together. [L *ars, artis*]

art */ärt/ n* that indefinable something that is at once everyday but untouchable and elusive. [L *ars, artis*]

art */ärt/ n* that mangled tower in the Olympic Park *(poss ref* The ArcelorMittal Orbit, *114.5m tall (376ft) sculpt and observation tower in the Queen Elizabeth Olympic Park in Stratford, London).* [L *ars, artis*]

art */ärt/ n* that one thing which makes sense when everything else fails. [L *ars, artis*]

art */ärt/ n* that outer expression of us which imitates life's inner impressions within us. [L *ars, artis*]

art */ärt/ n (opthalmol or poss educ)* that piece of light in your pupils. [L *ars, artis*]

art */ärt/ n* that sacred event *(or thing)* which loosens us from the shackles of the humdrum. [L *ars, artis*]

art */ärt/ n* that space between calm and outraged, black and white, right and wrong. [L *ars, artis*]

art */ärt/ n (poss fig)* that uncomfortable warm of sitting in seat just abandoned. [L *ars, artis*]

art */ärt/ n* that weird stuff with the squares and a bunch of old paintings that people pretend to like to seem important. [L *ars, artis*]

art */ärt/ n* that which awakens in

us a sense of wonder. [L *ars, artis*]

art */ärt/ n* that which can be seen in the result of a spark of inspiration, *a moment of improvisation and years and years of practice beforehand, during which the artist has developed an individual voice and unique aesthetic disposition.* [L *ars, artis*]

art */ärt/ n* that which comes FROM the 'soul' and speaks TO the 'soul'… *and if people need that explaining any more then they will probably never get it… and that makes me worry about the future of our species; end of rant.* [L *ars, artis*]

art */ärt/ n* that which delights the eye and excites the mind. [L *ars, artis*]

art */ärt/ n* that which delves deeply into the life around the artist; *life which he/she has pondered deeply, no matter how painful the subject and in doing so has inspired others to take up the cause to right a situation that they were not fully aware.* [L *ars, artis*]

art */ärt/ n* that which evolves from what we actually experience. [L *ars, artis*]

art */ärt/ n* that which has the characteristic we recognize art as having. [L *ars, artis*]

art */ärt/ n* that which is beautiful *or ugly.* [L *ars, artis*]

art */ärt/ n* that which is crafted by an artist. [L *ars, artis*]

art */ärt/ n* that which is created for creation's sake. [L *ars, artis*]

art */ärt/ n (derog)* that which is enjoyed by snobs. [L *ars, artis*]

art */ärt/ n* that which is made with the intention of stimulating thoughts and emotions. [L *ars, artis*]

art */ärt/ n* that which is static and repetitive is boring; that which is dynamic and random is confusing; in between lies art. [L *ars, artis*]

art */ärt/ n* that which is understood to be created for the unique purpose of translating non-empirical information into empirical form: *this dance is a work of art because it was choreographed to symbolize sexual frustration.* [L *ars, artis*]

art */ärt/ n (pers)* that which keeps me searching for and interpreting *(through my images)* – the meaning of life – *until there is no longer the necessity to do so and* *hence, no more breathing.* [L *ars, artis*]

art */ärt/ n* that which reminds us of age-old truths that we have forgotten. [L *ars, artis*]

art */ärt/ n* that which the collective artistic establishment – *and the wealthy patrons who purchase from it* – consider to be art. [L *ars, artis*]

art */ärt/ n* that which touches the soul. [L *ars, artis*]

art */ärt/ n* that which we decide to deem as such. [L *ars, artis*]

art */ärt/ n* the 3-dimensional expression of the human perception of the 4th dimension. [L *ars, artis*]

art */ärt/ n* the ability to cause emotion indirectly through a visible or obvious medium; *rather than through what is commonly understood as direct living, such as person-to-person interactions or watching strangers.* [L *ars, artis*]

art */ärt/ n* the ability to communicate that what is real from what is not. [L *ars, artis*]

art */ärt/ n* the ability to create something. [L *ars, artis*]

art */ärt/ n* the ability to create what you are feeling; eg *if you are feeling happy draw something that makes you feel good like a rainbow or flowers.* [L *ars, artis*]

art */ärt/ n* the ability to draw in and hold the viewer with an implied narrative. [L *ars, artis*]

art */ärt/ n* the ability to express the rhythm and spirit of life; *to show that all things spiritual are more corporeal than that which is physical.* [L *ars, artis*]

art */ärt/ n* the ability to invoke emotion in a way that is not easily replicated. [L *ars, artis*]

art */ärt/ n* the ability to make something recognizable as art. [L *ars, artis*]

art */ärt/ n* the ability to not only think WAY outside the box but the ability to take the esoteric and execute it into this plane. [L *ars, artis*]

art */ärt/ n* the ability to see past one's own self-imposed limitation and strive beyond what is expected, beyond excellence, beyond yourself. [L *ars, artis*]

art */ärt/ n* the absence of fear. [L *ars, artis*]

art */ärt/ n* the abstract stuff humans create to evoke emotion in others and ideally to control that emotion; *what the Impressionists were consciously working on – but it applies to the whole field (***Impressionism**, *c19th art movement that originated with a group of Paris-based artists).* [L *ars, artis*]

art */ärt/ n* the act of doing something; *inasmuch, most people can generally agree that, as artistic realms go, they are all a form of creative expression; be it a writer with a pen, singer with a guitar, painter with a brush, or athlete with a set of skis; all these acts are the explosion of a creative nature from the inside out; they are expressions of something from within to the greater cosmos; if we operate from this definition, then we have to accept that art requires action.* [L *ars, artis*]

art */ärt/ n* the act of doing something you enjoy. [L *ars, artis*]

art */ärt/ n* the act of living; *doing what you do well with confidence and joy.* [L *ars, artis*]

art */ärt/ n* the act of sharing. [L *ars, artis*]

art */ärt/ n* the act of turning something ordinary into the extra-ordinary. [L *ars, artis*]

art */ärt/ n* the activity of painting, drawing and making sculpture. [L *ars, artis*]

art */ärt/ n* the activity of painting, drawing or creating sculptures. [L *ars, artis*]

art */ärt/ n* the actual production or construction of objects beautiful in form, colour or sound. [L *ars, artis*]

art */ärt/ n* the adaptation of things in the natural world to the uses of life. [L *ars, artis*]

art */ärt/ n* the aesthetic exploitation of familiarity vs. surprise. [L *ars, artis*]

art */ärt/ n* the aesthetic exploitation of tension vs. release. [L *ars, artis*]

art */ärt/ n* the aesthetic rendering of thought. [L *ars, artis*]

art */ärt/ n* the aggrandizement of self or others. [L *ars, artis*]

art */ärt/ n* the amalgamation of creativity, skill, the presence of an objective and the use of artistic principles. [L *ars, artis*]

art */ärt/ n* the answer that humanity gives to our unsatisfied needs. [L *ars, artis*]

art */ärt/ n* the antithesis of whatever becomes popular in the cultured world. [L *ars, artis*]

art */ärt/ n* the application of knowledge or power to practical purposes. [L *ars, artis*]

art */ärt/ n* the application of knowledge or power to practical purposes; *blest with each grace of nature and of art.* [L *ars, artis*]

art */ärt/ n* the application of reason confined only by practical aspects; *and oriented towards the perfect realisation of an idea*. [L *ars, artis*]

art */ärt/ n* the application of skill to evoke or manipulate mood or emotion. [L *ars, artis*]

art */ärt/ n* the application of skill to the production of the beautiful by imitation or design; *or an occupation in which skill is so employed, as in painting and sculpture.* [L *ars, artis*]

art */ärt/ n* the application of understanding and educational value to a medium to which an individual can enjoy. [L *ars, artis*]

art */ärt/ n (obs)* the appreciation of beauty. [L *ars, artis*]

art */ärt/ n* the arrangement of the subject in provocative pose. [L *ars, artis*]

art */ärt/ n* the *art* [in any given case] proposes to itself an end to be attained, defines the end and hands it over to the *science*; *the* science *receives it, considers it as a phenomenon or effect to be studied and having investigated its causes and conditions, sends it back to* art *with a theorem of the causes and combinations by which it could be produced;* art *then examines these combinations of circumstances and according as any of them are or are not in human power, pronounces the end attainable or not; the only one of the premises, therefore, which* art *supplies, is the original major premise, which asserts that the attainment of the given end is desirable;* science, *then, lends to* art *the proposition (obtained by a series of inductions or deductions) that the performance of certain actions will attain the end; from these premises* art *concludes that the performance of these actions is desirable and finding it also practicable, converts the theorem into a rule or precept; the grounds, then, of every rule of art are to be found in the theorems of* science*; an* art, *or a* body of art, *consists of the rules, together with as much of the* *speculative propositions as comprises the justification of these rules; the complete art of any matter includes a selection of such a portion from the* science *as is necessary to show on what conditions the effects, which the* art *aims at producing, depend; and* art *in general consists of the truths of* science *arranged in the most convenient order for practice, instead of the order which is most convenient for thought;* science *groups and arranges its truths so as to enable us to take in at one view as much as possible of the general order of the universe;* art, *though it must assume the same general laws, follows them only into such of their detailed consequences as have led to the formation of rules of conduct and brings together from parts of the field of* science *most remote from one another, the truths relating to the production of the different and heterogeneous causes necessary to each effect which the exigencies of practical life require to be produced.* [L *ars, artis*]

art */ärt/ n (m)* the artist who creates a work of art must will it as part of his intention that the work should fundamentally be a work of art; ie *as having aesthetic value as its prime achievement.* [L *ars, artis*]

art */ärt/ n* the artist's view of spirituality and perfectness; *nirvana.* [L *ars, artis*]

art */ärt/ n* the attempt to capture that which cannot be described. [L *ars, artis*]

art */ärt/ n* the attempt to convey the nature of ideal form by the use of transient form; *or to use the materials of illusion to glimpse reality.* [L *ars, artis*]

art */ärt/ n* the attempt to create beautiful objects. [L *ars, artis*]

art */ärt/ n* the attempt to define ourselves. [L *ars, artis*]

art */ärt/ n* the attempt to depict a truth beautifully. [L *ars, artis*]

art */ärt/ n* the attempt to depict an emotion or thought; *or combination thereof.* [L *ars, artis*]

art */ärt/ n* the attempt to express something unspeakable; *something we've all tried to get at for thousands of years, but have been unable to, due to technological limitations.* [L *ars, artis*]

art */ärt/ n* the attempt to mimic life as nearly as possible. [L *ars, artis*]

art */ärt/ n* the attributes of free individual skill and invention; *ex-*

pressing themselves in ever new combinations of pleasurable contrivance and seeking perfection not as a means towards some ulterior practical end but as an ideal end in itself. [L *ars, artis*]

art /*ärt*/ *n* the authentic expression of any and all individuality. [L *ars, artis*]

art /*ärt*/ *n* the autobiography of the universe. [L *ars, artis*]

art /*ärt*/ *n* the barometer of a culture. [L *ars, artis*]

art /*ärt*/ *n* the bastion of subjectivity. [L *ars, artis*]

art /*ärt*/ *n (comput)* the battle against commonsense; *it rebuilds universal knowledge using a 'warm boot' into an alternate operating system.* [L *ars, artis*]

art /*ärt*/ *n* the beautiful way of doing things. [L *ars, artis*]

art /*ärt*/ *n* the beautifully tooled leather on a saddle. [L *ars, artis*]

art /*ärt*/ *n* the beauty and anger felt and seen within each and everyone of us. [L *ars, artis*]

art /*ärt*/ *n* the beauty of nature. [L *ars, artis*]

art /*ärt*/ *n* the beauty of that single fleeting moment; *it lasts only for a brief moment before it disappears.* [L *ars, artis*]

art /*ärt*/ *n* the beauty of that single fleeting moment of explosion. [L *ars, artis*]

art /*ärt*/ *n* the beauty that surrounds us. [L *ars, artis*]

art /*ärt*/ *n* the beauty, the ugly, the weak and the strong. [L *ars, artis*]

art /*ärt*/ *n* the becoming and happening of truth. [L *ars, artis*]

art /*ärt*/ *n* the becoming of truth. [L *ars, artis*]

art /*ärt*/ *n* the beginning of nothing and the end of forever. [L *ars, artis*]

art /*ärt*/ *n* the BEST expression of a society or an artist; *it has to be done with the most sublime of our inner feelings.* [L *ars, artis*]

art /*ärt*/ *n* the best place to do unpredictability. [L *ars, artis*]

art /*ärt*/ *n* the best thing you can do. [L *ars, artis*]

art /*ärt*/ *n* the best way for one to express all the feelings and emotions he or she is keeping. [L *ars, artis*]

art /*ärt*/ *n* the (best) way of doing something; *the art of conversation/*

war. [L *ars, artis*]

art */ärt/ n* the bit on Dead Space® 2 where the skull spider climbs up your body, bites your head off, sticks its legs down your neck stump and starts moving you around like a puppet with a skull face (Dead Space® 2, *a third-person shooter survival horror video game developed by Visceral Games™ and published by Electronic Arts™ for Microsoft® Windows™, PlayStation™ 3 and Xbox™ 360).* [L *ars, artis*]

art */ärt/ n* the body of human thoughts. [L *ars, artis*]

art */ärt/ n* the body of rules, the written code or manual, which lays down the discipline and regulates the dexterity. [L *ars, artis*]

art */ärt/ n* the breath of muses, through the human vehicle. [L *ars, artis*]

art */ärt/ n* the brick sidewalks I see every morning and walk on. [L *ars, artis*]

art */ärt/ n (derog)* the bullshit of the interested sociopaths involved. [L *ars, artis*]

art */ärt/ n* the catching and caging of William Blake's tiger; *or, at least, its fleeting tail; and we admire the artist who achieves it (*The Tyger*, poem by Eng poet William Blake published in 1794 as part of the Songs of Experience collection).* [L *ars, artis*]

art */ärt/ n* the child of Nature. [L *ars, artis*]

art */ärt/ n* the child of Nature; *yes, her darling child, in whom we trace the features of the mother's face, her aspect and her attitude.* [L *ars, artis*]

art */ärt/ n (poss fig)* the choice of spices entering the palate. [L *ars, artis*]

art */ärt/ n* the class of objects subject to aesthetic criteria; *as paintings, sculptures or drawings.* [L *ars, artis*]

art */ärt/ n* the cognition and evaluation of reality. [L *ars, artis*]

art */ärt/ n* the cognition of life. [L *ars, artis*]

art */ärt/ n* the combination or modification of things to adapt them to a given end. [L *ars, artis*]

art */ärt/ n* the communication by artifice of an essential truth that could only be found in nature. [L *ars, artis*]

art */ärt/ n* the communication of a response to an experience. [L *ars,*

artis]

art */ärt/ n* the communication of anything more than a mere fact. [L *ars, artis*]

art */ärt/ n* the communication of some feeling, sense, idea or emotion; *I get that from Rothko, from Far Cry® 2, from Doctor Who, from Vermeer, even from Guinness® adverts* (**Marcus Yakovlevich Rothkowitz** *(1903–1970), Am painter of Latvian Jewish descent;* **Far Cry® 2**, *open world first-person shooter developed by Ubisoft® Montreal and published by Ubisoft®;* **Doctor Who**, *Brit science-fiction television programme produced by the British Broadcasting Corporation;* **Johannes, Jan** *or* **Johan Vermeer**, *Du painter;* **Guinness®**, *popular Irish dry stout that originated in the brewery of Arthur Guinness at St. James's Gate, Dublin).* [L *ars, artis*]

art */ärt/ n* the complement of science; *science is concerned wholly with relations, not with individuals; art, on the other hand, is not only the disclosure of the individuality of the artist but also a manifestation of individuality as creative of the future, in an unprecedented response to conditions as they were in the past.* [L *ars, artis*]

art */ärt/ n* the complete expression of the artist's values. [L *ars, artis*]

art */ärt/ n* the concept, the subject and the arrangement. [L *ars, artis*]

art */ärt/ n* the conscious attempt to either create or recreate an emotion via the conduit of one or more of our senses. [L *ars, artis*]

art */ärt/ n* the conscious, expressive production of beauty. [L *ars, artis*]

art */ärt/ n* the conscious production or arrangement of sounds, colours, forms, movements or other elements in a manner that affects the sense of beauty; *specifically the production of the beautiful in a graphic or plastic medium; the study of these activities; the product of these activities; human works of beauty considered as a group.* [L *ars, artis*]

art */ärt/ n* the conscious use of skill and creative imagination; *esp in the production of aesthetic objects.* [L *ars, artis*]

art */ärt/ n* the conscious use of the imagination in the production of objects to be contemplated or appreciated as beautiful; *as in the arrangement of forms, sounds or words*. [L *ars, artis*]

art */ärt/ n* the conscious utterance of thought, by speech or action, to any end. [L *ars, artis*]

art */ärt/ n (pers)* the constant urge to find out more about myself, what I can do, what I feel. [L *ars, artis*]

art */ärt/ n* THE CONTINUATION OF OUR LIFE & ALL THOSE WHO COME AFTER US. [L *ars, artis*]

art */ärt/ n* the creation and destruction of what's expected. [L *ars, artis*]

art */ärt/ n* the creation of a self-explanatory and complete definition without any participation by a viewer; *they are only there to experience it.* [L *ars, artis*]

art */ärt/ n* the creation of a work of beauty; *or a work of some other special significance.* [L *ars, artis*]

art */ärt/ n* the creation of beautiful or significant things; *art does not need to be innovative to be good.* [L *ars, artis*]

art */ärt/ n* the creation of beautiful or significant things; *he said that architecture is the art of wasting space beautifully.* [L *ars, artis*]

art */ärt/ n* the creation of beauty from nothing. [L *ars, artis*]

art */ärt/ n* the creation of illusions. [L *ars, artis*]

art */ärt/ n* the creation of significant form. [L *ars, artis*]

art */ärt/ n* the creation of something designed to inspire emotion and invoke passion within the human spirit. [L *ars, artis*]

art */ärt/ n* the creation of things with the intent to express or produce emotion by stimulation of any or all of the five senses and/or the mind's eye. [L *ars, artis*]

art */ärt/ n* the creation of works of beauty or other special significance. [L *ars, artis*]

art */ärt/ n* the creation or expression of what is beautiful. [L *ars, artis*]

art */ärt/ n* the creation or pre-existence of something that is created by one person; *or through a collaborative effort that, based solely on aesthetics, is pleasing to the senses of one or more people.* [L *ars, artis*]

art */ärt/ n* the creative creation of

aesthetic objects; *often with a message, story or perspective.* [L **ars, artis**]

art */ärt/ n* the creative expression of existing contrasts of both societal and natural influences; *not of the surrealist abstraction of illusion.* [L **ars, artis**]

art */ärt/ n* the creative freedom which draws itself from an inexhaustible source within our own personal spirits, our cores. [L **ars, artis**]

art */ärt/ n* the creative output of the artist; *any and all recordings of the art; and the actual work performed by the artist; and the recordings of said work.* [L **ars, artis**]

art */ärt/ n* the creative preserving of truth in the work. [L **ars, artis**]

art */ärt/ n* the creative use of a medium to express an idea or feeling; *wherein the expression is a valuable end in and of itself.* [L **ars, artis**]

art */ärt/ n* the creative use of a medium to express ideas or feelings; *characterized by feelings closely associated with exquisiteness, wonder and the sublime; these ideas, feelings and their expression are an end in and of themselves; (hmm, I also think we should say something about subtlety, indirectness and richness – layers of meaning expressed indirectly and subtly; on the other hand, some art may not be subtle, indirect or rich; we may say good or great art has these qualities, but I don't think these are necessary properties).* [L **ars, artis**]

art */ärt/ n* the cultivation of the imagination beyond the practical and utilitarian. [L **ars, artis**]

art */ärt/ n (inf)* the curve of a good curl; *I'm talkin' about liften weights.* [L **ars, artis**]

art */ärt/ n* the daughter of freedom. [L **ars, artis**]

art */ärt/ n* the deliberate arrangement of elements in order to achieve an emotional or intellectual goal. [L **ars, artis**]

art */ärt/ n* the demon sleeping within ourselves. [L **ars, artis**]

art */ärt/ n* the design of the iPhone® (*iPhone®, a line of smartphones designed and marketed by Apple™ Inc).* [L **ars, artis**]

art */ärt/ n* the desire to do something for the first time – to make a difference; *either in ourselves, our process, our perception, others, etc.* [L **ars, artis**]

art */ärt/ n* the desire to reflect the truth of the human experience in all of its reality. [L *ars, artis*]

art */ärt/ n* the developed and efficient use of a language to convey meaning with immediacy and/or depth. [L *ars, artis*]

art */ärt/ n* the dynamic experience of fusing materials and imagination in a waking dream; *the product of the dream 'art work' becomes a corpse to be studied for information leading to the next dynamic experience.* [L *ars, artis*]

art */ärt/ n* the effective work of memory. [L *ars, artis*]

art */ärt/ n* the elegant paintings of Edgar Degas with his ballerinas who float across the canvas, or maybe the gargantuan statue of David that Michelangelo so meticulously sculpted; maybe even the bizarre sketches of Salvador Dalí come to mind (Hilaire-Germain-Edgar De Gas *(1834–1917), Fr artist famous for his paintings, sculptures, prints and drawings;* David *(c1040–970BC), according to the Hebrew Bible, the second king of the United Kingdom of Israel;* Michelangelo di Lodovico Buonarroti Simoni *(1475–1564), It sculptor, painter, architect, poet and engineer of the High Renaissance;* Salvador Domingo Felipe Jacinto Dalí i Domènech, *1st Marqués de Dalí de Pubol (1904–89), prominent Sp surrealist painter).* [L *ars, artis*]

art */ärt/ n (sculpt)* the embellishments, the adornments that a mason puts into a piece of carved stone; *which would be functional without them, but dull.* [L *ars, artis*]

art */ärt/ n* the embodiment of emotions and opinions. [L *ars, artis*]

art */ärt/ n* the embodiment of meaning. [L *ars, artis*]

art */ärt/ n* the embodiment of the idea in the material. [L *ars, artis*]

art */ärt/ n* the emotion you feel inside when you sing a beautiful song or create a magnificent painting that the world is ready to hear and see. [L *ars, artis*]

art */ärt/ n* the emotional equivalent of science. [L *ars, artis*]

art */ärt/ n* the employment of given means to effect a purpose. [L *ars, artis*]

art */ärt/ n* the employment of means to accomplish some desired end. [L *ars, artis*]

art */ärt/ n* the employment of the powers of Nature for an end. [L *ars, artis*]

art */ärt/ n* the emptying of a tortured soul onto a page, a canvas or a stage. [L *ars, artis*]

art */ärt/ n* the encounter with beauty. [L *ars, artis*]

art */ärt/ n* the enhancement of all human activities and experiences. [L *ars, artis*]

art */ärt/ n* the essence of humanity; *not good or bad, just what's so about being a human.* [L *ars, artis*]

art */ärt/ n* the essence of life in any of its manifestations; *distilled and presented in various forms; once confined to painting and drawing, sculpting together with music and dance which required high levels of skill, it now encompasses skills possessed only in the imagination, for instance 'conceptual' art which requires equal mind-reading skills from the viewer.* [L *ars, artis*]

art */ärt/ n* the essential quality inherent in any aesthetic object which serves as an interface by which aesthetic principles of a given culture are transmitted and transformed from one generation to the next; *with the object serving as a time capsule for the aesthetic attitudes and response of the period in which it is produced; of course, some art can be said to be ephemeral, universal or timeless but, ultimately, such art can be said to be marked by a continuity that transcends mere superficial fashions of the times.* [L *ars, artis*]

art */ärt/ n* the essential quality that connects aesthetic principles of a culture to subsequent generations. [L *ars, artis*]

art */ärt/ n* the etching on a belt buckle. [L *ars, artis*]

art */ärt/ n* the everlasting desire to express praise for oneself. [L *ars, artis*]

art */ärt/ n (fig)* the evolving tapestry. [L *ars, artis*]

art */ärt/ n* the exclusive role of the arts is to intensify aesthetic and emotional response; *works of art communicate feeling directly from mind to mind, with no intent to explain why the impact occurs.* [L *ars, artis*]

art */ärt/ n* the exercise of human skill; *as distinguished from nature.* [L *ars, artis*]

art */ärt/ n* the exhibition of skill. [L *ars, artis*]

art */ärt/ n* the exhibition of the power of perceiving the beautiful and of expressing it in artistic forms: *as, a picture skilfully painted, but devoid of art.* [L ***ars, artis***]

art */ärt/ n* the experience that arouses within. [L ***ars, artis***]

art */ärt/ n* the expression of **1** one's self-reflections and **2** one's impressions of the surroundings. [L ***ars, artis***]

art */ärt/ n (m)* the expression of a man's joy in his work. [L ***ars, artis***]

art */ärt/ n* the expression of an idea, the manifestation of your search and the process of working through this idea. [L ***ars, artis***]

art */ärt/ n* the expression of an individual who records and captures the state of mind at a particular moment in time and will also be influenced by the outcome of the project. [L ***ars, artis***]

art */ärt/ n* the expression of feelings, experiences, of yourself and others; *it can have a visible meaning or not, it can be protest or the expression of joy, sadness…* [L ***ars, artis***]

art */ärt/ n* the expression of human creative skill and imagination. [L ***ars, artis***]

art */ärt/ n* the expression of human suffering, passion, imagination and creativity. [L ***ars, artis***]

art */ärt/ n* the expression of life. [L ***ars, artis***]

art */ärt/ n* the expression of meaning through form. [L ***ars, artis***]

art */ärt/ n* the expression of one vision; *and therefore can only be done by one person, for no two individuals have the same vision; even if multiple people share a canvas, each one of them would have their own piece (in short: it would not be single piece, but actually an assortment of pieces); besides, it should not take more than one person to make a paint stroke.* [L ***ars, artis***]

art */ärt/ n* the expression of one's emotions and ideas. [L ***ars, artis***]

art */ärt/ n (relig)* the expression of one's unique love, imagination, vision and interpretation of beauty through eyes, sensation, smell, sound, taste and God. [L ***ars, artis***]

art */ärt/ n* the expression of oneself; *done without any objective other than self-expression.* [L ***ars, artis***]

art */ärt/ n* the expression of ourselves from within and without.

[L *ars, artis*]

art */ärt/ n* the expression of self; *it can be from love-anger-joy-pain; it is how the artist sees or envisions certain aspects of life and puts it on a canvas – or molds it into a sculpture.* [L *ars, artis*]

art */ärt/ n* the expression of the artist, making a statement or not, to elicit an emotional response in the viewer. [L *ars, artis*]

art */ärt/ n* the expression of the artist's interpretation. [L *ars, artis*]

art */ärt/ n* the expression of the creative human spirit. [L *ars, artis*]

art */ärt/ n* the expression of the emotions within the self. [L *ars, artis*]

art */ärt/ n* the expression of the mind and the body. [L *ars, artis*]

art */ärt/ n* the expression of the soul. [L *ars, artis*]

art */ärt/ n* the expression of things through a non-linear representation; *thus often fulfilling either a personal or social function that does not reach beyond representation.* [L *ars, artis*]

art */ärt/ n* the expression of thoughts and feelings. [L *ars, artis*]

art */ärt/ n (interrog)* the expression or application of creativity and imagination; *well, isn't cooking the act of applying creativity and imagination?* [L *ars, artis*]

art */ärt/ n* the expression or application of human creative skill and imagination. [L *ars, artis*]

art */ärt/ n* the expression or application of human creative skill and imagination; *typically in a visual form such as painting or sculpture.* [L *ars, artis*]

art */ärt/ n* the expression or application of human creative skill and imagination; *typically in a visual form such as painting or sculpture, producing works to be appreciated primarily for their beauty or emotional power.* [L *ars, artis*]

art */ärt/ n* the expression or application of human creative skill and imagination; *typically in a visual form such as painting or sculpture, producing works to be appreciated primarily for their beauty or emotional power: the art of the Renaissance; great art is concerned with moral imperfections; she studied art in Paris.* [L *ars, artis*]

art */ärt/ n* the expression or application of human creative skill and imagination; *vs science – systematic study*. [L *ars, artis*]

art */ärt/ n* the expression or application of human creative skill or imagination. [L *ars, artis*]

art */ärt/ n* the external expression of internal longing. [L *ars, artis*]

art */ärt/ n* the eye, the ear, the mouth, the hands and the body we often exaggerate. [L *ars, artis*]

art */ärt/ n* the feedback system of society. [L *ars, artis*]

art */ärt/ n* the feeling that exists in the heart or (and) the thought that exists in the mind; *it leaves the artist, taking on a visual form that provokes feelings and thoughts to the spectator.* [L *ars, artis*]

art */ärt/ n* the field of visual works such as painting, drawing and the like. [L *ars, artis*]

art */ärt/ n* the fine arts collectively. [L *ars, artis*]

art */ärt/ n* the finely-ground seeds of life. [L *ars, artis*]

art */ärt/ n* the finest expression of the human condition. [L *ars, artis*]

art */ärt/ n* the fingerprint of our existence in the world that has its impact on things we transform through the use of our imagination. [L *ars, artis*]

art */ärt/ n* the following three (3) criteria must be met: first of all, there must be some sensory manifestation *(Rendering)*, fugitive or permanent, that is based upon a creative, intellectual process *(Thought)* with the intention of a beautiful or pleasurable *(Aesthetic* or *Anti-aesthetic)* action, *or reaction*, in one *or more* of the senses and/or psyche. [L *ars, artis*]

art */ärt/ n* the fragrance of the volatiles entering the nose. [L *ars, artis*]

art */ärt/ n (poss fig)* the free expression of a soul tied with barb wire and a lace ribbon. [L *ars, artis*]

art */ärt/ n* the game, illusion, beauty, imagination, emotional expression, wish fulfilment, enjoyment, technique, feeling, meaning, function, abstraction and aesthetic distance. [L *ars, artis*]

art */ärt/ n* the generation of unselfconscious experience. [L *ars, artis*]

art */ärt/ n* the genuine manifestation of spirit. [L *ars, artis*]

art */ärt/ n* the giving of meaning to life. [L *ars, artis*]

art */ärt/ n* the glimpses that carry the most interesting experiences with the highest fidelity. [L *ars, artis*]

art */ärt/ n* the great democrat. [L *ars, artis*]

art */ärt/ n* the great purifier. [L *ars, artis*]

art */ärt/ n* the greatest evidence of humanity. [L *ars, artis*]

Art */ärt/ n* the guy that works at the grocery store up the road. [Arthur]

art */ärt/ n (poss theol)* the half-effaced memory of who we were before our fall. [L *ars, artis*]

art */ärt/ n* the heightening of existence. [L *ars, artis*]

art */ärt/ n* the highest form of expression; *even if it is not always pretty, or politically, or religiously, correct.* [L *ars, artis*]

art */ärt/ n* the highest form of hope. [L *ars, artis*]

art */ärt/ n (philos)* the highest level of philosophy. [L *ars, artis*]

art */ärt/ n (hist)* the history we have never known. [L *ars, artis*]

art */ärt/ n* the human ability to physically manifest a thought, idea or concept abstractly or strategically in a way that influences the emotional state of another being; *while simultaneously stimulating one or more of the five senses.* [L *ars, artis*]

art */ärt/ n* the human contribution to an art form. [L *ars, artis*]

art */ärt/ n* the human contribution to nature; *enviously mirroring its beauty, but introducing human error.* [L *ars, artis*]

art */ärt/ n* the human disposition of sensible or intelligible matter for an aesthetic end. [L *ars, artis*]

art */ärt/ n* the human disposition of sensible or intelligible matter for an aesthetic end; *whereby the aesthetic end is determined by context, tradition (ie established evaluative criteria) and audience (ie critical appraisal) – not by the artist.* [L *ars, artis*]

art */ärt/ n* the humanities. [L *ars, artis*]

art */ärt/ n* the humour we sometimes forget and the severity we often avoid. [L *ars, artis*]

art */ärt/ n (psychol)* the id, the ego and the supernatural. [L *ars, artis*]

art /*ärt*/ *n* the imitation of nature. [L *ars, artis*]

art /*ärt*/ *n* the imitation of reality to communicate an idea. [L *ars, artis*]

art /*ärt*/ *n* the imposing of a pattern on experience; *and our aesthetic enjoyment is recognition of the pattern.* [L *ars, artis*]

art /*ärt*/ *n* the imposition of order on disorder. [L *ars, artis*]

art /*ärt*/ *n* the impulse acted upon, that bridge that takes the feeling *(need, fire, desperation, glorious joy)* and turns it into something directionable, with limits; *limits because what we make is made finite by its revelation, then becomes a platform for greater inspiration.* [L *ars, artis*]

art /*ärt*/ *n* THE INCARNATION OF A THOUGHT. [L *ars, artis*]

art /*ärt*/ *n* the indispensable medium for the communication of a moral ideal. [L *ars, artis*]

art /*ärt*/ *n* the inducement of aesthetic experience. [L *ars, artis*]

art /*ärt*/ *n* THE INNER BEAUTY OF OUR SOULS AND THE TORMENT OF OUR UNBORN PASSIONS. [L *ars, artis*]

art /*ärt*/ *n* the inside of the world. [L *ars, artis*]

art /*ärt*/ *n (interrog)* the instructions written out on the signed certificate, or the image rendered according to the instructions? [L *ars, artis*]

art /*ärt*/ *n* the intention not the result; *if a monkey painted the birth of Venus by pure coincidence it would not be art even though it was just as inspiring (perh ref* The Birth of Venus, *1486 painting by Sandro Botticelli).* [L *ars, artis*]

art /*ärt*/ *n* the intentional creation, or replication, of something in order to provoke thought *and/or provide pleasure.* [L *ars, artis*]

art /*ärt*/ *n* the interpretation and expression of the artist's reality. [L *ars, artis*]

art /*ärt*/ *n* the interpretation of expression. [L *ars, artis*]

art /*ärt*/ *n* the invention of ideas. [L *ars, artis*]

art /*ärt*/ *n* the invention of meaning. [L *ars, artis*]

art /*ärt*/ *n* the ironwork on an exquisitely-made fireplace screen. [L *ars, artis*]

art /*ärt*/ *n* the kind of thing that

depends for its existence upon theories; *without theories of art, black paint is just black paint and nothing more.* [L ***ars, artis***]

art /*ärt*/ *n* the kiss of my love. [L ***ars, artis***]

art /*ärt*/ *n* the language of feelings. [L ***ars, artis***]

art /*ärt*/ *n* the language of the soul. [L ***ars, artis***]

art /*ärt*/ *n (theol)* the laughter of God. [L ***ars, artis***]

art /*ärt*/ *n* the lender or the giver. [L ***ars, artis***]

art /*ärt*/ *n* the lie that tells the truth. [L ***ars, artis***]

art /*ärt*/ *n (fig)* the lifebuoy for the [ship] sinking slowly in the sea of slops. [L ***ars, artis***]

art /*ärt*/ *n* the locus of an ecosystem of power, money, fashion and history *driven by curators, critics, collectors, museums and other institutions.* [L ***ars, artis***]

art /*ärt*/ *n* the luxury of detachment while facing the incivility, crudeness and insensitivity of the coming century. [L ***ars, artis***]

art /*ärt*/ *n* the making of objects, images, music *etc* that are beautiful; *or that express feelings.* [L ***ars, artis***]

art /*ärt*/ *n* the making of things such as paintings or drawings; *or the things that are made: modern art, an art gallery.* [L ***ars, artis***]

art /*ärt*/ *n* the making or doing of something whose purpose is to bring pleasure to people through their enjoyment of what is beautiful and interesting; *or things often made for this purpose, such as paintings, drawings, or sculptures: an art museum.* [L ***ars, artis***]

art /*ärt*/ *n (hort)* the making well, or properly arranging, of anything whatever that needs to be made or arranged; *whether a statuette, automobile, or garden.* [L ***ars, artis***]

art /*ärt*/ *n* the manifestation and meeting place of our otherwise intangible selves. [L ***ars, artis***]

art /*ärt*/ *n* the manifestation of emotions using one's skills; *people who perceive such art may sympathize with, relate to and/or just witness it for temporary pleasure; the result can be in tangible or intangible form.* [L ***ars, artis***]

art /*ärt*/ *n* the manifestation of everything in the universe. [L ***ars, artis***]

art /ärt/ *n (obs)* the manifestation of genius. [L *ars, artis*]

art /ärt/ *n* the mastery of a practice and the ritual that goes with it. [L *ars, artis*]

art /ärt/ *n* the material expression of the desire to understand the meaning of creation. [L *ars, artis*]

art /ärt/ *n* the meaning and expression of human beings. [L *ars, artis*]

art /ärt/ *n (theol)* the means God gives human beings to express their impression of his creation. [L *ars, artis*]

art /ärt/ *n* the means in which the soul communicates. [L *ars, artis*]

art /ärt/ *n* the mechanism that an artist uses to share his/her transcendent vision of life with others. [L *ars, artis*]

art /ärt/ *n* the mediator between heart and soul; *to break the everyday pattern of life as we usually know it and touch an emotion, a memory, or tell us a story we may not have known before, visualized before, or allowed to be a part of ourselves.* [L *ars, artis*]

art /ärt/ *n* THE MEMORY OF ALL LIFE THAT HAS FLOWED BEFORE OUR TIME. [L *ars, artis*]

art /ärt/ *n* the method, process or technique for creating something; *or for achieving a useful result.* [L *ars, artis*]

art /ärt/ *n* the mind, body and spirit encompassed into anything that influences and satisfies without prejudice or pride. [L *ars, artis*]

art /ärt/ *n* the mirror of thoughts and emotions, driven by passion and inspiration, creating a masterpiece. [L *ars, artis*]

art /ärt/ *n* the mode of expression that entertainment is not. [L *ars, artis*]

art /ärt/ *n* the most beautiful deception of all; *and although people try to incorporate the everyday events of life in it, we must hope that it will remain a deception lest it become a utilitarian thing, sad as a factory.* [L *ars, artis*]

art /ärt/ *n* the most belligerent expression of political, spiritual or emotional conception known to man. [L *ars, artis*]

art /ärt/ *n* THE MOST ELEGANT WAY OF GETTING FROM POINT A TO POINT B. [L *ars, artis*]

art */ärt/ n* the most flawed perfection I have ever known. [L *ars, artis*]

art */ärt/ n* the most impactful thing imaginable. [L *ars, artis*]

art */ärt/ n* the most important thing in life; *because it gives us a way to be creative and express ourselves.* [L *ars, artis*]

art */ärt/ n* the most intense mode of individualism that the world has known. [L *ars, artis*]

art */ärt/ n* the most passionate orgy within man's grasp. [L *ars, artis*]

art */ärt/ n* the most powerful form of expression; *it can easily express and invoke emotions in ways 1000 words can't.* [L *ars, artis*]

art */ärt/ n* the most powerful protection against a sense of boredom; *and boredom, ultimately, is the most terrifying and most dangerous human experience because boredom creates a sense of meaningless, pointlessness; it destroys our sense of the power of time, of the finite character of mortality; it creates anger and resentment; and it's unnecessary: the finding or creating of beauty in the world is enormous protection against a sense of meaningless and resentment and pointlessness.* [L *ars, artis*]

art */ärt/ n* the most precious fruit of the most sensuous part of our perception; *and to define is to defy it.* [L *ars, artis*]

art */ärt/ n (econ, derog)* the most successful of all money making scams. [L *ars, artis*]

art */ärt/ n (fig)* the music of wind moving leaves. [L *ars, artis*]

art */ärt/ n* the name for a wide set of socially inherited tools that we may use to derive meaning from things. [L *ars, artis*]

Art */ärt/ n* the name of a guy my mom used to date. [Arthur]

Art */ärt/ n (photog)* the name of Sigma's new lens lineup; *these lenses are developed with an emphasis on artistic touch and are designed to meet the expectations of users who value a creative, dramatic outcome; along with landscapes, portraits, still-life, close-up and casual snaps, these lenses are perfect for the kind of photography that unleashes the inner artist; ideal for studio photography, they offer just as much of an expressive scope when capturing architecture, starry skies, underwater shots and many other scenes; this* *category will be comprised of many focal lengths and designs, such as large-aperture prime lenses, wide-angle lenses, ultra wide-angle lenses and macro and fisheye lenses* (Sigma Corporation, *a Japanese company, manufacturing cameras, lenses, flashes and other photographic accessories*). [L *ars, artis*]

art */ärt/ n* the narrow definition of art is one that says *'today we are making sock puppets'*. [L *ars, artis*]

art */ärt/ n (poss joc)* the nasty addiction of the artist. [L *ars, artis*]

art */ärt/ n* the nebulous perceptions of the mind that shape and appreciate the beauty of existence; *I suppose.* [L *ars, artis*]

art */ärt/ n* the necessity of life for someone who must create it. [L *ars, artis*]

art */ärt/ n* the objectification of feeling. [L *ars, artis*]

art */ärt/ n* the objectification of feeling; *and the subjectification of nature.* [L *ars, artis*]

art */ärt/ n* the objectification of human emotions and feelings presented in a stylized manner. [L *ars, artis*]

art */ärt/ n* the observing and classifying of facts and obtaining a systematic view of the order of the universe. [L *ars, artis*]

Art */ärt/ n* the old guy that lives down the street that I drink coffee with on Saturday mornings; *since it is Saturday morning I think I will leave now and go enjoy some time with Art over a hot cup of coffee on his deck and enjoy the beautiful art of nature that is his back yard.* [Arthur]

art */ärt/ n* the oldest profession. [L *ars, artis*]

art */ärt/ n* the one activity where a person chooses the problem, sets the constraints and solves it; *in all other activities we are given the problem and the constraints to solve it.* [L *ars, artis*]

art */ärt/ n* the one form of expression that allows the individual to express the truth – *theirs or someone else's* – without rebuttal, but simply to exist. [L *ars, artis*]

art */ärt/ n* the one form of expression that can capture a beautiful movement in such a way that even one's feelings naturally merge with it. [L *ars, artis*]

art */ärt/ n (pers)* the one thing I am

decent at. [L *ars, artis*]

art */ärt/ n (pers)* the one thing I trust myself with. [L *ars, artis*]

art */ärt/ n (pers)* the only reason I get out of bed in inclement weather. [L *ars, artis*]

art */ärt/ n (pers)* the only thing about the world that seems *prima facie* meaningful or life-affirming or Good to me; *and without it I'm literally not sure I'd have the will to live.* [L *ars, artis*]

art */ärt/ n (pers)* the only thing I breathe. [L *ars, artis*]

art */ärt/ n (pers)* the only thing I'm good at. [L *ars, artis*]

art */ärt/ n* the only thing in life worth pursuing. [L *ars, artis*]

art */ärt/ n* the only twin life has; *its only valid metaphysic.* [L *ars, artis*]

art */ärt/ n (inf, fig)* the only umbrella in the shitstorm of life. [L *ars, artis*]

art */ärt/ n* the only way to run away without leaving home. [L *ars, artis*]

art */ärt/ n* the only way you can let go of everything and create something for someone else or yourself to connect to and feel the meaning or message of what you created. [L *ars, artis*]

art */ärt/ n* the opium of the people, *I guess.* [L *ars, artis*]

art */ärt/ n* the opportunity for love between strangers. [L *ars, artis*]

art */ärt/ n* the origin of the artwork and of the artist. [L *ars, artis*]

art */ärt/ n* the original Silent Hill® trilogy (**Silent Hill®**, *survival horror video game series consisting of nine installments created by Keiichiro Toyama and published by Konami™ and its subsidiary Konami™ Digital Entertainment).* [L *ars, artis*]

art */ärt/ n (m)* the outlet in which a creator, writer, painter *etc* fulfils his social commitment to the people and to the unity and liberty of mankind. [L *ars, artis*]

art */ärt/ n* the outlets of cognitive abstraction: *imagination and creativity*. [L *ars, artis*]

art */ärt/ n (neurol)* the over-stimulation of evolutionary prefrontal dopermegenic disinhibition resulting in a 'go towards' behaviour due to desire. [L *ars, artis*]

art */ärt/ n* the oxygen of humanity. [L *ars, artis*]

art /*ärt*/ *n* the path of the melody to the ears. [L *ars, artis*]

art /*ärt*/ *n* the patternistic expression of a talent within a person; *which is pleasing to the senses of those that observe it.* [L *ars, artis*]

art /*ärt*/ *n* the perceptual sensing of the real in the unreal. [L *ars, artis*]

art /*ärt*/ *n* the perfection of nature. [L *ars, artis*]

art /*ärt*/ *n* the perpetual motion of illusion. [L *ars, artis*]

art /*ärt*/ *n* the physical expression of the ideals formed by the mind. [L *ars, artis*]

art /*ärt*/ *n* the physical manifestation of an idea, created to serve a purpose. [L *ars, artis*]

art /*ärt*/ *n* the physical medium between the viewer and the creator's mind; *and their experience of it is not necessarily the same, because the medium is actually a MINIMAL expression of the creator's emotions: so it is kind of dull and contains small amounts of information; therefore the viewer's mind AUTO-COMPLETES it with its own perceptions and experiences.* [L *ars, artis*]

art /*ärt*/ *n* the plaything of the intellectual rich. [L *ars, artis*]

art /*ärt*/ *n* the plethora of sensory creations created by man. [L *ars, artis*]

art /*ärt*/ *n* the portrayal of one's feelings. [L *ars, artis*]

art /*ärt*/ *n (pers)* the power for me to go on. [L *ars, artis*]

art /*ärt*/ *n* the power of doing something not taught by nature or instinct. [L *ars, artis*]

art /*ärt*/ *n* the power to transcend our own self-interest, our solipsistic zoom-lens on life and relate to the world and each other with more integrity, more curiosity, more wholeheartedness. [L *ars, artis*]

art /*ärt*/ *n* the practical application of aesthetic principles; *as in the departments of production specifically called the fine arts.* [L *ars, artis*]

art /*ärt*/ *n* the practice of creating an emotional or intellectual response in the audience. [L *ars, artis*]

art /*ärt*/ *n* the presentation of self. [L *ars, artis*]

art /*ärt*/ *n* the presentation of works that challenge the senses as expressions through visual, audible and written forms for observers to experience for the purpose of communicating a concept, feeling and ideas that excite, stir, even provoke, feelings that would not otherwise have been experienced. [L *ars, artis*]

art */ärt/ n* the prime mover of the consciousness. [L *ars, artis*]

art */ärt/ n* the principles or methods governing any craft or branch of learning: *the art of baking*. [L *ars, artis*]

art */ärt/ n* the process of deliberately arranging elements in a way that appeals to the senses or emotions. [L *ars, artis*]

art */ärt/ n* the process of developing your inner self so much so that it pours out all the wonders and goodness in your soul. [L *ars, artis*]

art */ärt/ n* the process of experiencing strong, imaginative and purified emotions. [L *ars, artis*]

art */ärt/ n* the process of making something special. [L *ars, artis*]

art */ärt/ n* the process of perfecting one's craft to their ultimate ability. [L *ars, artis*]

art */ärt/ n* the process or product of deliberately arranging elements in a way that appeals to the senses or emotions. [L *ars, artis*]

art */ärt/ n* the process through which people, ideas, feelings, relationships and societies reveal themselves. [L *ars, artis*]

art */ärt/ n* the process through which we understand. [L *ars, artis*]

art */ärt/ n* the produced result when an artist observes the world around him or her and makes a comment about it. [L *ars, artis*]

art */ärt/ n* the product of a human decision to make something called 'art' or to name something as 'art'. [L *ars, artis*]

art */ärt/ n* the product of a struggle. [L *ars, artis*]

art */ärt/ n* the product of conscious intention. [L *ars, artis*]

art */ärt/ n* the product of creative choice. [L *ars, artis*]

art */ärt/ n* the product of creative human effort. [L *ars, artis*]

art */ärt/ n* the product of creativity. [L *ars, artis*]

art */ärt/ n* the product of expressing feelings, emotions, stories *etc* in a way that is visual, audible or a combination of the two. [L *ars, artis*]

art */ärt/ n* the product of human consciousness; *and not just some random occurrence; otherwise it is just stuff.* [L *ars, artis*]

art */ärt/ n* the product of human creativity. [L *ars, artis*]

art */ärt/ n* the product of human endeavour for the sole purpose of reflection. [L *ars, artis*]

art */ärt/ n* the product of imagination and creativity; *particularly in a physical form.* [L *ars, artis*]

art */ärt/ n* the product of man's creative activity. [L *ars, artis*]

art */ärt/ n (pers)* the product of my connection to 'all that is' – *earth, spirit, heaven, life* – and through my heart-centred perspective I perspire, laugh and create to express this connection. [L *ars, artis*]

art */ärt/ n* the product of the artist's confidence in creating; *which allows them to become vulnerable.* [L *ars, artis*]

art */ärt/ n* the product of what you don't know what you're doing. [L *ars, artis*]

art */ärt/ n* the product or process of deliberately arranging items *(often with symbolic significance)* in a way that influences and affects one or more of the senses, emotions and intellect. [L *ars, artis*]

art */ärt/ n* the product, result, intent, reflection, emotion, or representation of expression created by humans. [L *ars, artis*]

art */ärt/ n* the production of visually-pleasing aesthetics, requiring some degree of skill and experience on the part of the artist. [L *ars, artis*]

art */ärt/ n* the production or expression according to the aesthetic principals of what is beautiful, appealing or an object of more than ordinary significance. [L *ars, artis*]

art */ärt/ n* the proper task of life. [L *ars, artis*]

art */ärt/ n* the provision of paradigms of order and/or disorder. [L *ars, artis*]

art */ärt/ n* the purpose of art is to create an emotional response in the person that is exposed to that art; *and there are three categories of* *art:* bad art, good art *and* great art; **bad art** *will elicit no emotional response in the person that is exposed to it* eg *a song you hear in an elevator and it does nothing to you, a picture on a wall that gives you the same emotional response as if the wall had been blank, a movie that chews up time;* **good art** *will make you feel an emotion that you have felt before* eg *you see a picture of a forest and you remember the last time you went fishing with your dad, you hear a song about love and you remember the last time you were in love;* **great art** *will make you feel an emotion you have never felt before* eg *seeing the Pieta, the world famous sculpture by Michelangelo, can cause someone to feel the pain of losing a child even if they've never had one; and when you're trying for these emotions the easiest one to trigger is anger; anyone can do it; go into the street, throw a rock at someone, you will make them angry; the emotions of love, empathy and laughter are much harder to trigger, but since they operate on a deeper level, they bring a much greater reward* (**Pietà**, *(1498–1499) a work of Renaissance sculpt by* **Michelangelo Buonarroti**, *housed in St. Peter's Basilica, Vatican City).* [L *ars, artis*]

art */ärt/ n (prob fig)* the pus forming in the wounds of life as we try to heal ourselves. [L *ars, artis*]

art */ärt/ n* the quality of communication. [L *ars, artis*]

art */ärt/ n* the quality of doing. [L *ars, artis*]

art */ärt/ n* the quality or state of being artful. [L *ars, artis*]

art */ärt/ n* the quality, production, expression or realm of what is beautiful or of more than ordinary significance. [L *ars, artis*]

art */ärt/ n* the quality, production, expression or realm, according to aesthetic principles, of what is beautiful, appealing, or of more than ordinary significance. [L *ars, artis*]

art */ärt/ n* the quality, production, expression or realm, according to aesthetic principles, of what is beautiful, appealing, or of more than ordinary significance: *collectors are discovering video art.* [L *ars, artis*]

art */ärt/ n* the question of execution, the direction of strokes and the mystery of values. [L *ars, artis*]

art /ärt/ *n* the realization of a mental concept, stimulated by a certain experience, with the intention to stimulate the other, with aesthetic characteristics. [L *ars, artis*]

art /ärt/ *n* the reflection and apprehension of the real world. [L *ars, artis*]

art /ärt/ *n* the reflection and creation of reality. [L *ars, artis*]

art /ärt/ *n* the reflection of the progress of human existence; *it involves different time periods and civilizations to educate the future; in this sense, things that are part of human development are part of art.* [L *ars, artis*]

art /ärt/ *n* the reflection of your soul. [L *ars, artis*]

art /ärt/ *n* the relationship between the concept and the expression of it. [L *ars, artis*]

art /ärt/ *n* the relationship forged between an artist and an audience in the process of contemplating any object created in any medium. [L *ars, artis*]

art /ärt/ *n* the representation of a subject in the form of a painting, a sculpture or a composition from materials such as rock, metal, glass, plastic *etc.* [L *ars, artis*]

art /ärt/ *n* the representation of an idea; *it does not have to be the artist's intended idea since there can be unintentional art; it does not exclude photography since a photograph is a representation of an idea.* [L *ars, artis*]

art /ärt/ *n* the representation of the human feelings embodied in different ways and techniques. [L *ars, artis*]

art /ärt/ *n (hist)* the representative of history. [L *ars, artis*]

art /ärt/ *n* the reproduction and symbolic representation of reality. [L *ars, artis*]

art /ärt/ *n* the reproduction of the thing's general essence. [L *ars, artis*]

art /ärt/ *n* the reproduction of what the Senses perceive in Nature through the veil of the soul. [L *ars, artis*]

art /ärt/ *n* the research and development wing of consumer culture. [L *ars, artis*]

art /ärt/ *n* the residue of the observational process. [L *ars, artis*]

art /ärt/ *n* the resonance between the perceiver and the piece; *re-*

gardless if it's coldly calculated construction, intuitive disgorgement or penciled outlines. [L ***ars, artis***]

art */ärt/ n* the response of man's creative soul to the call of the real. [L *ars, artis*]

art */ärt/ n* the response of man's creative soul to the call of the Real. [L *ars, artis*]

art */ärt/ n* the result of a creative act executed for the sake of itself. [L *ars, artis*]

art */ärt/ n (obs)* the result of having a great skill. [L *ars, artis*]

art */ärt/ n* the result of intentional creative exercise; *be it painting, literature, performance or music; today, neither can intentions behind art be defined nor its characteristics and mediums be listed, but art always carries traces of the artist; even art made with the intention of being completely detached from the artist speaks of those intentions; therefore, the artwork and the artist maintain a special connection; and every artwork invokes from its imagery, colour, sound or touch something within its viewer; thus, an artwork becomes the supernatural connection between two people.* [L *ars, artis*]

art */ärt/ n* the result of one's having been in danger; *of having gone through an experience all the way to the end, where no one can go any further.* [L ***ars, artis***]

art */ärt/ n* the result of projected expressions. [L *ars, artis*]

art */ärt/ n* the result of somebody being driven to creation. [L *ars, artis*]

art */ärt/ n* the result of successfully doing something purposefully skilfully. [L *ars, artis*]

art */ärt/ n* the result of the artist's work and vision. [L *ars, artis*]

art */ärt/ n (inf, vulg)* the result, and cause, of boners. [L *ars, artis*]

art */ärt/ n* the revealing of the thoughts in one's mind; *yet it is the sacred thing of the soul.* [L ***ars, artis***]

art */ärt/ n* the rich blood that runs through our bodies; *we may not all notice it but we live, dress, eat, live in, buy, sell, make, read, hear and see every day of our lives; there is no right or wrong as long as there is another that appreciates the statement.* [L *ars, artis*]

art */ärt/ n* the richness of life. [L *ars, artis*]

art */ärt/ n* the right way of making

things; *whether symphonies or aeroplanes.* [L *ars, artis*]

art */ärt/ n* the root of ALL human consciousness and IN-pressing is FAR more important than EX-pressing; *expression is for soda pop labels.* [L *ars, artis*]

art */ärt/ n* the satisfying experience that happens between an artefact and a person experiencing that artefact. [L *ars, artis*]

art */ärt/ n* the science of understanding music, theatre, plays. [L *ars, artis*]

art */ärt/ n* the search for harmony. [L *ars, artis*]

art */ärt/ n* the search for who we are. [L *ars, artis*]

art */ärt/ n* the search of perfection; *and not the object of it.* [L *ars, artis*]

art */ärt/ n* the searching of some kind of experience that will change or confirm our own reality. [L *ars, artis*]

art */ärt/ n* the seeking for ideal truth. [L *ars, artis*]

art */ärt/ n* the self-expressions of *Homo sapiens.* [L *ars, artis*]

art */ärt/ n (relig)* the separation between man and God. [L *ars, artis*]

art */ärt/ n (inf)* the 'shit' of our perception of our world. [L *ars, artis*]

art */ärt/ n* the shortest distance between two points. [L *ars, artis*]

art */ärt/ n* the single most useless word in the English language; *anything or nothing can be art, when viewed from the proper perspective: 'That isn't art!' 'Why not?'* [L *ars, artis*]

art */ärt/ n* the skilful presentation of concepts and/or emotions in a form that is structurally satisfying and coherent. [L *ars, artis*]

art */ärt/ n* the skilful presentation of concepts and/or emotions *(ideas and feelings)* in a form that is structurally *(compositionally)* satisfying and coherent. [L *ars, artis*]

art */ärt/ n* the skill to think about as many as possible means to describe an object, feeling, scene *etc* and to choose out of those the most appropriate one in terms of time and space. [L *ars, artis*]

art */ärt/ n* the slightest graceful movement. [L *ars, artis*]

art */ärt/ n (inf)* the smartest kind of bullshit in the world. [L *ars,*

artis]

art /*ärt*/ *n* the soul of all things. [L *ars, artis*]

art /*ärt*/ *n* the soul of an artist shown in the physical world. [L *ars, artis*]

art /*ärt*/ *n* the soul that remains after all the skills, materials and hard work are removed from the object. [L *ars, artis*]

art /*ärt*/ *n* the soul's outlet. [L *ars, artis*]

art /*ärt*/ *n* the soul's truth. [L *ars, artis*]

art /*ärt*/ *n* the source of being. [L *ars, artis*]

art /*ärt*/ *n* the special human voice or language we call upon when communicating in ordinary ways seems to fall short of conveying our observations and inner reflections. [L *ars, artis*]

art /*ärt*/ *n* the spectrum of colours entering the eyes. [L *ars, artis*]

art /*ärt*/ *n* the stimulus of the touch. [L *ars, artis*]

art /*ärt*/ *n* *(fig)* the stored honey of the human soul. [L *ars, artis*]

art /*ärt*/ *n* the striving for beauty; *most of us have forgotten this: this act of constantly striving for beauty, for some, is the highest, most worthwhile activity we can engage in – as life is short – and beauty makes life worth living.* [L *ars, artis*]

art /*ärt*/ *n* the striving to learn what it means to be human. [L *ars, artis*]

art /*ärt*/ *n* the study of creativity in someone's mind. [L *ars, artis*]

art /*ärt*/ *n* the stuff that has been hanging or sitting around in museums for a very long time. [L *ars, artis*]

art /*ärt*/ *n* the stuff that we do when we're not doing the stuff that keeps us alive. [L *ars, artis*]

art /*ärt*/ *n* the stuff you'd hang on the walls to show off to guests. [L *ars, artis*]

art /*ärt*/ *n* *(joc)* the subjective expression and appreciation of form; *hey like porn; excellent, I'm an art addict.* [L *ars, artis*]

art /*ärt*/ *n* the suitably technical, creative and intentional embodiment of aesthetically engaging thought or emotion in any publicly accessible medium. [L *ars, artis*]

art /*ärt*/ *n* the symbol of the two

noblest human efforts: *to construct and to refrain from destruction.* [L *ars, artis*]

art */ärt/ n* the symbolic representation of any number of things that intends to evoke a specific feeling or otherwise titillate the senses, *oftentimes drawing upon the archetypal impulses or images common to our species in order to articulate or relay something profoundly human, such as a subtle emotion, that would otherwise be difficult if not impossible to explain in a more forthright and common manner.* [L *ars, artis*]

art */ärt/ n* the symbolic residue of personal reflection. [L *ars, artis*]

art */ärt/ n* the system of rules or principles governing a particular human activity; *the art of government.* [L *ars, artis*]

art */ärt/ n* the systematic application of knowledge or skill in effecting a desired result. [L *ars, artis*]

art */ärt/ n* the systematic application of knowledge or skill in effecting a desired result; *also, an occupation or business requiring such knowledge or skill.* [L *ars, artis*]

art */ärt/ n* the talent of making a skill look effortless. [L *ars, artis*]

ART */ärt/ n* the term referring to the various techniques used to achieve pregnancy by artificial or partially artificial methods (Assisted Reproductive Technology). [acronym]

art */ärt/ n* the term that describes different ranges of human activities as well as the resulting products of activities *such as painting, film, dances, singing and a lot more.* [L *ars, artis*]

art */ärt/ n* the thing that people make that has no immediate practical relevance. [L *ars, artis*]

art */ärt/ n (pers)* the thing that wakes me up in the morning and puts me to bed at night. [L *ars, artis*]

art */ärt/ n (fig, milit)* the touch of a beautiful woman and the wounds of war. [L *ars, artis*]

art */ärt/ n* the Tracey Emin bed *(prob ref* My Bed *(1998), a work by Brit artist* Tracey Emin CBE RA *(1963–)).* [L *ars, artis*]

art */ärt/ n (relig)* the transfiguration of Nature into Cosmos, performed by a human; *thus displaying the latter as having the properties of God the Creator.* [L *ars, artis*]

art */ärt/ n* the transformation of the ordinary into the EXTRAORDINARY. [L *ars, artis*]

art */ärt/ n* the translation medium between the mind and matter. [L *ars, artis*]

art */ärt/ n* the triumph over chaos. [L *ars, artis*]

art */ärt/ n* the true vision of the heart, body and soul. [L *ars, artis*]

art */ärt/ n (bot)* the unceasing effort to compete with the beauty of flowers; *and never succeeding.* [L *ars, artis*]

art */ärt/ n* the unique quality which can be developed and presented to the world in a unique way. [L *ars, artis*]

art */ärt/ n* the unique result of a unique temperament. [L *ars, artis*]

art */ärt/ n* the unknown maelstrom where our ability to divide the universe fails and for a brief moment, all too brief, everything joins back up and we feel whole; *this can be through any form of art: music, painting, sport, anything.* [L *ars, artis*]

art */ärt/ n* the unspoken language of an experience. [L *ars, artis*]

art */ärt/ n* the untamed abandonment of the soul, *communicating through others, piercing concepts their rational minds can only weep to understand yet their souls yearn to covet again and again and again.* [L *ars, artis*]

art */ärt/ n* the uplifting of the beautiful so that all may see and enjoy. [L *ars, artis*]

art */ärt/ n* the use and application of imagination to create objects and experiences that can be shared with others. [L *ars, artis*]

art */ärt/ n* the use of characteristic methods of a discipline to criticize the discipline itself. [L *ars, artis*]

art */ärt/ n* the use of decoration on objects. [L *ars, artis*]

art */ärt/ n* the use of human creative skill. [L *ars, artis*]

art */ärt/ n* the use of skill and creative imagination in the production of film/theatre. [L *ars, artis*]

art */ärt/ n* the use of skill and imagination in the creation of aesthetic objects, environments or experiences that can be shared with others. [L *ars, artis*]

art */ärt/ n* the use of the brain

without limits; *guided by limits towards an idea in the brain.* [L *ars, artis*]

art */ärt/ n* the utilization of intentional rhetorical techniques to communicate an idea important to its creator about the current times they live in *(social problems, a close relationship, a historic event),* or about eternal truths *(the nature of existence, people, the future of mankind, feelings).* [L *ars, artis*]

art */ärt/ n* the utilization of love's exhaust. [L *ars, artis*]

art */ärt/ n* the value of the work of art is determined by its capacity to transcend the limits of its chosen medium in order to strike some universal chord by the rarity of the skill of the artist or in its accurate reflection in what is termed *the zeitgeist.* [L *ars, artis*]

art */ärt/ n* the various branches of creative activity; *such as painting, music, literature and dance.* [L *ars, artis*]

art */ärt/ n* the vengeance of the *ideal* on the *real.* [L *ars, artis*]

art */ärt/ n* the visible and convincing expression of fundamental truth. [L *ars, artis*]

art */ärt/ n* the visual aesthetic appeal and the individuality of the art piece; *a true artist can take a rock or a piece of dirt and find an artistic composition within and preferably tell a story.* [L *ars, artis*]

art */ärt/ n* the visual arts, drawing and painting and *usu* sculpture. [L *ars, artis*]

art */ärt/ n* the visual communication of some aspect of the philosophy of the artist making the work of art. [L *ars, artis*]

art */ärt/ n* the visual expression of life. [L *ars, artis*]

art */ärt/ n* the visual inspiration and the emotions of the artist. [L *ars, artis*]

art */ärt/ n* the visual measuring stick to measure in part the unmeasurable as imparted to mankind by the unfathomable as a means to ensure such beings maintain a sense of humanity, self-worth and dignity; *to furthermore stimulate investigation and contemplation in the midst of societal upheavals and change by which the discoverer finds cause and evidence that life regardless is to be celebrated and the heart filled with thankfulness.* [L *ars, artis*]

art */ärt/ n* the visual *(normally)* expression of an idea. [L *ars, artis*]

art */ärt/ n* the visualization of the intangible imagination of the soul. [L *ars, artis*]

art */ärt/ n* the voice of the artist baring his soul and ours; *that's why it is sad or beautiful or disturbing; if we are stirred by a work, then it is truly art.* [L *ars, artis*]

art */ärt/ n* the voluntary prostitution of one's own soul and conscience. [L *ars, artis*]

art */ärt/ n* the way a leaf lands down on a ground, where it lands and what details are specific to that very leaf, that's art; *perhaps sometimes not impressive because of its ordinariness, but still impressive because of the millions of possibilities that emerged out of it; each leaf has a personal identity based on the how, where and when of the specificities of its landing on the ground.* [L *ars, artis*]

art */ärt/ n (m)* the way for someone to express his own feelings in a way that they feel is creative enough for them. [L *ars, artis*]

art */ärt/ n* the way humans differ from all other living things. [L *ars, artis*]

art */ärt/ n (m)* the way man defines the indefinable. [L *ars, artis*]

art */ärt/ n* the way people see things. [L *ars, artis*]

art */ärt/ n* the way that we perceive something. [L *ars, artis*]

art */ärt/ n* the way we see something and feel compelled to represent it so as to share it as to convey a message. [L *ars, artis*]

art */ärt/ n (poss fig)* the way you put mustard on your burger. [L *ars, artis*]

art */ärt/ n* the word we use to describe things created for the primary purpose of eliciting an emotion within the audience. [L *ars, artis*]

art */ärt/ n* the work of art is by definition not merely created but creation itself. [L *ars, artis*]

art */ärt/ n* the works produced by painters, sculptors, writers, musicians, filmmakers and the like. [L *ars, artis*]

art */ärt/ n* the world (in all its glory) 'talks' to me and my response to it is 'art'. [L *ars, artis*]

art */ärt/ n* the world **1** passing through any mind **2** being apprehended by any mind; *for this definition, the mind includes the body;*

the category of mind includes: children, animals, computers, complex natural processes; the category of mind may or may not include God; not all minds can apprehend the world passing through minds; mind (1) can be the artist while mind (2) is the audience; mind (1) can be the audience while mind (2) can be the artist; mind (1) can be at the same time mind (2); this experience compels the second mind to emotional response, wonder, awe, a feeling of magic, thoughts of transcendence or loss of self, animal spirits, dreams, horror – also novelty, humour, playfulness, simplicity, happiness. [L *ars, artis*]

art */ärt/ n (poss fig)* the wrinkle in a river. [L *ars, artis*]

art */ärt/ n (psychol)* therapy. [L *ars, artis*]

art */ärt/ n* there really is no such thing as art; *there are only artists.* [L *ars, artis*]

art */ärt/ n* things I like to look at; examples: Wyoming, sexy girls. [L *ars, artis*]

art */ärt/ n* things or actions that aim to cause emotion or feelings. [L *ars, artis*]

art */ärt/ n* things that are found in galleries. [L *ars, artis*]

art */ärt/ n* things that have no purpose other than to exist and be art. [L *ars, artis*]

art */ärt/ n (pers)* things that I can relate to. [L *ars, artis*]

art */ärt/ n (pers)* things that I find beautiful or interesting or provocative to look at. [L *ars, artis*]

art */ärt/ n* things that people don't need to have. [L *ars, artis*]

art */ärt/ n (pers)* things that truly astound me *and better me as a person.* [L *ars, artis*]

art */ärt/ n (inf, photog)* this talk about what is art and what isn't reminds me of a kind of off-topic story I will share: *I did one art show in my life; didn't sell anything; the photos I presented were mainly of rock musicians performing or 'rocker lifestyle' type of subjects; the exhibitor next to me was presenting his black and white, out-of-focus pictures of women bound, gagged and tied up; he looked over and sneered at me and I heard him comment out loud to someone, while clearly looking my way, that 'some of this crap here isn't even art'...; make what you will of that story; carry on...* [L *ars, artis*]

art */ärt/ n* those branches of learning which are taught in the academical course of colleges. [L *ars, artis*]

art */ärt/ n* those things we do *(or perh the works that we create)* that do not specifically contribute to our safety or our property. [L *ars, artis*]

art */ärt/ n* thought expressed orally or physically. [L *ars, artis*]

art */ärt/ n* three little letters that just can't hold it in any longer. [L *ars, artis*]

art */ärt/ n* thrives in the unconfined lawlessness of ridiculous unreasonableness. [L *ars, artis*]

art */ärt/ n* thrives on democratic ideals, freedom of expression and rugged individualism. [L *ars, artis*]

art */ärt/ n (hort)* tilling the soil of culture. [L *ars, artis*]

art */ärt/ n* timeless. [L *ars, artis*]

art */ärt/ n* timeless, emotive, special *and never tiring of viewing it.* [L *ars, artis*]

art */ärt/ n* to be in the ears, eyes and feelings of the beholders. [L *ars, artis*]

art */ärt/ n* to cause the viewer to partake in introspective thought. [L *ars, artis*]

art */ärt/ n* to challenge preconceptions. [L *ars, artis*]

art */ärt/ n* to evoke in oneself a feeling one has experienced and having evoked it in oneself, then, by means of movements, lines, colours, sounds or forms expressed in words, so to transmit that feeling that others may experience this same feeling. [L *ars, artis*]

art */ärt/ n* to find beauty and something worth taking the time to pay close attention to, in everything that surrounds us. [L *ars, artis*]

art */ärt/ n* to find solutions; *from source and not from the schemes.* [L *ars, artis*]

art */ärt/ n* to fit; *in an aesthetic and emotional sense.* [L *ars, artis*]

art */ärt/ n* to make us look at the world with fresh eyes, I think; *she said that day.* [L *ars, artis*]

art */ärt/ n* to mislead in any way. [L *ars, artis*]

art */ärt/ n* to not be correct. [L *ars, artis*]

art */ärt/ n* to provoke some reaction or feeling or mood in the viewer. [L *ars, artis*]

art /ärt/ *n* to put things together. [L *ars, artis*]

art /ärt/ *n* to reproduce to others the inner truth of some matter as truthfully as possible from the artist's point-of-view. [L *ars, artis*]

art /ärt/ *n* to satisfy the artist's own desire to create an idea which evokes feelings and thought. [L *ars, artis*]

art /ärt/ *n* to use various elements such as light, sound, colour and words to convey a greater truth or understanding; *one that goes beyond just the physical element of the art.* [L *ars, artis*]

art /ärt/ *n (m)* too lofty for mortal men in any medium. [L *ars, artis*]

art /ärt/ *n* too serious to be taken seriously. [L *ars, artis*]

art /ärt/ *n* too-smart gimmicks. [L *ars, artis*]

art /ärt/ *n* torment and evil. [L *ars, artis*]

art /ärt/ *n* touching. [L *ars, artis*]

art /ärt/ *n tra* spelled backwards. [L *ars, artis*]

art /ärt/ *n* trained ability or mastery of a medium. [L *ars, artis*]

art /ärt/ *n* training in the perception of reality. [L *ars, artis*]

art /ärt/ *n* transcendent. [L *ars, artis*]

art /ärt/ *n* transcends all the barriers we like to hold against people; *like age, race, religion, lifestyle, gender, political view or whatever; when you hold a piece of pottery in your hands you have no idea if it was made by a 98–year-old southern Baptist black man or a 17–year-old emo high school white girl from Seattle – and that's cool.* [L *ars, artis*]

art /ärt/ *n* transfigures the ordinary. [L *ars, artis*]

art /ärt/ *n* transformative and is placed within a 'frame'; ie *gallery, studio, museum, collection.* [L *ars, artis*]

art /ärt/ *n* transformative, sites are moving; *and when I get that feeling I need to pass it on.* [L *ars, artis*]

art /ärt/ *n* transformed from the real to the unreal. [L *ars, artis*]

art /ärt/ *n* transformed reality. [L *ars, artis*]

art /ärt/ *n* transforming one's most inflamed personal sentiments and perceptions into a tangible creation, designed for no other purpose than the architect's own personal satisfaction; *anything else is a marketing scheme: Renoir was an artist; Hugh Hefner is a salesman (***Pierre-Auguste Renoir** *(1841–1919), Fr artist;* **Hugh Hefner** *(1926–), Am magazine publisher, as well as founder and chief creative officer of Playboy™ Enterprises).* [L *ars, artis*]

art */ärt/ n* transforming reality and thus nature through human imagination and emotion and realised by skill and technique. [L *ars, artis*]

art */ärt/ n* transforms the everyday into art; *such as Warhol with his soup cans and Lichtenstein with his comic books (***Andrew Warhola** *(1928–87), Am artist;* **Roy Fox Lichtenstein** *(1923–97), Am pop artist).* [L *ars, artis*]

art */ärt/ n* translates on all levels and with all mediums. [L *ars, artis*]

art */ärt/ n* translates the language of the human experience. [L *ars, artis*]

art */ärt/ n* translating imagination into physical objects; *without necessarily having a purpose; maybe not even physical objects, just taking your imagination and expressing it through anything perceptible should be enough.* [L *ars, artis*]

art */ärt/ n* translating the rational to sensual beauty in the factory of imagination. [L *ars, artis*]

art */ärt/ n* transmits ideas and values inherent in every culture across space and time. [L *ars, artis*]

art */ärt/ n (interrog)* tries to define a number of things *(paintings, music, movies, books, clothing, television, theatre etc)* all under one term; *isn't this a bit ridiculous? paintings share no characteristics with the written word, yet they are under the same term.* [L *ars, artis*]

art */ärt/ n* tries to demonstrate things. [L *ars, artis*]

art */ärt/ n* tries to have a certain feel, a certain movement or a certain flow. [L *ars, artis*]

art */ärt/ n* truth. [L *ars, artis*]

art */ärt/ n* truth is out there; *art is in your own head.* [L *ars, artis*]

art */ärt/ n* trying to convey meaning by means other than straight narration; *so a technical document, or an ideogram at an airport for baggage claim wouldn't meet the test.* [L *ars, artis*]

art */ärt/ n* trying to express and reach out to something greater than just the form of whatever medium the artist uses. [L *ars, artis*]

art */ärt/ n* trying to make something out of the chaos of existence. [L *ars, artis*]

art */ärt/ n* trying to say something *and it's trying to evoke some kind of emotional response.* [L *ars, artis*]

art */ärt/ n (neg)* turning a urinal upside-down and writing your name on it or whatever, is NOT complicated and does NOT really serve a purpose, so that is NOT art *(prob ref* Fountain *(1917), a work by Marcel Duchamp (1887–1968)).* [L *ars, artis*]

art */ärt/ n* two things: **1** the transformation of a person's *(creator's)* thoughts given form in the real world **2** the transformation back from the real world into another person's *(observer's)* mind. [L *ars, artis*]

art */ärt/ n* typically what one might find in an art museum of some kind. [L *ars, artis*]

art */ärt/ n* ubiquitous; *and transcends the contrived exposition of the post-war art industry.* [L *ars, artis*]

art */ärt/ n* ugly. [L *ars, artis*]

art */ärt/ n* una forma de comunicación que se produce a través de un admirable nivel de habilidad técnica que puede ser apreciado por su mensaje, alto nivel de conocimientos técnicos ni de impacto emocional. [L *ars, artis*]

art */ärt/ n* unapologetic. [L *ars, artis*]

art */ärt/ n* undefinable. [L *ars, artis*]

art */ärt/ n* undefinable in any absolute way. [L *ars, artis*]

art */ärt/ n (inf)* undefined now; *it has a place and a measure which affects, and has effect; I asked my friend Ray the other day, but he was piss-assed drunk; perhaps it is swearing where it is legal; I think then that it is all around us, but it is undefined; art does have an inner-meaning; It comes, … it also goes; because art may come and go, it keeps nameless (without definition); there is a time and place for everything; and art has both, time and place; to define art as a time, or a place would eliminate all of the art coming before and after, wouldn't it; deciphering the wishes of the world cannot be served in either a date or a month, a time, or a place,* *but when it does, it is the individual which decides; which is one definition to art, a sense that can be shared; yeah* (**Ray** *– ref not known*). [L *ars, artis*]

art */ärt/ n* unlimited. [L *ars, artis*]

art */ärt/ n* unusual things that catch your interest and curiosity. [L *ars, artis*]

art */ärt/ n* used to be a hell of a lot more clear cut before the whole Modern Art thing kicked into gear. [L *ars, artis*]

art */ärt/ n (inf)* useful; *be it a painting to a nude figure in Florence; though there are some kinds of art that are utterly crazy, like the bathroom sculpture – ugh.* [L *ars, artis*]

art */ärt/ n* useless; *all you can do is hang it on your wall and look at it.* [L *ars, artis*]

art */ärt/ n* useless and admired. [L *ars, artis*]

art */ärt/ n* useless and priceless. [L *ars, artis*]

art */ärt/ n* useless, boring, impotent, elitist and very, very beautiful. [L *ars, artis*]

art */ärt/ n* useless-looking. [L *ars, artis*]

art */ärt/ n* useless yet essential J *(J. In the Wingdings font by Microsoft®, the letter 'J' is rendered as a smiley face (note this is distinct from the Unicode code point U+263A)).* [L *ars, artis*]

art */ärt/ n* uses a medium to make a statement to an abstract principle. [L *ars, artis*]

art */ärt/ n* using your hands to generate something you want to see or portray. [L *ars, artis*]

art */ärt/ n* usually about an almost conscious thought. [L *ars, artis*]

art */ärt/ n* usually beautiful; *but it takes a true artist to see the potential in the ugly and make it beautiful.* [L *ars, artis*]

art */ärt/ n* usually the creation of one artist. [L *ars, artis*]

art */ärt/ n (neg)* utterly useless. [L *ars, artis*]

art */ärt/ n* value, design and aesthetics. [L *ars, artis*]

art */ärt/ n* varies from person to person; *from culture and history to time and space; yes, even space.* [L *ars, artis*]

art */ärt/ n* variety of expertise gained from experience that allows a person have the skills to create, organize and plan things systematically with the purpose of expressing psychological meaning and to achieve good results in accordance with the principles of aesthetics, *both intuitively and cognitively.* [L ***ars, artis***]

art */ärt/ n* verbal, neurological, emotional, visual splendour. [L ***ars, artis***]

art */ärt/ n* very subjective; *something that appears to have zero artistic value for one may have substantial value for another.* [L ***ars, artis***]

art */ärt/ n* via its art-historical relationship to some set of earlier artworks. [L ***ars, artis***]

art */ärt/ n* video games. [L ***ars, artis***]

art */ärt/ n* video games; *whether they have stories or not.* [L ***ars, artis***]

art */ärt/ n* video games are art by definition; *however, there is still the debate as to whether or not they are GOOD art.* [L ***ars, artis***]

art */ärt/ n* visual and acoustic man-made creations *which require unusual talent to produce and which are pleasing to the eye or ear of non-perverse humans.* [L ***ars, artis***]

art */ärt/ n* visual essence of the collective consciousness. [L ***ars, artis***]

art */ärt/ n* visual passion. [L ***ars, artis***]

art */ärt/ n* visual poetry. [L ***ars, artis***]

art */ärt/ n* visual sensation that transcends emotion. [L ***ars, artis***]

art */ärt/ n* vital for the cultural health of the society. [L ***ars, artis***]

art */ärt/ n* wakes something in you; *something essential and important; not always pleasant but always alive.* [L ***ars, artis***]

art */ärt/ n* wakes up sleepers. [L ***ars, artis***]

art */ärt/ n* wallets, belts, a car, an iPhone® (iPhone®, *a line of smartphones designed and marketed by Apple™ Inc).* [L ***ars, artis***]

art */ärt/ n* warrior Russ Reyes sitting across the table, under an umbrella, rooster nearby and me captivated by his passionate eyes and glowing soul; *my fantasy finally realized after 25 years of searching (poss ref* @boyband_russell*: I'm just a kid who loves music).* [L ***ars, artis***]

art */ärt/ n* washes away from the soul the dust of everyday life. [L ***ars, artis***]

art */ärt/ n* washing the dust of daily life off our souls. [L *ars, artis*]

art */ärt/ n* we don't know what it is until it is no longer that which it was. [L *ars, artis*]

art */ärt/ n (hist)* we identify works as artworks – where the question of whether or not they are art arises – by means of historical narratives which connect contested candidates to art history in a way that discloses that the mutations in question are part of the evolving species of art; *I call these stories 'identifying narratives'.* [L *ars, artis*]

art */ärt/ n* weird. [L *ars, artis*]

art */ärt/ n (inf)* weird; *I've been trying to think of something more eloquent than that but meh.* [L *ars, artis*]

art */ärt/ n* well-defined, objective *and has nothing to do with what anyone necessarily likes.* [L *ars, artis*]

art */ärt/ n (interrog)* well, we still haven't decided have we? [L *ars, artis*]

art */ärt/ n (derog)* what a small group of pretentious twats label as art. [L *ars, artis*]

art */ärt/ n (interrog)* what about acting, writing, poetry, music… *are those not art?* [L *ars, artis*]

art */ärt/ n (interrog)* what about Etch A Sketch™ art is that art? (Etch A Sketch™, *mechanical drawing toy invented by André Cassagnes of Fr and subsequently manufactured by the Ohio Art Company).* [L *ars, artis*]

art */ärt/ n (interrog)* what about quantum art? *It's only art when you're not looking at it.* [L *ars, artis*]

art */ärt/ n (interrog)* what about the artistic imaginings of the machines that draw ever closer to artificial intelligence? [L *ars, artis*]

art */ärt/ n (interrog, zool)* what about the paintings done by elephants or chimpanzees? [L *ars, artis*]

art */ärt/ n (m)* what affects the senses; *that means that every piece of art is 'touching' one of more of our five senses – hearing, seeing, tasting, feeling (haptic) and smelling;* eg *a perfumer is an artist in that he creates something that's designed to affect a sense in us; which in turn affects us as humans and creates* eg *an emotional reaction towards the smell; a musician affects our hearing sense, a cook's art affects our smell-*

ing, tasting and feeling etc. [L *ars, artis*]

art */ärt/ n* what an artist does. [L *ars, artis*]

art */ärt/ n (m)* what an artist sees when he opens his eyes. [L *ars, artis*]

art */ärt/ n* what any single person considers to be art. [L *ars, artis*]

art */ärt/ n* what art is; *and nothing less.* [L *ars, artis*]

art */ärt/ n (pers)* what comes from inside me, *my psyche.* [L *ars, artis*]

art */ärt/ n* what comes from natural fluidity; *and only has to make sense to you.* [L *ars, artis*]

art */ärt/ n* what develops out of the mind's eye. [L *ars, artis*]

art */ärt/ n* what doesn't make me yawn. [L *ars, artis*]

art */ärt/ n* what dogs like. [L *ars, artis*]

art */ärt/ n* what feelings look like. [L *ars, artis*]

art */ärt/ n* what gives another human a special kind of experience. [L *ars, artis*]

art */ärt/ n* what hangs in galleries; *everything else is entertainment.* [L *ars, artis*]

art */ärt/ n* what happens when painters stop looking at girls and persuade themselves that they have a better idea. [L *ars, artis*]

art */ärt/ n* what happens when you dream. [L *ars, artis*]

art */ärt/ n* what humans use to express things that cannot be expressed. [L *ars, artis*]

art */ärt/ n (educ)* what I did to get expelled from the Sydney College of the Arts (**Sydney College of the Arts**, *the University of Sydney's school of contemporary art; we respond creatively to the major issues driving contemporary society; teach people how to become leading artists, curators and writers active in national and international visual culture; value intelligence, innovation, creative thinking, research and problem-solving; generously engage with the world beyond our campus through collegiality, exhibitions and collaborations; draw and build on the heritage of academic rigour and research intensity of the University of Sydney to provide an enriched learning experience for our undergraduate, postgraduate and research students; our* *work, our openness and our philosophy reflect our view that art is a wide-ranging concept that allows many viewpoints, approaches and backgrounds).* [L *ars, artis*]

art */ärt/ n (pers)* what I do to unwind. [L *ars, artis*]

art */ärt/ n (inf, pers)* what I enjoy; *then I don't give a toss about the efforts it took to create it or what anyone else thinks.* [L *ars, artis*]

art */ärt/ n (pers)* what I feel it is: *The Haywain; Macbeth; The Sistine Chapel; Requiem for a Dream; The Physical Impossibility of Death in the Mind of Someone Living; single or collaborative; talent or happenstance; unique or mass-produced; tangible or intangible; the only common grounds they have is that someone has done at least something – and that they are labelled art (*The Hay Wain*, painting by John Constable, finished in 1821, which depicts a rural scene on the River Stour between the Eng counties of Suffolk and Essex;* Macbeth*, written by William Shakespeare, considered one of his darkest and most powerful tragedies;* Sistine Chapel*, a large and renowned chapel of the Apostolic Palace, official residence of the Pope in Vatican City;* Requiem for a Dream *(2000), Am drama film dir Darren Aronofsky and starring Ellen Burstyn, Jared Leto, Jennifer Connelly and Marlon Wayans;* The Physical Impossibility of Death in the Mind of Someone Living*, artwork created in 1991 by Damien Hirst, Eng artist and leading member of the 'Young British Artists').* [L *ars, artis*]

art */ärt/ n (pers)* what I perceive when I look at things around me. [L *ars, artis*]

art */ärt/ n (pers)* what I see. [L *ars, artis*]

art */ärt/ n* what is done by regular and disciplined methods. [L *ars, artis*]

art */ärt/ n (prob joc)* what I've got between my legs. [L *ars, artis*]

art */ärt/ n (inf)* what knucklehead says is art (**knucklehead**, *ref not known).* [L *ars, artis*]

art */ärt/ n* what makes life more interesting than art. [L *ars, artis*]

art */ärt/ n (pers)* what makes me happy. [L *ars, artis*]

art */ärt/ n* what makes the world

go round. [L *ars, artis*]

art */ärt/ n* what makes us human. [L *ars, artis*]

art */ärt/ n (pers)* what motivates me to get out of bed in the morning. [L *ars, artis*]

art */ärt/ n* what occurs when you do something well for its own sake. [L *ars, artis*]

art */ärt/ n* what one individual thinks is beautiful. [L *ars, artis*]

art */ärt/ n* what people accept as such. [L *ars, artis*]

art */ärt/ n* what people label as 'art'. [L *ars, artis*]

art */ärt/ n* what separates us from animals. [L *ars, artis*]

art */ärt/ n* what some run from and the factors that others run to. [L *ars, artis*]

art */ärt/ n* what speaks to your heart and soul. [L *ars, artis*]

art */ärt/ n* what the artist intends to impression on the admirers of the work of art. [L *ars, artis*]

art */ärt/ n* what the artist says is art. [L *ars, artis*]

art */ärt/ n* what the avant garde art phenomenon does. [L *ars, artis*]

art */ärt/ n (milit)* what the military and the police are there to defend. [L *ars, artis*]

art */ärt/ n* what touches your soul; *and not just your senses.* [L *ars, artis*]

art */ärt/ n* what used to be a visual medium of expression; *now a pop-culture fad.* [L *ars, artis*]

art */ärt/ n* what we create, partake and explore in order to itch at the void and celebrate humanity. [L *ars, artis*]

art */ärt/ n* what we do when we do something for the first time, do it uniquely and do it to touch someone else. [L *ars, artis*]

art */ärt/ n* what we make when we really mean what we do. [L *ars, artis*]

art */ärt/ n* what we're doing when we do our best work. [L *ars, artis*]

Art */ärt/ n (joc)* what you call a guy with no arms and no legs hanging on the wall. [Arthur]

art */ärt/ n* what you can get away with. [L *ars, artis*]

art */ärt/ n* what you choose to frame and put on your wall. [L *ars, artis*]

art /ärt/ *n* what you desire most. [L *ars, artis*]

art /ärt/ *n* what you draw on paper with pencil or paint. [L *ars, artis*]

art /ärt/ *n* what you feel is most precious and beautiful in your life. [L *ars, artis*]

art /ärt/ *n (poss pharmacol)* what you go to when a clinical description [perh *prescription*] fails you. [L *ars, artis*]

art /ärt/ *n* what you like; *the rest is somebody's mistake.* [L *ars, artis*]

art /ärt/ *n* what you love yourself to be; *discover your art and discover life.* [L *ars, artis*]

art /ärt/ *n* what you make of it. [L *ars, artis*]

art /ärt/ *n* what you think it is; *and if you ask what I think it is ask me later.* [L *ars, artis*]

art /ärt/ *n* what you think it is personally. [L *ars, artis*]

art /ärt/ *n* what you want the world to be like *and your way of showing it.* [L *ars, artis*]

art /ärt/ *n (prob joc)* what your Mom looks like naked. [L *ars, artis*]

art /ärt/ *n* whatever an artist comes up with and enough authorities support. [L *ars, artis*]

art /ärt/ *n* whatever an artist comes up with and enough authorities support; *now please don't ask me who gets to be an artist or an authority, or how many authorities are enough.* [L *ars, artis*]

art /ärt/ *n* whatever is at some point arranged in some way. [L *ars, artis*]

art /ärt/ *n* whatever is described as having undergone a deliberate process of arrangement by an agent. [L *ars, artis*]

art /ärt/ *n* whatever is made in an artistic process and consumed as art. [L *ars, artis*]

art /ärt/ *n* whatever lends to the observer deep sensation; *either physical, mental, emotional or spiritual: any one of these or a combination thereof.* [L *ars, artis*]

art /ärt/ *n* whatever one does to express themselves when they aren't forced into it. [L *ars, artis*]

art /ärt/ *n (joc)* whatever Sister Wendy tells me it is *(Wendy Beckett (b 25 Feb 1930), better known as* **Sister Wendy***, Brit hermit, consecrated virgin, and* *art historian who became well known internationally during the 1990s when she presented a series of documentaries for the BBC on the history of art).* [L *ars, artis*]

art */ärt/ n (derog)* whatever some super-egotistical clown who deems him/herself to be an art critic, tells the masses; *most normal people would not recognize it for anything but garbage; however, the snobs and super-elite, of course, know better.* [L *ars, artis*]

art */ärt/ n* whatever someone claims to be art; *there are no precise definitions, boundaries or litmus tests as to what deserves to be titled as art; the art might be amateurish or disgusting or tacky and my opinion might differ from the next person's opinion as to it's worth, but that doesn't mean it isn't art.* [L *ars, artis*]

art */ärt/ n* whatever someone says is art; *this is why we have so much pornography in art lately: the 'artists' there think that's 'beauty'; the reason we have a 1st Amendment is to avoid fistfights over defining that.* [L *ars, artis*]

art */ärt/ n* whatever the artist says it is. [L *ars, artis*]

art */ärt/ n* whatever the eye beholds in an artful frame of mind; *an artful frame of mind is a readiness to see beyond apparently stable boundaries of physical objects and actions, into the dynamic relationships between objects and actions.* [L *ars, artis*]

art */ärt/ n (inf)* whatever the fuck you want it to be. [L *ars, artis*]

art */ärt/ n (inf)* whatever the hell you want it to be. [L *ars, artis*]

art */ärt/ n (econ)* whatever the public or any other patron is willing to pay an artist to produce. [L *ars, artis*]

art */ärt/ n* whatever we as artists, institutions or organisations say it is. [L *ars, artis*]

art */ärt/ n* whatever we do after the chores are done. [L *ars, artis*]

art */ärt/ n (derog)* whatever you are told it is; *these days often by effete parasites who make money from dissected and embalmed animals, or an unmade bed; if these parasites tell you it is art, then you better believe it because otherwise you are fascist reactionary scum; oh, but I forgot, the real fascists also liked to tell people what 'art' is; so, generally, 'art' is for parasites with their heads up in the* *clouds, or perhaps up somewhere else…* (**dissected and embalmed animals**, *perh ref Mother and Child (Divided) or related work by Brit artist Damian Hirst (1965–);* **unmade bed**, *perh ref My Bed (1998), a work by Brit artist Tracey Emin (1963–)).* [L *ars, artis*]

art */ärt/ n* whatever you believe, imagine or think it to be. [L *ars, artis*]

art */ärt/ n* whatever you can get away with. [L *ars, artis*]

art */ärt/ n* whatever you make of it; *it could be an oil painting like that of the old masters, it could be a drawing made with Photoshop®, it could even be 'snow flowers' sculpted with only the artist's urine (*Adobe Photoshop™*, graphics editing program developed and published by Adobe Systems; poss ref* Piss Flowers, *by Helen Chadwick and her partner David Notarius).* [L *ars, artis*]

art */ärt/ n* whatever you think. [L *ars, artis*]

art */ärt/ n* (*inf, perh joc*) whatever you think is art and can get somebody to agree; *I'm toying with the idea that if you get someone else to recognise your pile of dog shit as art, you two have engaged in a minimal act of art criticism – and lo and behold, a tiny local art field with its own participants (artist, critic, audience) and its own criteria for art has been born.* [L *ars, artis*]

art */ärt/ n* whatever you think is nice to look at. [L *ars, artis*]

art */ärt/ n* whatever you think it is, basically; *which is why I tend to stay away from it, as it annoys me and that's exactly what art is supposed to do.* [L *ars, artis*]

art */ärt/ n* whatever you want it to be; *a decapitated horse, a painting with some swirls or just a collage of your cat (poss ref Maurizio Cattelan,* 'Untitled' *(2007) and* Paul Jackson Pollock *(January 28, 1912 – August 11, 1956), known professionally as Jackson Pollock, Am painter and a major figure in the abstract expressionist movement, well known for his unique style of drip painting).* [L *ars, artis*]

art */ärt/ n* whatever you want it to be; *as long as it's you and creative; it can be a sculpture, painting, abstract work; even photographs are art.* [L *ars, artis*]

art */ärt/ n* when a human uses a

medium to express an idea or emotion to a viewer using representational means. [L *ars, artis*]

art */ärt/ n* WHEN ANY KIND OF ELEMENTS WHETHER PHYSICALLY EXISTING OR CONCEIVABLE IN THIS WORLD *(widest definition)* ARE PUT TOGETHER FORMING A SYSTEM AS CAPTIVATING AND LOGICAL *(and this is the subjective component about it)* IN ITSELF THAT ITS SURROUNDINGS ARE NO LONGER NEEDED TO ITS UNDERSTANDING AND FUNCTIONING. [L *ars, artis*]

art */ärt/ n* when anyone in the world takes any sort of material and fashions a deliberate statement with it. [L *ars, artis*]

art */ärt/ n (inf)* when beauty, complexity, philosophy, genius and sensuality all have a gang bang together, this misbegotten but wondrous creation ensues. [L *ars, artis*]

art */ärt/ n (interrog)* when Bob Rauschenberg dumped a pile of trash on a museum floor; *however, when the garbage collection guys accidentally dump a pile of trash onto the street, it's just a pile of trash; but what if the garbage men dumped the pile of trash there as a sardonic artistic statement regarding suburban consumerism – sort of like a neo-dadaist pop meets an expressionist social statement; what if Bob Rauschenberg was riding in the truck (or was part of the trash)? (Milton Ernest* "Robert" Rauschenberg *(October 22, 1925 - May 12, 2008), Am painter and graphic artist whose early works anticipated the pop art movement).* [L *ars, artis*]

art */ärt/ n* when desire overtakes reason. [L *ars, artis*]

art */ärt/ n (pers)* when I can't function properly until I spit out whatever mess I'm feeling. [L *ars, artis*]

art */ärt/ n (pers)* when I pour all of my heart and soul into a piece of craft, flash fiction, travel article, poem or photograph. [L *ars, artis*]

art */ärt/ n* when it goes beyond pretty and becomes beautiful, or when it goes beyond a street scene and becomes a comment on the urban environment; *so it is the 'beyond' bit that matters.* [L *ars, artis*]

art */ärt/ n* when man manages to touch what Plato described as the 'Good'; *this 'everything is art be-*

cause I said so' BS is just man's egocentric and pretentious hubris at work; Dada is the death of art (**Plato** *(427–347BC), philos in Classical Gr;* **BS**, *prob bullshit;* **Dada**, *art movement of the Eur avant-garde in the early c20th).* [L *ars, artis*]

art */ärt/ n* when someone shows you the world from their point of view. [L *ars, artis*]

art */ärt/ n* when something takes a lot of creativity and effort and the end product is a highly enjoyable [experience] for the person experiencing it. [L *ars, artis*]

art */ärt/ n* when you become homeless and roll around in your own pee in a crowded subway train singing Christmas carols in falsetto on repeat whilst drawing a penis, then you suddenly stop and do a spin after three hours and take a bow. [L *ars, artis*]

art */ärt/ n* when you go into seclusion for six months, let your hair grow, never shower, get arrested a few times and on the last day fling paint randomly at a canvas and smear it around; *and if anyone calls you on it, just say 'that's what I'd expect from you'.* [L *ars, artis*]

art */ärt/ n* when you illustrate *(through music, drawing, painting, speaking* etc*)* just whatever you feel connected with, to show a certain way you feel towards something/someone. [L *ars, artis*]

art */ärt/ n* when you put some paint on the end of a toothbrush and flick it on to a bit paper. [L *ars, artis*]

art */ärt/ n* where a deep message or meaning can be found. [L *ars, artis*]

art */ärt/ n* where form and function come together in beauty, colour and shape. [L *ars, artis*]

art */ärt/ n (pers)* where I can ride upon on the storms of my oh so blind and fallible emotions and know that whatever shore I wash up on is one that is right for me; *I love that I can stand upon that strand and shout 'this is right!' in a way that brooks no argument whatsoever; because art is the one beautiful, shining exception where the subjective is in fact everything.* [L *ars, artis*]

art */ärt/ n* where personal interpretation is not just possible, but perfectly valid; *and as such I'd have to say that it would be hypocritical to* *define it beyond the subjective opinions of the creator, with a big caveat.* [L *ars, artis*]

art */ärt/ n* where we expose ourselves. [L *ars, artis*]

art */ärt/ n* while it may borrow from prior work, must innovate. [L *ars, artis*]

art */ärt/ n* who you deeply are. [L *ars, artis*]

art */ärt/ n* wholeness, harmony and radiance. [L *ars, artis*]

art */ärt/ n (interrog)* why isn't the photocopier sitting next to me in an art museum? *what about the mouse in your hand? how about the shirt you're wearing, the rocks in the ground, the trees in the park, the sound of a honking horn? why hasn't someone put them in a museum? why aren't they art?* [L *ars, artis*]

art */ärt/ n* wildly subjective; *there are those who like paintings of the ocean, others may enjoy sculpture, perhaps even exquisitely crafted Easter eggs.* [L *ars, artis*]

art */ärt/ n* will bring a heightened experience of truth; *although it isn't literally manifested.* [L *ars, artis*]

art */ärt/ n* will evoke an emotion and cause a stirring in the spirit. [L *ars, artis*]

art */ärt/ n (interrog, neg, poss relig)* wind, rain, glaciers and all manner of natural phenomena can be considered beautiful, *but since no creative process was used, they surely could not be considered art, unless you invoke a creator, the ultimate artist, of course?* [L *ars, artis*]

art */ärt/ n* wine can be art; *I think this is obvious.* [L *ars, artis*]

art */ärt/ n* with internet memes, people are creating images and sharing them with strangers for the purpose of communicating their personal experiences; *that, my friends, is art, plain and simple.* [L *ars, artis*]

art */ärt/ n* wondrous and paradoxical. [L *ars, artis*]

art */ärt/ n* work created with the intention of being art. [L *ars, artis*]

art */ärt/ n* working. [L *ars, artis*]

art */ärt/ n* works of art collectively; *an art exhibition.* [L *ars, artis*]

art */ärt/ n* works of art collectively; *an art exhibition, a fine collection of art.* [L *ars, artis*]

art */ärt/ n* works of art collectively; as *paintings, sculptures or drawings.*

[L *ars, artis*]

art */ärt/ n* works of art collectively, *esp of the visual arts, sometimes also music, drama, dance and literature.* [L *ars, artis*]

art */ärt/ n* works of art collectively; *esp of the visual arts, sometimes also music, drama, dance and literature*; *excellence or aesthetic merit of conception or execution as exemplified by such works.* [L *ars, artis*]

art */ärt/ n* works of art, *in categorical contrast with mere representations,* use the means of representation in a way that is not exhaustively specified when one has exhaustively specified what is being represented. [L *ars, artis*]

art */ärt/ n* works primarily appreciated for their beauty or emotions; *whether we like it or not.* [L *ars, artis*]

art */ärt/ n* works produced by human creative skill and imagination. [L *ars, artis*]

art */ärt/ n* would cease to exist if any one definition could be found to perfectly articulate and contain the whole nature of it. [L *ars, artis*]

art */ärt/ n (lit)* writing. [L *ars, artis*]

art */ärt/ n (lit)* writing can be art. [L *ars, artis*]

art */ärt/ n* written about in a magazine, exhibited in a museum or bought by a private collector; *it seems pretty clear by now that more or less anything can be designated as art; the question is, has it been called art by the so-called 'art system'?; in our century, that's all that makes it art.* [L *ars, artis*]

art */ärt/ n (philos)* x is an artwork if and only if x is an object which a person or persons non-passingly intends for regard as a work of art; ie *regard in any way (or ways) in which prior artworks are or were correctly (or standardly) regarded.* [L *ars, artis*]

art */ärt/ n (philos)* x is art if and only if someone created x to be an imitation or representation of some other thing. [L *ars, artis*]

art */ärt/ n (philos)* x is art to you if you interpret x in a particular aesthetic way. [L *ars, artis*]

art */ärt/ n* you and what you give. [L *ars, artis*]

art */ärt/ n (neg)* you do not have to be an artist to make art. [L *ars, artis*]

art */ärt/ n* you know it when you

feel it; *it doesn't involve the eyes alone, if at all; it can be a total body or out of body experience.* [L *ars, artis*]

art */ärt/ n* your emotional signature in action. [L *ars, artis*]

art */ärt/ n* your hair in your avi (**avi**, *an avatar used on Twitter™ and other social media platforms).* [L *ars, artis*]

art */ärt/ n* your imagination personified through your physical efforts. [L *ars, artis*]

art */ärt/ n* your mind's flirtation with an external fantasy. [L *ars, artis*]

art */ärt/ n* your potion. [L *ars, artis*]

art */ärt/ n* yours for the taking. [L *ars, artis*]

art */ärt/ n* yourself; *it represents yourself; it tells all about yourself; it defines yourself.* [L *ars, artis*]

art */ärt/ n* zeroing in on colour with design. [L *ars, artis*]

art */ärt/ n* הזו ךיתח ןוסרדנא טרב יכ (**Brett Lewis Anderson** *(b 29 September 1967), Eng singer-songwriter, best known as the lead vocalist of the band Suede).* [L *ars, artis*]

art */ärt/ vt* a verb – *an action word and I am compelled to do it.* [L *ars, artis*]

ABBREVIATIONS USED IN THE DICTIONARY

abbrev	abbreviation
Am	American
appar	apparently
approx	approximately
Aust	Australia, Austria
b	born
biog	biography
biol	biology
bot	botany
Brit	British
©	copyright
c	about *(L circa)*
cf	compare *(L confer)*
comput	computing
derog	derogatory
dir	director
Du	Dutch
econ	economics
educ	education
eg	for example *(L exempli gratia)*
Eng	English
esp	especially
etc	& so on *(L et cetera)*
Eur	European
euphem	euphemism
f	feminine
fig	figurative(ly)
fl	flourished *(L floruit)*
Fr	French
gen	generally
geog	geography
geol	geology
geom	geometry
Ger	German
Gr	Greek
hist	historical
hort	horticulture
ie	that is *(L id est)*
imit	imitative
incl	including
inf	informal
interj	interjection
interrog	interrogative
It	Italian
joc	jocular
L	Latin
lit	literal(ly)
m	masculine
math	mathematics
meteorol	meteorology
milit	military
mus	musical
myth	mythology
n	noun

neg negative
neurol neurology
Nor Norwegian
obs obsolete
OE Old English
opp opposite, opposed
opthalmol opthalmology
orig originally
perh perhaps
pers personal
pharmacol pharmacology
philos philosophy
photog photography
phys physics
physiol physiology
pl plural
pos positive
poss possibly
prob probably
prof professional
psychol psychology
® registered trademark
ref reference
relig religion
Rom Roman, Romanian
Russ Russian
sic thus (L)
sculpt sculpture
sociol sociology
sl slang
Sp Spanish
stat statistics
theol theological
™ trademark
urol urology
usu usually
vt verb transitive
vulg vulgar
zool zoology

DETAILED CHART OF PRONUNCIATION

Examples:

ä	as in	art
r	"	art
t	"	art

ABOUT

Robert Good is an artist who works with text to consider the frailties of language and the problems of knowledge. Deconstructing texts, systems and structures, Good's meticulous doubt combined with a desire for certainty sets up a fault line of both tension and humour throughout his work.

www.robertgood.co.uk

Jane Glennie is an artist and typographer who works with installation and poetry film, while remaining fervent on the finer points of typesetting.

www.janeglennie.co.uk

Professor Derek Matravers joined the Open University in 1994, having spent the previous three years as a Research Fellow at Darwin College, Cambridge. His particular interests are in aesthetics and the philosophy of mind, as well as the philosophical aspects of twentieth-century art. He is currently working on a book on axiology (the metaphysics of value), and a number of articles in ethics and aesthetics.

www.open.ac.uk/people/dcm4

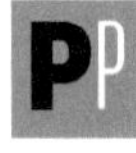

www.peculiaritypress.com

ISBN 978-1-912384-00-6

This work first published 2017.
by Peculiarity Press, an imprint of Leigh & Glennie Ltd.
The Business Centre, Greys Green Farm, Henley-on-Thames RG9 4QG, UK.

Design by Jane Glennie.
Typeset in Myriad and Aleo.

www.ingramcontent.com/pod-product-compliance
Ingram Content Group UK Ltd.
Pitfield, Milton Keynes, MK11 3LW, UK
UKHW041951190726
13854UKWH00005B/1908

9 781912 384006